HONEST CHRISTIANITY
For America Today

Affirming Faith Through Action

By Richard G. Leahy

ISBN 978-0-578-76838-0

This book is dedicated to the life and example of Heather Heyer, killed on August 12, 2017, while marching peacefully to protest White supremacy on Charlottesville's pedestrian mall, as well as to the many other marchers injured in that attack, all Americans standing up for social justice, and all Christians who are affirming their faith through action.

The Heather Heyer Foundation, established in her honor, awards scholarships awarded to those who have already proven themselves to be activists in positive non-violent social change. "Scholarships are awarded to those seeking a degree or certification in, but not limited to, law, paralegal studies, social work, social justice and education, and who intend to promote peaceful social change using those skills in their profession. This scholarship recognizes Heather's devotion to positive social change, and hopes to support the education and empowerment of activists, advocates, and allies in promoting positive non-violent social change." For more information, visit
https://www.heatherheyerfoundation.com/scholarships.

"For I know how many are your transgressions, and how great are your sins— you who afflict the righteous, who take a bribe, and push aside the needy in the gate. Seek good and not evil, that you may live; and so the LORD, the God of hosts, will be with you, just as you have said. Hate evil and love good, and establish justice in the gate; it may be that the LORD, the God of hosts, will be gracious to the remnant of Joseph. **But let justice roll down like waters, and righteousness like an ever-flowing stream."**

Harper Bibles. NRSV Bible, Amos 5:12-15, 24. Kindle Edition.

Then Amos answered Amaziah, "I am no prophet, nor a prophet's son; but I am a herdsman, and a dresser of sycamore trees, and the LORD took me from following the flock, and the LORD said to me, 'Go, prophesy to my people Israel.'"

Harper Bibles. NRSV Bible, Amos 7, 14-15. Kindle Edition.

"If I say, 'I will not mention him, or speak any more in his name,' then within me there is something like a burning fire shut up in my bones; I am weary with holding it in, and I cannot."

Harper Bibles. NRSV Bible, Jeremiah 20:9. Kindle Edition.

"God made us all...We've got to love each other; we've just got to do that. We are all one race, and we need to love each other."[1]

"To love is to act."[2]

Honest Christianity for America Today

Affirming Faith Through Action

Prologue: Two Months
That Shook the Nation

"To say that everything is in God's hands, and not take action, is just a cop-out." –Corina Newsome, #BlackBirdersWeek[3]

On Sunday May 24th, 2020, the nation prepared for a somber Memorial Day in the midst of the coronavirus pandemic that was on the verge of claiming 100,000 American lives. President Trump went to his golf course in Sterling, Virginia, dividing his time between golfing and tweeting insults at House speaker Nancy Pelosi and Stacey Abrams, a Black former minority leader of the Georgia House of Representatives who was considered a potential Vice-Presidential candidate for Joe Biden. He finally had the flags at the White House lowered to half-staff after being hectored by critics, and otherwise made no mention of the crisis.[4]

On Memorial Day, Christian Cooper, a Black man, was birding in Central Park, New York City, when he encountered a White woman named Amy Cooper (no relation). He politely asked her to leash her dog, per Park regulations. Instead, she called the police to report that "an African American man" was threatening her life.[5] Later that day, Minneapolis police arrested George Floyd for allegedly using counterfeit bills to buy cigarettes. Floyd submitted peacefully to arrest and was handcuffed without incident, but resisted being put into a squad car, saying he was claustrophobic.

The incident was recorded by multiple witnesses. When the third squad car arrived, officer Derek Michael Chauvin told the others he would take charge. According to prosecutors, Floyd told the officers he could not breathe while they tried to force him into the car. Chauvin dragged Floyd across the backseat of the car and, still handcuffed, he fell to the street, lying on his chest with his cheek to the ground.

Multiple videos record that at 8:20 p.m. Chauvin put his knee on Floyd's neck while two other offices held him in place, and a fourth watched passively. Floyd can be heard repeatedly saying "I can't breathe", "Please", and "Mama"; Floyd repeated at least 16 times that he could not breathe.

By 8:25, Floyd appeared unconscious. An ambulance arrived at 8:27 and even while the technicians checked Floyd's pulse and he remained unconscious; Chauvin kept his knee on Floyd's neck for almost another minute. When he finally did lift his knee, it had been there for eight minutes and forty-six seconds. [6] Particularly chilling is both the unconcern for Floyd's life by the other officers on the scene, and the defiant, proud sadism of Chauvin's expression and body language in the video taken by a bystander.

Chauvin has been charged with second-degree murder, and he and the other three police officers involved were fired by the Minneapolis police department. In the week following Floyd's killing, all four living previous American presidents released statements that not only expressed sorrow for Floyd's death but all of which acknowledged systemic failures in American criminal justice and police behavior that must be addressed. President Trump expressed his condolences to Floyd's family via Twitter, promising that "Justice will be done!" and calling the death "sad and tragic."

However, four days later, amidst reports of rioting, violence and looting occurring during nationwide protests over Floyd's death, Trump tweeted: "These THUGS are dishonoring the memory of George Floyd, and I won't let that happen. Just spoke to Governor Tim Walz and told him that the Military is with him all the way. Any difficulty and we will assume control but, when the looting starts, the shooting starts.[7] Thank you!" [8]On June 1, in response to continued protests, President Trump threatened to deploy the military against protesters by invoking the Insurrection Act of 1807.

Floyd's death, which could be called not only tragically unnecessary but an execution, triggered some 2,000 protests (including some looting in Minneapolis) and demonstrations against systematic police brutality against African Americans. The protests continued through June, and also spread around the world.

On June 1st, President Trump was making a televised speech in the Rose Garden in which he called himself the "president of law and order, and an ally of all peaceful protesters."⁹ When he finished his remarks, he said he was going to "pay my respects to a very, very special place." Meanwhile, just north of the White House in Lafayette Square, military police began to abruptly disperse a peaceful group of protesters, with riot gear, tear gas and rubber bullets. A CNN video showed Attorney General William Barr talking with officials and gesturing to the north shortly before the action began.

As reported in the *Washington Post,* Rev. Virginia Gerbasi, an Episcopal priest, was in Lafayette Square to deliver water and snacks to demonstrators who had gathered to protest the killing of George Floyd. "Around 6:15 or 6:30, the police started really pushing protestors off of H Street...the street between the church and Lafayette Park, and ultimately, the White House," Gerbasi wrote on her Facebook page.

She then described tear gas filling the area, sending people running toward the church for eyewashes, water and paper towels. "I was coughing, her [friend Julia's] eyes were watering, and we were trying to help people as the police — in full riot gear — drove people toward us." Gerbasi, who once served as assistant rector at St. John's in Lafayette Square, was stunned by the police aggression and how quickly it escalated. She and others, including clergy members and volunteer medics from Black Lives Matter, were soon overrun.

"Around 6:30, there was more tear gas, more concussion grenades, and I think I saw someone hit by a rubber bullet — he was grasping his stomach and there was a mark on his shirt," Gerbasi wrote in the post, which had been shared more than 125,000 times on Facebook by early Tuesday afternoon. "The police in their riot gear were literally walking onto the St. John's, Lafayette Square patio with these metal shields, pushing people off the patio and driving them back. People were running at us as the police advanced toward us from the other side of the patio."

Lafayette Square now emptied of protesters, President Trump strode across it to the front of St. John's Episcopal Church, known as the "church of presidents" from its proximity to the White House (Mr. Trump does not worship there). Mr. Trump did not pray or bow his head. Scowling, he held up a bible in front of the church and said simply, "This is a great country."

Richard G. Leahy

President Trump's daughter, Ivanka gave him the idea for the bible/church photo op and even provided a bible, carried in her designer Max Mara purse.[10] Later on Fox News, Trump said "I think it was a beautiful picture. I'll tell you, I think Christians think it was a beautiful picture."[11] The following day the president proceeded to the Saint John Paul II National Shrine in Northeast Washington with his wife, for another photo opportunity.

Lafayette Square is named in honor of the Marquis de Lafayette, a French nobleman whose military and financial aid were instrumental in securing the American victory in the Revolutionary War. Ironically, Lafayette believed in emancipation of enslaved Africans and even wrote to Washington to urge him to emancipate his own enslaved workers.

The outrage of Gerbasi's first-person account of the attack on the clergy and peaceful protesters struck a chord with tens of thousands of readers, Gerbasi said in an interview Tuesday afternoon, because it "tapped into something that was so universally offensive. That church people got driven off of church grounds by riot police for a photo op for the president in front of a church holding a Bible is offensive to the core."

Gerbasi wrote that the crowd had been peaceful all day and had not thrown anything at the police until after they began deploying flash-bangs and chemical irritants. The incident, she wrote, was deeply troubling.

"I am DEEPLY OFFENDED on behalf of every protestor, every Christian, the people of St. John's, Lafayette square, every decent person there, and the Black Lives Matter medics who stayed with just a single box of supplies and a backpack, even when I got too scared and had to leave. I am ok. But I am now a force to be reckoned with."[12]

In what was likely a surprise to President Trump, Rev. Gerbasi was not the only Christian who was appalled by his actions. Rev. Mariann Budde, bishop of the Episcopal Diocese of Washington which includes St. John's church, posted the following statements on Twitter: "Tonight President just used a Bible and a church of my diocese as a backdrop for a message antithetical to the teachings of Jesus and everything that our church stands for. To do so, he sanctioned the use of tear gas by police officers in riot gear to clear the church yard."

"The President did not come to pray; he did not lament the death of George Floyd or acknowledge the collective agony of people of color in our nation. He did not attempt to heal or bring calm to our troubled land. We are followers of Jesus. In no way do we support the President's incendiary response to a wounded, grieving nation. We stand with those seeking justice for the death of George Floyd through the sacred act of peaceful protest."[13]

Washington's Catholic Archbishop Wilton Gregory, who had clearly not been informed of the President's visit in advance, criticized him for attempting to politicize a visit to a Catholic shrine. He read the following statement as the President and Mrs. Trump arrived at the site: "I find it baffling and reprehensible that any Catholic facility would allow itself to be so egregiously misused and manipulated in a fashion that violates our religious principles, which call us to defend the rights of all people, even those with whom we might disagree."[14]

Even televangelist Pat Robertson, a longstanding political and religious conservative, criticized the president's decision to clear Lafayette Square of peaceful demonstrators with riot police, as well as his calling state governors "jerks." At the beginning of the 700 Club on Tuesday June 2nd, he said "It seems like now is the time to say, 'I understand your pain, I want to comfort you, I think it's time we love each other. But the president took a different course. He said, 'I am the "president of law and order,' and he issued a heads-up. He said, 'I'm ready to send in military troops if the nation's governors don't act to quell the violence that has rocked American cities.' As matter of fact, he spoke of them as being 'jerks. You just don't do that, Mr. President. It isn't cool!"

Robertson also spoke out about racism, saying "we are one" and "God made us all." "We've got to love each other, we just got to do that," Robertson said. "We are all one race, and we need to love each other."[15]

Starting May 28 through the end of July 2020, demonstrations over the police killing of George Floyd were held in the city of Portland, OR, concurrent with protests in other cities. Some protests drew crowds from 1,000 to 10,000 people. People and groups engaging in the protests have since identified a number of Black people killed by local police, with local victims including Kendra James, Aaron Campbell, Quanice Hayes, and Patrick Kimmons, in addition to others around the country like Breonna Taylor and Elijah McClain.[16]

Some of the protests in Portland were peaceful, but some involved injury, vandalism, arson looting, and heated confrontations with police, sometimes involving injury to protesters and police, declaration of riot, and use of tear gas and other non-lethal weapons.

On June 8th, Orange County's chief health officer Dr. Nichole Quick resigned after several intense weeks defending her countywide face mask order in response to the coronavirus pandemic. The mask order, which requires that people wear face coverings while in public, faced immediate resistance after mandated it in late May. Some residents and elected officials have challenged the need for the widespread use of face coverings as businesses in the region reopen. That ire at times was directly aimed at Quick.

The Orange County Sheriff's Department provided a security detail for Quick after she received what officials deemed to be a death threat during a county Board of Supervisors meeting. During the meeting, a woman who identified herself as an attorney disparaged Quick's experience in the medical field and read her home address aloud, saying she planned to take a group to Quick's home and "do calisthenics in masks on her front doorstep" in an attempt to prove that face coverings are unsafe.[17]

On June 11th, USA Today reported that the U.S. had surpassed 2 million cases of COVID-19 -19, the disease caused by the novel coronavirus. The number of cases had doubled in six weeks; on April 28th it had been one million.

Less than a month after Floyd's death, on June 12th, Rayshard Brooks, another African American, was shot and killed by a White officer of the

Atlanta police who tried to arrest him for failing a sobriety test after falling asleep in his car while in a drive-in line. Brooks had resisted arrest and ran from the police after grabbing an officer's taser. Officer Garrett Rolfe shot Brook in the back, killing him. An autopsy from the county medical examiner said Brooks suffered two gunshot wounds to his back and listed his cause of death as a homicide. Officer Rolfe was fired from the force and charged with murder and faces 11 total charges. [18]

During a heightened state of national trauma, President Trump took the opportunity to ignore Pat Robertson's advice and instead, went on Fox News with Sean Hannity, where he defended Officer Rolfe and seemed to criticize Brooks.

"You can't resist a police officer, and if you have a disagreement, you have to take it up after the fact," Trump said. "It was out of control – the whole situation was out of control."

Trump also said police had been treated unfairly in the U.S. "It's up to justice right now. It's going to be up to justice. I hope he [Rolfe] gets a fair shake, because police have not been treated fairly in our country. But again, you can't resist a police officer like that."[19] Mr. Trump seemed to be saying that resisting arrest and running away excuses a policeman shooting someone in the back twice, and killing them.

On Saturday June 20th, president Trump held a rally in Tulsa, Oklahoma, which had originally been scheduled for the day before, which happened to be the 101st anniversary of a White massacre of an estimated 300 Blacks in Tulsa. June 19th is also Juneteenth, on which the last enslaved persons in Galveston, Texas were notified by Union troops that they were free, and has traditionally been a day of celebration by Black Americans. During the rally Mr. Trump contemptuously referred to the coronavirus pandemic as "kung-flu", as if diseases had nationalities, or could be insulted into oblivion.

Although the management of the BOK center in Tulsa where the rally was held had put "Do not sit here" stickers throughout the arena on every other seat to promote social distancing, Trump campaign workers were documented on video removing the stickers, apparently to create better optics for a crowded rally to please Trump.[20]

Also on July 20th, Homeland Security officials said they were making preparations to deploy federal agents to Chicago, while President Trump threatened to send U.S. law enforcement personnel to other Democratic-led cities experiencing spates of crime.

Trump made the pronouncement as he defended his administration's use of force in Portland, OR, where agents have clashed nightly with protesters and made arrests from unmarked cars. Calling the unrest there "worse than Afghanistan," Trump's rhetoric escalated tensions with Democratic mayors and governors who have criticized the presence of federal agents on U.S. streets, telling reporters at the White House that he would send forces into jurisdictions with or without the cooperation of their elected leaders. "We're looking at Chicago, too. We're looking at New York," he said. "All run by very liberal Democrats. All run, really, by the radical left."[21]

On June 23rd, four doctors including Dr. Anthony Fauci, the nation's top infectious disease expert, testified before the House Energy and Commerce Committee about the COVID-19 pandemic. Dr. Robert Redfield, director of the Centers for Disease Control, said the coronavirus has "brought this nation to its knees." [22]

At that time, the United States had more than 2.3 million confirmed cases and more than 121,000 deaths. With about 4% of the world's population, the United States has had about 25% of the world's deaths from COVID-19 -19.[23] In less than a month, the U.S. saw its death toll from the pandemic jump by 21,000; it had taken three months from February to May, to reach 10,0000.

In his testimony before Congress, Fauci warned that "the virus is not going to disappear," referencing Trump's statement to Fox News Channel personality Sean Hannity last week that the coronavirus is "fading away," as the states reopen. "We are starting up and it's going to be very, very strong," the president said. "We're very close to a vaccine and we're very close to therapeutics, really good therapeutics. But even without that, I don't like to talk about that because it's fading away. It's going to fade away, but having a vaccine would be really nice and that's going to happen."[24]

On June 23rd, president Trump addressed some 3,000 students at the Dream City megachurch in Phoenix, Arizona, where, despite pleas from the mayor, they crowded in, with few wearing masks. Trump told the crowd that "someday" his work on coronavirus testing would "be recognized by history. Someday." Referring to COVID-19 as "the plague" and the "China flu," he told the crowd in Arizona, a state experiencing a deadly spike: "It's going away."[25]

Just before midnight on June 25th, 2020, in the midst of a global pandemic in which the U.S. is seeing the highest national rate of infections in the industrialized world, the Department of Justice filed a brief asking the Supreme Court to invalidate the Affordable Care Act, a k a Obamacare, the health care law that has enabled millions of Americans to get health insurance who otherwise were left out of the existing for-profit system, and despite nine states expanding the ACA to the uninsured in March to enable them to get medical coverage during the pandemic.

In 2020, about 11.4 million people signed up for Obamacare policies, while nearly 12.7 million adults are covered by the law's expansion of Medicaid. The law has increased the number of Americans covered by health insurance and slowed the rise of health care costs across the board.[26]

By Sunday June 28, total U.S. coronavirus cases surpassed 2.4 million, with nearly 125,000 deaths.[27] Texas, Arizona and Florida (all with Republican governors) became new epicenters of the pandemic. The day before, Texas set a record for coronavirus-related hospitalizations for the 16th day in a row with 5,523 patients being treated. Arizona health officials also reported a record, with 2,577 current hospitalizations. On June 26, Florida had reported its highest number of new cases in one day, with close to 9,000;[28] by Sunday state officials said the south Florida beaches of Miami-Dade, Broward and Palm Beach counties would be closed for the July 4th weekend. Notably, all three states had among the shortest times of official shutdown in March-April and fastest re-openings; now they were pulling back from further re-opening.

As Karen Attiah, Global Opinions Editor of the *Washington Post* reported on June 26, "Texas Governor Greg Abbott was an early champion of rushing to reopen the state, despite saying that he knew doing so would put lives at risk. He barred mayors in Texas from fining people who failed to wear masks. In late April, when a Dallas salon owner was jailed for violating Abbott's own executive order to shut down nonessential businesses, he called for her release. Several days later, he eased restrictions on restaurants, malls, and nail and hair salons."[29]

On June 26th, Governor Abbott dramatically ordered a reversal of the state's re-opening, due to a dramatic spike in coronavirus cases there. He ordered bars be shut back down and scaled back restaurant capacity to 50%. He also shut down river-rafting trips and banned outdoor gatherings of over 100 people unless local officials approve.[30]

On June 29 Arizona Governor Doug Doucey followed Abbott's example, ordering the state's bars, gyms, movie theaters and water parks to shut down for at least 30 days, as thousands of new cases of the coronavirus appear daily.[31]

On Friday June 26, the *New York Times* reported that U.S. intelligence officials have concluded that a Russian military intelligence unit secretly offered bounties to Taliban-linked militants for killing coalition forces in Afghanistan, including targeting American troops, amid peace talks to end the 18-year war, saying the Trump administration has been deliberating for months about how to respond.[32] Initially, White House Press Secretary Kayleigh McEnany said that the president and Vice President Mike Pence had not been briefed on the issue, while president Trump dismissed the story as "fake news" in a tweet Sunday June 28th.[33]

That same day, president Trump re-tweeted a video of one of his supporters saying "White power", setting off a "five-alarm fire" in the White House, according to two officials there. Aides couldn't reach the president quickly to get him to delete the offending tweet because he was on the golf course at his club and had put down his phone; the tweet remained on the president's Twitter page for more than three hours.[34]

According to historian and blogger Heather Cox Richardson, "White House aides immediately recognized they had a problem, but it took them three hours to delete the tweet, and even then, no one in the White House denounced it. White House Deputy Press Secretary Judd Deere simply said that the president did not hear the "White power" slogan on the video. Today, McEnany said that Trump had retweeted the video 'to stand with his supporters, who are oftentimes demonized.'"[35]

On June 30th, the Associated Press reported that "Top officials in the White House were aware in early 2019 of classified intelligence indicating Russia was secretly offering bounties to the Taliban for the deaths of Americans, a full year earlier than has been previously reported, according to U.S. officials with direct knowledge of the intelligence.

The assessment was included in at least one of President Donald Trump's written daily intelligence briefings at the time, according to the officials."[36] That day Susan Rice, president Obama's National Security Advisor, wrote an editorial in the *New York Times* blasting president Trump for a pattern of deferring to Putin and Russia, of which his silence on the bounty scandal was typical: "Most recently, we have learned that even Russian efforts to slaughter American troops in cold blood do not faze this president."

"Mr. Trump brushes off the information, evades responsibility and fails to take action — not even lodging a diplomatic protest. Now Mr. Putin knows he can kill Americans with impunity. At best, our commander in chief is utterly derelict in his duties, presiding over a dangerously dysfunctional national security process that is putting our country and those who wear its uniform at great risk. At worst, the White House is being run by liars and wimps catering to a tyrannical president who is actively advancing our arch adversary's nefarious interests."[37]

The same day, Republican party leaders had conceded that wearing masks was necessary for public health; both former Vice President Dick Cheney and his daughter Liz, a Wyoming congresswoman, said that wearing masks was "manly." Even Sean Hannity and Steve Doocy, two of

Trump's most fervent and loyal boosters on Fox News Channel, endorsed wearing masks. "I think that if the president wore one, it would just set a good example," Doocy said Tuesday on "Fox & Friends" as he interviewed Republican National Committee Chairwoman Ronna McDaniel. "MAGA should now stand for 'masks are great again.'"[38]

Also on June 30th, the world count of COVID-19 cases was just under 10,500,000, with deaths at over half a million (510,646). During the month of June in the U.S., the total infection grew by 800,000, led by Florida, Arizona, Texas and California, and the total count was just under 2.6 million,[39] with 129,075 deaths,[40] with 16 states pausing their re-opening plans as 36 states' infection rates were trending upward compared to the previous week.[41] On June 30th, Dr. Fauci and other public health experts testified before Congress on the pandemic.

The U.S. is seeing about 50,000 new cases daily, a national average of 1,000 per state, while the E.U. is only seeing 6,000. According to CNN, Fauci said he was "very concerned" with the increase in cases in some parts of the country and said he wouldn't be surprised if the US begins to see daily new cases coming in at 100,000[42] a day given current trends. He said he couldn't make an accurate prediction of the number of deaths the country will see before the pandemic is over, but noted that "it's going to be very disturbing; I will guarantee you that."[43]

On July 1st, with about 130,000 American deaths so far from the pandemic, President Trump said on Fox News, "I think we're gonna be very good with the coronavirus. I think that at some point that's going to sort of just disappear, I hope."[44]

On July 3rd, as detailed by the *Washington Post,* the Anderson County Review, a rural Kansas newspaper, posted a cartoon to Facebook in response to a new statewide mask order from Gov. Laura Kelly (D). The image showed Kelly in a face covering emblazoned with the Star of David over a photo of Jews in Nazi Germany, with the caption: "Lockdown Laura says: Put on your mask ... and step onto the cattle car." After a weekend of stinging rebukes, the paper's owner and publisher, who is also a GOP county chairman, pulled the cartoon and apologized on Sunday.[45]

On July 5th, the *New York Times* reported that over the weekend, President Trump had falsely and fantastically claimed that while the testing of tens of millions of Americans had identified many cases, "99 percent" of them were "totally harmless." At that point, at least 2.8 million Americans were known to be infected, and public health officials have said the real number of infections may be 10 times higher since testing so many Americans have yet to be tested.[46] Infections announced across the United States the previous week totaled more than 330,000 — a record high that included the five highest single-day totals of the pandemic.

On the same day, more than 40,000 new cases had been announced nationally by evening. That day, former F.D.A. commissioner Dr. Scott Gottlieb said that "certainly more than one percent of people get serious illness" if they are infected. Speaking on the CBS program "Face the Nation," he estimated that when all cases were counted, including asymptomatic ones, between 2 and 5 percent of infected people become sick enough to require hospitalization.[47]

The next day, in the span of just a week and a half, the number of coronavirus cases in the U.S. had doubled, to nearly 3 million infections, and more than 130,000 deaths, with some survivors grappling with long-term complications. In 32 states, the rates of infection were still rising. "We're accelerating nationally...the number of cases still continues to accelerate," said Dr. Peter Hoetz, deal of the National School of Tropical Medicine at the Baylor College of Medicine in Houston. "We're breaking records almost every day here in the state of Texas. People are piling into hospitals, into ICUs. We really can't keep going at this rate."[48]

On July 6th, consistent with President Trump's "Putting America First" posture, his administration notified the World Health Organization that the U.S. would withdraw from that organization effective immediately, although according to a 1948 treaty, the U.S. would need to give a year's notice and pay its debts to the agency to leave.

When President Trump first threatened to withdraw from the WHO, Democratic lawmakers argued that doing so would be illegal and vowed to push back. Trump's push to withdraw in the middle of a pandemic has alarmed health specialists and put America at odds with traditional allies. Joe Biden, the presumptive Democratic nominee, said Tuesday that, if elected, he would immediately rejoin the organization and "restore our leadership on the world stage." "Americans are safer when America is engaged in strengthening global health," he tweeted.[49]

In early July, President Trump sent in law enforcement officers, including some not easily identified as such and some in unmarked vehicles, to Portland to "safeguard federal property", but engaged in tactics–such as seizing protesters not on or near federal property–that were criticized by Portland's mayor and most of the state's congressional delegation. Several lawsuits were filed, including suits by and on behalf of journalists and legal observers against local and federal law enforcement, and suits by the state against several federal agencies. [50]

On July 21, after three months without holding a coronavirus news briefing, President Trump suddenly did. Changing his previously dismissive tone on the topic, he said "It will probably, unfortunately, get worse before it gets better. Something I don't like saying about things, but that's the way it is". Trump also recommended wearing face coverings, something he has not done and had publicly doubted as an effective way to fight the spread of the virus. However, at the same time, he repeated his claim that, contrary to all evidence, the coronavirus will "just disappear."[51]

On July 23, President Trump announced that he had canceled the Republican national convention scheduled for August in Jacksonville, FL, saying he wanted to keep his supporters safe from the coronavirus pandemic and protesters. That day, the *Washington Post,* which has been tracking coronavirus infection statistics, announced that the U.S. has reached a grim milestone of four million people infected with the novel coronavirus, doubling the total number of infections in just six weeks as deaths and hospitalizations continue a sharp rise in many states. The same day, 1,000 new deaths were reported, a record for a single day, bringing the total at that point to 141,000 deaths.[52]

Sunday July 26 capped the deadliest week in the United States since the end of May, as more than 6,300 new coronavirus-related deaths were added to the national toll, with nearly half a million Americans newly reported infections in the past week.[53]

On July 30, the Bureau of Economic Analysis reported that the US economy contracted at a 32.9% annual rate from April through June, its worst drop on record. America plunged into its first recession in eleven years, putting an end to the longest economic expansion in US history and wiping out five years of economic gains in just a few months. Between January and March, GDP declined by an annualized rate of five percent. [54]

On July 31, the $600 weekly unemployment benefits under the CARES act passed by Congress, for those left jobless due to the pandemic expired, leaving millions without a way to pay for rent or food. Senate Republicans refused to vote on an extension of those benefits already passed by the House.

October 31, 2020

On October 25, White House chief of staff Mark Meadows said that the US is "not going to control" the coronavirus pandemic, as cases surge across the country and nearly 225,000 Americans have died from the virus. "We are not going to control the pandemic. We are going to control the fact that we get vaccines, therapeutics and other mitigation areas," Meadows told CNN's Jake Tapper on "State of the Union."[55]

The United States reported 99,321 new coronavirus cases on October 30, the second consecutive day it has seen the highest number of daily infections since the pandemic began, according to Johns Hopkins University (JHU).[56] By Halloween, the US was just shy of adding 100,000 new coronavirus cases, while deaths tallied the day before totaled over 1,000. In the big picture, the US had added nearly a million new cases of COVID-19 in just two weeks, with 230,000 total deaths from COVID-19 by October 30, and over nine million US infections.

Meanwhile, President Trump has been packing his campaign rallies with enthusiastic supporters, most wearing no masks, standing closely together against CDC recommended guidelines, while he claimed at a rally in Wisconsin that the country is "rounding the turn" on the pandemic.[57] An influential model of the coronavirus pandemic has predicted 399,000 total coronavirus deaths in the US by Feb. 1. The US is averaging 74,000 new coronavirus cases daily. [58]

By the end of October, negotiations ended on a second economic stimulus and relief package for the unemployed whose benefits had run out. Senate majority leader Mitch McConnell had told the White House not to conclude a deal before the election,[59] but he ensured that the Senate voted on, and confirmed, President Trump's nominee for the Supreme Court, Amy Barrett, just days before the election.[60]

In 2016, McConnell had refused to allow a senate vote on Merrick Garland, President Obama's nominee for the Supreme Court, claiming that it was inappropriate to confirm a Court nominee in a presidential election year.

Introduction

It's the natural human instinct during awful times to want to retreat like a turtle into one's shell; the home, the church, the circle of friends in your hometown (while trying to maintain safe social distancing in the COVID-19 pandemic), and try to ignore anything outside. However, the time for magical thinking and escapism ("I think that at some point that's going to sort of just disappear, I hope.") is over.

As Abraham Lincoln said in his message to Congress in 1862, "My friends, we cannot escape history. We [of this Congress and this administration] will be remembered, in spite of ourselves."[61] We are Americans, and Americans of conscience (of any or no religion) have always made a difference for this country, and even for the world, by having the courage to affirm the principles on which this country was founded.

In the Declaration of Independence, Thomas Jefferson declared that "We hold these truths to be self-evident; that all men are created equal, that they are endowed by their Creator with certain unalienable Rights, that among these are Life, Liberty and the pursuit of Happiness." He did not say, as many assumed, that "all *White* men are created equal", he said *all* men, although he was unable to stand by his principles by freeing his enslaved workers. We had to endure a terrible Civil War to make clear that distinction, and a century ago we had to further make clear that "men" should have been "persons", and thankfully women are now citizens of equal rights with men.

Jefferson was not an evangelical Christian, but his distillation of Enlightenment philosophy in the Declaration has inspired Americans and oppressed persons the world over for 250 years.

Since 2015 however, covert and systemic racism has broken out in more frequent and violent ways. On the evening of June 17, 2015, Dylann Roof shot and killed nine African American members of the Emanuel African Methodist Episcopal Church in downtown Charleston, South Carolina, while they were meeting for a bible study there, saying that he was trying to ignite a race war.[62]

Eleven days later, Pastor Mike Huckabee, a leading Evangelical voice and sometime Presidential candidate, was asked by a supporter at the Western Conservative Summit how he felt about values in America at that time. This came just after the Supreme Court had ruled that states cannot keep same-sex couples from marrying and must recognize their unions.

Now, a question on "values" could offer a chance to speak on many things, but Huckabee knew the man meant "values" as a code for opposition to gay marriage. Huckabee no doubt pleased the audience when he said that the Supreme Court had tried to "unwrite the laws of nature and the laws of nature's God" with its decision. However, although he could have added something about the problem of violent White supremacists gunning down African Americans in church, he failed to mention the massacre at that time.

You would think a Christian minister would be able to prioritize an answer about values, and at least include a racially motivated massacre of Christians in their church, while speaking on values, which had happened just 11 days prior, but apparently it wasn't as important as a chance to deplore gay marriage. Now, imagine the races had been reversed and a Black man had massacred nine Whites in their church during a bible study. Do you suppose Huckabee would have overlooked that 11 days later in a question about "values"?

Especially with our long and unresolved history of institutional racism, and continuing violence against women, it's very disturbing to this writer to see these things normalized and even encouraged, especially by persons whose lives are of no moral example.

Although I myself have not been a victim of racial violence, I am a long-time resident of Charlottesville, Virginia, where on August 11-12 2017, hundreds of White supremacists, neo-Nazis and affiliated thugs descended on the University of Virginia and the Downtown area, many with riot gear, swastikas, Confederate flags and firearms, for a "Unite the Right" rally to protest the planned (now scrapped) removal of Confederate equestrian statues from public parks, shouting "Jews will not replace us!"

Initially, President Trump (reading from a prepared statement) condemned the violence. Two days later (back on his home turf of Trump Tower), he insisted that there were "very good people on both sides" of the demonstration, creating an alleged, and outrageous, moral equivalency between the opponents of racism and those who came armed and prepared to enact violence on behalf of their racist views.

Heather Heyer, a local resident, had joined a crowd of others protesting the racist rally. According to her mother, Susan Bro, Heather was with the crowd that was peacefully walking down Water Street from the Federal Building. That crowd was chanting in support of Black Lives Matter but stayed away from Lee Park where a confrontation between white supremacists and counter-demonstrators was becoming violent.

"They were joined by some of the activists who were in McGuffey Park and ran down to assist the Friendship Court neighborhood because they had heard that a White militia was there. Word came to them that the residents were handling it themselves, so they joined the marchers, who decided to head up Fourth Street to celebrate the neo-Nazis and others leaving town. They were singing and chanting. Her friends tell me the mood was one of relief and celebration," recounts Bro.

That's when James Alex Fields Jr., a self-styled neo-Nazi, drove his car down Fourth Street and into the crowd of peacefully marching counter-protesters marching up that street, hitting and injuring nearly three dozen people, and killing Heyer. A photo taken at the time showed people thrown off their feet, into the air from the force of the impact. On her Facebook page, Heyer had posted "If you're not outraged, you're not paying attention." Sadly, two state police troopers who were circling the town in a helicopter also died, when it crashed. Many of those who were hit in the deadly car attack sustained painful, long-term injuries.

The failure of the president to condemn not only the violence but the racism that led to it, has encouraged White supremacists to understand that the president is standing with them, which he does nothing to discourage. As of this writing (July 2020), the president has only made his racist rhetoric more strident, in a desperate attempt to energize and motivate his base, although everyone agrees this is only diminishing, not increasing, his support.

On March 15, 2019, Brenton Tarrant, an Australian-born White man launched two well-planned, coordinated attacks in Christchurch, New Zealand on the Al Noor mosque during Friday prayers, then at the Linwood Islamic Center nearby. Using semi-automatic weapons, Tarrant allegedly killed 50 people and injured 50 more, and live-streamed the first attack on Facebook. After arresting him, police found a 74-page manifesto he wrote in which he praised President Trump as "a symbol of renewed White identity and common purpose".[63]

While Trump condemned the killings and offered sympathy for the victims "in places of worship turned into scenes of evil killing," he pointedly did not distance himself from the praise of the alleged mass killer, or condemn White supremacy and the violence done in its name.

When asked about whether he thought violent White nationalism was a problem, he said "I don't, really" when asked whether it was a rising threat around the world. "I think it's a small group of people that have very, very serious problems, I guess," Trump said. Questioned about the accused gunman's reference to him, Trump claimed ignorance. "I didn't see it. I didn't see it," he said. "But I think it's a horrible event ... a horrible, disgraceful thing and a horrible act."[64] During the first 2020 presidential debate on September 30th, Trump also refused to condemn White supremacy (he finally did the next day in an interview on Fox News).

Why does President Trump dodge any responsibility for inspiring this deranged killer? Why did he not condemn White supremacy outright until weeks before the 2020 election? What kind of moral leadership is this from someone who is the leader of the free world and who claims to be a Christian, and why hasn't the (White) evangelical community spoken out against his encouragement of White supremacy and its resulting violence?

However, I'm not concerned just for the safety of my own hometown.

The President has called migrants at our borders an "infestation", and has ordered children to be separated and incarcerated, separately from their parents, then told the parents to "leave with or without your children." His administration failed to meet a deadline set by a judge for the week of July 23rd 2018 to re-unite all families whose children had been taken from them; over 700 children were still unaccounted for when the deadline passed.

On October 22, 2020, a story on CNN explained that this "zero tolerance" policy towards migrants with children has left advocates unable to reach the parents of 545 children still separated from their families -- and that hundreds of those parents were likely deported without their children.[65]

"The problem here is that when the Trump administration decided to separate families back in July of 2017, there was no plan to keep track of the families or ever reunite them," says Nan Schivone, legal director of Justice In Motion, an advocacy organization.

The evangelical community in America has long wanted to brand itself as being for "family values." What kind of "family values" policy is this? Do families have to be White, and legal U.S. citizens, to rate basic Christian (or indeed human) kindness? Although Trump's executive order separating family members (struck down by the courts) was rescinded, the crisis at the border continues, as does Trump's rage at the migrants whose countries are so overrun by gang violence, they walked all the way from Central America to our southern border.

Inside our borders, anti-Semitism has broken out in the kind of violence that we used to associate only with Nazi Germany; on October 27th, 2018, a disturbed gunman burst into the Tree of Life Synagogue in Pittsburgh during Shabbat services and opened fire, killing eleven and wounding six, in the deadliest attack against the Jewish community in American history. [66]Sadly, this was followed only a few months later by another synagogue shooting in San Diego, killing one worshipper and wounding three others.

Roy Moore was a Republican senate candidate from Alabama in 2018. He spent his career as a judge defying the courts on the separation of church and state by refusing to remove the Ten Commandments he ostentatiously installed in his courtroom (violating the Establishment clause of our Constitution), and posturing publicly on his Christian values. During his senate campaign he was called out by *five* ordinary women, for very similar, predatory sexual behavior against them when he was married, in his thirties, and they were all underage.

Far from ending his career with the evangelical community in Alabama, many of them rallied around him, refusing to consider the testimony of five separate, ordinary women in the equation of whether Moore was as much of a moral example as he himself claimed. Although he ultimately lost the race, it was noted that his alleged behavior had seemed to make no difference for his supporters.

On November 13, 2017, Miguel De la Torre wrote in the *Baptist News Global* "Christianity has died in the hands of Evangelicals. Evangelicalism ceased being a religious faith tradition following Jesus' teachings concerning justice for the betterment of humanity when it made a Faustian bargain for the sake of political influence."

A day later, Cal Thomas, a long-time conservative columnist writing for Fox News, pointed out how evangelicals quoting the Bible became corrupted by political goals over the Gospel; he noted that Jim Ziegler, the state auditor of Alabama, had claimed there are many instances in the Bible where older men had sexual relations with young girls, and cited Mary and Joseph as one example! This kind of perversion of scripture is no better than using the book of Exodus[67] to justify the hanging of the victims of the Salem witch trials in 1692-93.

"There is an unstated conceit among some evangelicals that God is only at work when a Republican is elected, even a Republican who does not share their view of Jesus, or practice what He taught. It is the ultimate compromise, which leads to the corruption and dilution of a message more powerful than what government and politics offer," continues Thomas.

In the U.S. (at least during recent Democratic administrations) it had become fashionable to talk about resisting the government, as if it were tyrannical, and lots of hysteria was whipped up about Democratic Presidents (or candidates) intent on seizing citizens' guns. Now, on the other extreme, it has become fashionable (even in some Christian circles) not to challenge anything the Trump administration says or does, even when it's blatantly un-Christian.

When Attorney General Jeff Sessions announced the Trump Administration's policy of "zero tolerance" for migrants arriving at our borders without legal approval, and then separating the children of these unfortunates from their parents to discourage others from following them (without so much as a paper or digital trail with which to track or retrieve them), Sessions quoted Paul's letter to the Romans as a way of claiming some moral high ground which could not be challenged:

"I would cite you to the Apostle Paul and his clear and wise command in Romans 13, to obey the laws of the government because God has ordained the government for his purposes," Sessions said, *The Washington Post* reported. "Orderly and lawful processes are good in themselves. Consistent, fair application of the law is in itself a good and moral thing, and that protects the weak and protects the lawful." The actual verse, Romans 13:1-2 is, "Let every person be subject to the governing authorities; for there is no authority except from God, and those authorities that exist have been instituted by God. Therefore, whoever resists authority resists what God has appointed, and those who resist will incur judgment."[68]

This passage, used by itself in isolation, can (and has) been an excuse for any ungodly power to tell citizens to obey it since that's what the apostle Paul said. It was used by Loyalist preachers to discourage American patriots from revolution, by Southern preachers as a justification for allowing the institution of slavery, and by the Nazis to justify obedience to their rule.

How would you react if you were living in the South at the time of the Civil War and some union officer quoted this passage to you to justify obeying their occupation? How would you feel if you were a German citizen during the Second World War and you were told to obey the Nazi government because of this passage? Whom would you serve, Hitler or

Jesus?

If we continue to read Paul's letter to the Romans, however, we see that he assumes that secular authorities act to protect everyone from wrongdoers. "For rulers are not a terror to good conduct, but to bad. Do you wish to have no fear of the authority? Then do what is good, and you will receive its approval; for it is God's servant for your good. But if you do what is wrong, you should be afraid, for the authority does not bear the sword in vain! It is the servant of God to execute wrath on the wrongdoer."[69]

But don't all Christians have a duty to challenge, and even resist the government, if it uses force to pull families apart for partisan political ends? In Acts 5, the chief priests challenge Peter and the apostles, whom they had told not to speak of Jesus or the Resurrection; "But Peter and the apostles answered, 'We must obey God rather than any human authority.'"[70]

How do you feel about our government seizing children and separating them from their parents, just because the president wants to teach migrants some kind of a lesson, especially since some 545 remain separated from their parents at the time of this writing? Many of these children were so young at the time of separation it is difficult for them to tell advocates where and how to find their parents.

How would you feel if you were visiting some foreign country with your family and the authorities separated you from your children just to send a message to the American president? Would you be willing to "obey the authorities?" If you voted for the President, how would you feel if these foreign authorities told you they would hold your children hostage to teach *you* what it feels like to be on the other side of such a policy?

Things have gotten to the point where some people claim that President Trump is more of an authority for them than Jesus. On November 20th 2017, on CNN's "New Day" program which featured a panel of Trump supporters, one supporter said he likes that the President's cabinet is filled with millionaires and that he would take the President's word even if Jesus were to contradict it. I have not heard that the President reprimanded this man or reminded everyone that he is not God.

The migrant crisis at the border continues with terrible disregard to human suffering by our Trump administration. Although the forced separation of family members was discontinued, our nation still bears actual and moral responsibility for re-uniting 545 children with their families. By May 2019, we knew of at least six children taken from their migrant parents who had died in custody.[71]

At the end of March 2019, the U.S. Customs and Border Protection Commissioner Kevin McAleenan said that the "breaking point has arrived this week" for the US immigration system. McAleenan announced that nearly 40,000 migrant children had been taken into custody at the U.S./Mexico border in March alone (in December 2018, two Guatemalan children died after they were detained with their fathers after crossing the border). How can this kind of inhumanity be defended, and biblically justified, by *any* American administration, and what will you do about it, in your life and your public witness?

As 2020 has shown us, (largely) peaceful protests have been met with increasingly violent action from White supremacy groups, under the name of "law and order." 2019 was the deadliest year for domestic extremist violence since the Oklahoma City bombing of 1995. White supremacists were responsible for most of such deaths in 2019, 39 out of 48.[72]

On October 6th 2020, Chad Wolf, the acting Secretary of Homeland Security, released his department's annual assessment of violent threats to the nation. In a foreword, Wolf wrote that he was "particularly concerned about white supremacist violent extremists who have been exceptionally lethal in their abhorrent, targeted attacks in recent years. [They] seek to force ideological change in the United States through violence, death, and destruction."[73]

Just two days later, the FBI arrested 13 right wing extremists in an alleged plot to kidnap Michigan governor Gretchen Whitmer and put her on trial for imposing pandemic safety precautions on the public.

There are some signs of hope. On Dec. 19th, 2019, editor Mark Galli of *Christianity Today*, founded by the late Rev. Billy Graham, wrote in an editorial for that magazine that President Trump's actions and behavior regarding his attempt to force President Zelensky of Ukraine to open a phony investigation into Joe Biden by withholding nearly $4 million of congressionally-approved military aid, warranted his impeachment and removal from office.

Despite loud condemnations of Galli by Trump and some evangelical leaders, subscriptions to *Christianity Today* actually increased despite some cancellations. Progressive Christians all around the country were encouraged and excited by Galli's brave example, although he stepped down as editor.

I believe I have a calling through this book, in dark, chaotic and confusing times, to invite other Christians to ask themselves what Christianity is and should be, and what it is not, here and now in the United States of America.

Daring to speak honestly about Christianity can hopefully guide us to practice honest Christianity, now in this life, and to see the difference that makes in the world around us. Since the 500th anniversary of the start of the Reformation was marked in 2017, considering what I've outlined above, I believe it's time to examine the contradictions between what we say Christianity is and how it is practiced, especially in the U.S. today, and to call for a new Reformation, in the country with more active Protestant churches than any other in the world.

I welcome readers of any or no faith. For faithful Christians of any denomination, this book is a call to take your faith seriously as a commitment where your relationship with Christ becomes one where you hear and can answer His call. Too often, for Americans, merely "believing" in Christ has been enough. Christ did ask us to believe in Him, but he also issued a call to all his disciples and to us, "Follow me."

Chapter One

Martin Luther and the Legacy of the Reformation (A Lutheran Perspective)

You probably know that 2017 was the 500th anniversary of the start of the Protestant Reformation, which had a lasting religious, cultural and political influence on Western civilization to the present. In the United States, Protestant denominations still hold the majority of religious affiliations (although religious affiliation is now less than 50% of all adults), with 70.6% of American adults self-identifying as Christians, 46.5% of them Protestant (and 55% of those self-identifying as evangelicals), and 20.8% of them Catholic, in a 2014 study.[74]

Interestingly, although the percentage of evangelical Protestants has grown by four percent since 2007 while the percentage of "mainline" Protestants (such as Lutherans and Methodists) and Catholics has shrunk over three percent, the number of "unaffiliated" American adults (think "spiritual but not religious") has grown the most, from 16.1% in 2007 to 22.8% in 2014.[75]

Although I welcome readers of any interest and faith background (including none), this book is primarily addressed to American Protestants, since they are the largest group of Christians in the U.S. and since many of them are politically engaged. Since this is my own faith tradition, I want to speak from that tradition to others within it about a common heritage and purpose.

With the 500th anniversary of the Reformation just behind us, it's appropriate to look at what it was and what its founder, Martin Luther, did and said that became such an important and enduring part of the Christian faith. This can help us clarify how Protestantism began, and help us ask ourselves if what is being called Protestant Christianity in America today remains true to its original intentions.

Richard G. Leahy

Martin Luther was an extraordinary man who had an extraordinary influence beyond his lifetime, although he was not a braggart and claimed that it was not him, but the Word of God (which he translated into everyday German) that accomplished any change people credited him with. He disagreed with calling his followers "Lutherans" ("What is 'Luther'? he asked") and insisted that "Christian" or "evangelical" were the only proper names for those who professed Christ as their savior.[76]

Luther was born in 1483 in Saxony, Germany to a father who was a member of the rising class of proto-merchants. Hans Luther realized his son was intelligent, and being ambitious, saw that he got good primary schooling, so he would eventually become a lawyer. He was educated at Erfurt University where he received a master's degree in 1505.

His life changed dramatically when, in July 1505, he was on his way to university on horseback when he was overtaken by a violent thunderstorm which struck him as the wrath of God, he later told his father. When a lightning bolt struck near him, he cried out, "Help! Saint Anna, I will become a monk!" [77] (Saint Anna was the patron saint of miners; his father began as one before becoming a refiner, so it was natural for him to call on the family's patron saint.)

Luther was nothing if not stubborn and sincere, and considered his vow to become a monk as something he could not break.[78] Despite his father's anger of what he saw as a wasted opportunity, Luther left law school and entered St. Augustine's Monastery in Erfurt on 17 July 1505.

Far from achieving inner peace, Luther's time in the monastery was a period of despair, he later reflected. He said, "I lost touch with Christ the Savior and Comforter, and made of him the jailer and hangman of my poor soul."[79] Despite a regimen of self-denial, prayer, and penance, he felt he stood condemned before God, probably due to post-traumatic stress after imagining the thunderstorm and lighting bolt he had been caught in were meant for him and his sins.

Fortunately for Luther, his superior, Johann von Staupitz, was a kind man who helped Luther understand that true repentance is about a change of heart, not outward actions. After Luther was ordained in 1507, von Staupitz had the foresight to have Luther sent to teach theology in the new university of Wittenburg (also in Saxony). By 1512 Luther had received his doctorate of theology, and succeeded von Staupitz as the chair of theology, where he spent the rest of his career.

Moving from solitary (and perhaps obsessive) contemplation, Luther was able to challenge his intellect in the university, and serve both his students and his Augustinian order. As was common in university faculties, he would engage in debates with other scholars.

In 1517, when events took place that led to the Reformation, Leo X was the Pope. While a noted patron of the arts, Leo X was a lavish spender. He rebuilt St. Peter's basilica and bankrolled the Sistine Chapel by Michelangelo and works by Raphael, He also led a costly war in the Marche region of Italy to install his nephew as Duke of Urbino, in addition to fighting a war against the (Catholic) King of France.

In short, the Pope was spending a great deal of money on things that Jesus would not have considered necessary for the care of the faithful. At this point, opportunism met necessity in the form of the most notorious commission-based traveling salesman in Western history: Johann Tetzel, a Dominican friar and preacher. His employer, Albrecht von Brandenburg, the Archbishop of Mainz, was himself deeply in debt to Rome and was obliged to raise money to pay for the building of St. Peter's basilica.

"Indulgences" were basically a gimmick to buy forgiveness of sins. You could buy them for yourselves, your family, or even deceased relatives. Their sale even had the 16th century equivalent of a commercial jingle, to the effect that

> "As soon as the coin in the coffer rings,
> The soul out of Purgatory springs."

Tetzl had already been selling indulgences for the building of St. Peter's for seven years and was noted as a successful salesman. Accordingly, von Brandenburg obtained permission from the Pope to conduct the sale of a special indulgence, half of the proceeds of which would be given to von Brandenburg to pay his debts to Rome, while Tetzel and his subordinates pocketed the rest. Perhaps it was their idea of the "Great Commission."

Luther was offended as much by the jingle as by the insinuation that salvation could be bought for a buck. He was by this time used to making detailed academic arguments on theology, and on October 31, 1517 he (according to popular legend) posted his list of complaints on the church door of Wittenburg, enclosing a copy in a letter to his bishop (who happened to be Tetzel's employer, von Brandenburg). His complaint was formally titled "Disputation of Martin Luther on the Power and Efficacy of Indulgences", which came to be known as the *Ninety-five Theses*.

Scholars like Hans Hillerbrand point out that it is unlikely Luther thought he would be confronting and challenging the entire authority of the Catholic church, but was merely pointing out a fundamental breach of Christian doctrine.[80] "Luther firmly declared that, since forgiveness was God's alone to grant, those who claimed that indulgences absolved buyers from all punishments and granted them salvation were in error. At the same time, he said that Christians could not absolve themselves from the responsibilities of following Christ on account of such false assurances."[81]

Luther's theological challenge might have gone very differently, had not another group with its own financial agenda not taken advantage of the situation: printers, who, as they are today, were looking for something salacious that would sell copy, thanks to Gutenberg and his invention of the moveable type printing press circa 1440.

When word got out that there was a challenge to the sale of indulgences by the head of theology at the university of Wittenburg, the opportunistic printers took Luther's public posting and did the 16th century equivalent of making it "go viral"; they printed them without his knowledge or permission, and the cat was out of the bag with the Catholic authorities.

Luther had written his 95 theses in Latin, the language of the church, but within three months, friends of Luther had translated the theses from Latin into German, and the printers found this material, accessible to any educated German, a hot item. Within two weeks of their translation, copies of the theses had spread throughout Germany; within two months, they had spread throughout Europe.[82] The Reformation, without anyone planning to do so, had been launched.

In 1520, as he continued to study the scriptures, Luther published three of his best-known works: *To the Christian Nobility of the German Nation, On the Babylonian Captivity of the Church*, and *On the Freedom of a Christian*.

Through these studies, Luther became convinced that the Catholic Church had lost sight of the essential truth of the Gospel: a Christian could only be granted salvation by God's grace alone, not through actions like penance, or giving alms, or buying indulgences. His source for this (to show it was not something he just made up) was Paul's letter to the Ephesians; "For by grace you have been saved through faith, and this is not your own doing; it is the gift of God—not the result of works, so that no one may boast."[83]

"This one and firm rock, which we call the doctrine of justification", he wrote, "is the chief article of the whole Christian doctrine, which comprehends the understanding of all godliness," Luther explained.[84] He further elaborated based on scripture as follows:

The first and chief article is this: Jesus Christ, our God and Lord, died for our sins and was raised again for our justification (Romans 3:24–25). He alone is the Lamb of God who takes away the sins of the world (John 1:29), and God has laid on Him the iniquity of us all (Isaiah 53:6). All have sinned and are justified freely, without their own works and merits, by His grace, through the redemption that is in Christ Jesus, in His blood (Romans 3:23–25). This is necessary to believe. This cannot be otherwise acquired or grasped by any work, law or merit. Therefore, it is clear and certain that this faith alone justifies us ... Nothing of this article can be yielded or surrendered, even though heaven and earth and everything else falls (Mark 13:31). [85]

The bishop Albrecht von Brandenburg did not reply to Luther's 95 theses, but forwarded them to Rome. Luther was summoned to Rome by Pope Leo to explain himself. Fortunately for Luther, Friedrich, the Elector of Saxony (so called because as a leading German prince, he held a hereditary right to elect the Holy Roman Emperor from amongst other peers) looked kindly on Luther. Friedrich also realized that if Luther went to Rome, he would most likely be martyred there as a heretic.

Accordingly, Friedrich arranged for Luther's examination to be held in Augsburg, where the Imperial Diet was held. Luther was examined for three days by the papal legate, Cardinal Cajetan, in December 1518. Rather than risk arrest by the Cardinal, Luther, with the help of a Carmelite monk, left the city during the night.

Luther was not looking for further confrontation, and in early 1519 when he was examined in Saxony by the papal *nuncio* Karl von Miltitz (a relative of Elector Friedrich), he agreed that he would remain silent on his doctrine of justification by faith, if his opponents would not challenge him openly.[86]

Once again, the course of history might have been very different, but for the fervent opposition to Luther from the Catholic theologian Johann Eck. He not only viewed Luther as a heretic but wanted to expose his doctrine in a public forum, where the Catholic Church would be forced to deal with it. In June and July 1519, he arranged a public disputation with Luther's colleague Andreas Karlstadt at Leipzig, and invited Luther to speak.[87]

Luther took the bait; during the disputation, he made an implacable enemy of Eck by claiming that there was no scriptural basis for the idea that popes had exclusive right to interpret scripture, and that therefore neither popes nor church councils were infallible.[88] In response, Eck called Luther a new "Jan Hus" (a Czech reformer who, a century earlier, had been burned at the stake as a heretic), and Eck then decided to devote himself to Luther's defeat.[89]

From this point, a formal break with Rome was all but inevitable. In 1520 the Pope sent Luther a papal edict warning him that unless he recanted his 95 theses and 41 other writings within 60 days, he would be excommunicated. Luther, who had sent the Pope a copy of *On the Freedom of a Christian* in October 1519, reacted by publicly set fire to the edict at Wittenberg on December 10th 1520, an act he defended by writing *Why the Pope and his Recent Book are Burned* and *Assertions Concerning All Articles*.[90] Unsurprisingly, the Pope responded with a bull (edict) titled *Decet Romanum Pontificem* on January 3rd, 1521 that formally excommunicated Luther. Far from being contrite, when Luther received the bull, he invited friends in Wittenburg over, then publicly set the bull on fire.

The civil authorities were to enforce Rome's ban on the publication of the 95 theses, so the Diet of Worms (a town on the Rhine) was called into session on the matter from January to May of 1521. Friedrich the Elector of Saxony, mindful of the danger Luther was in, asked for safe transport for him to and from the Diet.

The Diet was an assembly of the princes of the Holy Roman Empire who, since the days of Charlemagne, had been charged with safeguarding both the Pope and the Catholic Church. In addition to the regular German princes, the Holy Roman Emperor Charles V attended, though he was just 17 at the time.

Luther's nemesis Johann Eck asked him if he still stood by his contentious writings. Luther's famous reply, which formally marked the start of a "conscious" Reformation, was:

> Unless I am convinced by the testimony of the Scriptures or by clear reason (for I do not trust either in the pope or in councils alone, since it is well known that they have often erred and contradicted themselves), I am bound by the Scriptures I have quoted and my conscience is captive to the Word of God. I cannot and will not recant anything, since it is neither safe nor right to go against conscience. May God help me. Amen.[91]

It is important to note that Luther raised the importance of Christian conscience in his refusal to recant what he had said. Since the Diet was a secular meeting, it was the Emperor who would decide what would happen. Five days after Luther's affirmation, on May 25, 1521, The Emperor issued the Edict of Worms which declared Luther an outlaw and a "notorious heretic", banning his literature, and requiring his arrest. It also made it a crime for anyone in Germany to give Luther food or shelter, and permitted anyone to kill Luther without legal consequence.[92]

Friedrich the Elector knew what he was doing when he extracted a promise of safe conduct for Luther both to and from the Diet. The Elector had Luther intercepted on his way home in the forest near Wittenberg by masked horsemen impersonating highway robbers. They escorted Luther to the security of the Wartburg Castle at Eisenach,[93] free from vigilante fanatics who now had the Emperor's permission to kill Luther without punishment. You could say Luther was taken into "protective custody".

To further protect Luther, he was given the identity of a knight while living at Wartburg Castle. He stayed at the castle for ten months, which gave him the time, security and means to devote himself to one of his greatest achievements; translating the New Testament from Greek into everyday German. He spent a lot of care in choosing the German words of his translation, with the intention that every German household would be capable of understanding them without difficulty.

His translation was so admired that it became the foundation of the standard modern German vocabulary. Luther's translation was not the first, but it quickly became a popular and influential Bible translation. It included notes and prefaces by Luther, and with woodcut illustrations by Lucas Cranach, and played a major role in the spread of Luther's doctrine throughout Germany.[94] The Luther Bible influenced other vernacular translations, such as William Tyndale's English Bible, a precursor of the King James Bible.[95] Luther then turned to a translation of the Old Testament, with collaborators, which was completed and published in 1534.

In November 1521, Luther wrote *The Judgement of Martin Luther on Monastic Vows*. He assured monks and nuns that they could break their vows without sin, because vows were an illegitimate and vain attempt to win salvation.[96] As a result, men and women in holy orders began to abandon their convents and monasteries. This presented a social problem for the women however, since there was no socially respectable place for a single woman in early modern European society outside their family home.

In April 1523, Luther helped 12 nuns escape from the Nimbschen Cistercian convent by hiding them in empty herring barrels leaving the convent. One of them, a noblewoman named Katharina von Bora, decided that if she had to marry someone, she might as well marry Luther himself. This was not on Luther's mind, but as he later wrote to Wenceslaus Link, "Suddenly, and while I was occupied with far different thoughts, the Lord has plunged me into marriage."

Marriage made Luther a better Christian, putting him the position of both husband and father, and it also made him a better person. It gave him the perspective of the ordinary husband with duties and responsibilities, as well as the discipline and sometimes humbling experience of marriage. He had written to a friend that he had decided to resist marriage because he "daily expected the fate of a heretic,"[97] but after probably initially refusing Kate for that reason, she probably said she'd be content to take her chances.

Although it had its trials, and he was 41 at the time while she was 26, Martin and Kate seemed to have had a happy marriage, for the times and circumstances. She bore him six children, two of whom died as children. He wrote his Small Catechism in 1529 intended for parents to teach core Christian principles to their children while they were growing up, no doubt influenced by his experience in raising and instructing his own children (his larger Catechism was intended for pastors and church leaders.

The catechisms provided easy-to-understand instructional and devotional material on the Ten Commandments, the Apostles' Creed, the Lord's Prayer, baptism, and the Lord's Supper.[98] Luther wrote questions and answers on these subjects into the catechism so that the basics of Christian faith would not just be learned by rote, "the way monkeys do it", but understood.[99] Luther had hated the rote learning he had had to endure as a young student and wanted to communicate the faith in a more meaningful way.

In this way, Luther also designed a new church service to be conducted in German, and in which the congregation fully participated. He had found, surveying the churches in Saxony, that both the pastors and the laity understood next to nothing of Christian doctrine; "Merciful God, what misery I have seen," Luther wrote, "the common people knowing nothing at all of Christian doctrine ... and unfortunately many pastors are well-nigh unskilled and incapable of teaching."[100]

Luther's liturgy included congregational recitation of the Creed and the Lord's Prayer, so that each person would affirm their belief in their own words. Instead of a private confession to a priest, Luther designed a corporate confession, where everyone would jointly, aloud, confess that they had sinned and needed God's forgiveness.

I personally like this corporate confession for several reasons. First, consistent with Luther's theology, forgiveness is not in the hands of another person to give or withhold. Second, it should keep everyone honest. Public, joint confession lets everyone hear themselves and their neighbors admitting that they cannot save themselves, and calling on God for forgiveness. The pastor then reminds the congregation that Christ died for their sins, and that our faith in his redemption makes it available to us as a gift of grace; we have not earned it.

The text is from First John: "If we say that we have no sin, we deceive ourselves, and the truth is not in us. If we confess our sins, he who is faithful and just will forgive us our sins and cleanse us from all unrighteousness. If we say that we have not sinned, we make him a liar, and his word is not in us."[101]

An important change Luther brought to the new service was the role of music, and how it was performed. In the traditional Catholic Church, the choir sat in front of the congregation, facing one another across the aisle, and sang to God. In Luther's new format, the congregation sang hymns, creating and sharing the music, with words in the vernacular.

Luther also reduced the number of sacraments from seven, in the Catholic Church, to two. His criteria were that a sacrament needed to have been instituted by Christ himself, and that it has both physical and spiritual components. This gave both simplicity and focus to the Lutheran worship. Baptism and Holy Communion are the two Lutheran sacraments.

Luther could be superstitious; like most people of that age, he believed that devils and demons roamed the countryside. The sound of sacred music, he believed, helped drive them away. He wrote many hymns himself, some adapted from chants he remembered from his Augustinian order, but some of his own creation. His most famous, "A mighty fortress is our God", based on Psalm 46, is widely used by Protestant churches and is very inspirational to both hear and sing.

The use of hymns sung by the congregation in their own language is now used by all Protestant churches, and even the Catholic church lists "A mighty fortress" in its hymnal. Luther also used hymns as a way to teach articles of the faith, such as the Apostle's Creed, the Ten Commandments and the Lord's Prayer.[102]

Luther's natural musical talents, and the use of hymns as instruments of religious instruction, inspired classical composers to follow his example. The most prolific, and (now) famous of these, was Johann Sebastian Bach, who wrote cantatas, masses, chorales and organ works setting the Scriptures to music, or adapting Luther's own hymns.

Franz Schubert wrote a "German Mass", quite simple and straightforward, where the performance was done by the church congregation and both performing and listening were affirmations of faith, with the text in German; interestingly, Schubert was Catholic. Perhaps the most famous example for the layman is the "Messiah" oratorio by George Friedrich Handel.

Luther developed a view of the world known as the doctrine of the "Two Kingdoms." The world was to be ruled by temporal authorities, to which a Christian was subject as a good citizen, but ultimately, he believed that the world was doomed, and Christians should have as their primary allegiance the Lord Jesus Christ, while they awaited his Second Coming. In his view, the temporal authorities were useful for enforcing civil laws, but did not have authority to advise or compel Christians on matters of faith. This could keep the civil authorities from using their power to enforce religious views. The kingdom of God on earth was the church and its living members, which Luther called "God's 'right hand;'" the rest of creation and human institutions were "God's 'left hand.'"

Luther had a dark side. He was bold, stubborn, passionate, and could be obstinate and ornery (bad health exacerbated his bad moods). He was also prone to fits of depression which he called "attacks" (*anfechtungen*) which could immobilize him for days. He was dismayed, then shocked, when the German peasants saw in his challenge to Rome's authority a sign that they should also challenge the feudal order.

To be sure, the peasantry had many legitimate complaints. Luther however had not challenged the secular authorities; his argument lay with the Pope and the Catholic Church. He was appalled at the consequences of challenging or removing the rule of law which he believed would result in chaos and catastrophe. In his "Kingdom of the Two Worlds" thinking, he believed that a Christian lived in the world and should obey secular authority, in the way that St. Paul had justified it in Romans 13: 1-4, but that the world was doomed and a Christian's true spiritual home was with Christ in paradise.

Accordingly, if people invited chaos by challenging the secular authorities in the way the peasants and their allies (some nobles in deep debt) were, they threatened civil society itself. In 1524, peasant revolts broke out in Franconia, Thuringia and Swabia (southern Germany). Touring Thuringia himself, Luther was shocked to see monasteries, libraries, and bishop's palaces burned and looted.

Luther's response was, to put it ironically, "over-kill." He wrote in *Against the Murderous, Thieving Hordes of Peasants* that the violence was the devil's work, and called for the nobles to put down the rebels like mad dogs.[103] The peasant army was defeated in the battle of Frankenhausen in 1525 and their radical leader Müntzer was executed. The next year, Luther wrote: "I, Martin Luther, have during the rebellion slain all the peasants, for it was I who ordered them to be struck dead."[104]

Luther was also possibly the most influential and extreme anti-Semite until the rise of racial anti-Semitism in the late 19th century. In 1523, his book *That Jesus Christ was Born a Jew,* Luther argued that they should be treated kindly by Christians, to turn them from the error of their ways and convince them to convert.

When this failed, he hardened his attitude. In 1543, he wrote two polemics; *On the Jews and Their Lies*, and *On the Holy Name and the Lineage of Christ*. In them he claimed that the Jews were no longer the chosen people but "the devil's people" because they had rejected Christ. Luther advocated setting synagogues on fire, destroying Jewish prayer books, forbidding rabbis from preaching, seizing Jews' property and money, and smashing up their homes, so that these "envenomed worms" would be forced into labor or expelled "for all time".[105]

On the Jews and Their Lies is a baffling title until you realize that the German words for "lies" and "Jews" rhyme. Reportedly, Luther started writing it just after his daughter Magdalena died in his arms, and this was how he dealt with his grief and bitterness. Still, this is no excuse for constructing a religious justification for persecution, robbery and murder against an entire people, especially the people of Jesus. Understandably, Luther's writings were enthusiastically embraced and cited by Hitler and the Nazis as respectable justification for their extermination of the Jews, not to mention expropriation of their property, goods and money.

Since the 1994, the Evangelical Lutheran Church in America and other Lutheran denominations such as the Missouri Synod have formally repudiated Luther's religious arguments for anti-Semitism and their use to justify persecution of the Jews[106] but all Protestants should be aware of the danger of uncritically buying into anti-Semitic conspiracy theories, and the shameful history and consequences of Luther's anti-Semitism for the last 500 years, and repudiate it. As a graduate student of modern German history, I was told by my Jewish professor (with evident glee) that the Protestant clergy of Germany were, as an occupational group, some of Hitler's most reliable supporters.

Richard G. Leahy

The Legacy of Luther and the Reformation

Luther was a complex, and highly influential man. He never claimed to be a "good" man, saying before he died "Truly, we are all beggars". I'm not trying to make him a hero; he is much like St. Peter who on the one hand told Jesus in front of the other disciples that he believed him to be the Son of God, and then was rebuked by Jesus minutes later for telling him that his rejection and crucifixion should never happen.

Luther's insight and doctrine of "Justification by Faith" was what opened the door to the Protestant Reformation in all its many denominations. This is not only an important legacy, but something every Protestant should embrace. After all, if we are saved by works, then we cannot really be saved at all. When a certain ruler asked Jesus, "Good Teacher, what must I do to inherit eternal life?" Jesus said to him, "Why do you call me good? No one is good but God alone."[107] Indirectly, Jesus was showing the ruler that he was acknowledging Jesus' divinity.

Luther's doctrine of "Two Kingdoms" gave a place of honor to temporal civil authorities while affirming that the Christian belonged first, and ultimately, to God. His separation of these two kingdoms was practical, but also avoided the trap of temporal authorities being given authority over religious matters, to avoid religious wars and persecution for dissenting religious views by the state.

The Two Kingdoms doctrine would have a big impact on the men who influenced the building of the American Constitution. James Madison, the main author of the First Amendment, explicitly credited Martin Luther as the theorist who "led the way" in providing the proper distinction between the civil and the ecclesiastical spheres.[108]

Luther's distinction was also adopted by John Milton and John Locke, the latter being much admired by Thomas Jefferson. Locke had echoed the "two kingdoms" doctrine:

There is a twofold society, of which almost all men in the world are members, and from that twofold concernment they have to attain a twofold happiness; viz. That of this world and that of the other: and hence there arises these two following societies, viz. religious and civil.[109]

The thoughts of Madison and Locke were echoed by those of Thomas Jefferson, third President and author of the *Statutes for Religious Freedom in Virginia,* which dis-established the Episcopal Church in that state, meaning that the state would not tax its citizens for that church's benefit. This was the model subsequently reflected in the First Amendment, prohibiting the "establishment of religion", or in other words that neither the federal government nor the states could officially favor, and support, one religion over any other (including denominations of Christianity).

Luther's rejection of the Catholic Church hierarchy as a necessary intermediary for Christian souls to receive salvation, and his belief in the sainthood of all believers, anticipated the democratization of secular government and the ideals of the Enlightenment of the mid and late 18th century.

Luther's primacy of the conscience as a spiritual guide was taken up after World War II by UNESCO (United Nations Educational, Scientific and Cultural Organization) in its Memorandum on Human Rights cited the Reformation, because of its "appeal to the absolute authority of the individual conscience, as one of the historical events most responsible for the development of human rights."[110]

This chapter was sub-titled "A Lutheran perspective", both in general and specifically from a Lutheran individual. This is not meant to suggest that Lutheran teachings are "better than" those of other Christian denominations, but as an opportunity to connect us with the roots of the Reformation so we can take stock of how faithful Protestant Christianity in America may or may not be. Luther always pointed towards the scriptures, and we need to be sure we are taking our moral cues from them, rather than political or cultural influences.

We need to safeguard our faith from opportunistic political and cultural forces that would have us believe that Christians need to follow particular candidates or parties. God is not a Republican (or a Democrat)[111], and we should consider how Luther framed the Christian conscience; as being bound by scripture. With a sincere devotion to scripture (meaning you can't just pick and choose what is convenient for you, but are bound to the whole), Luther recognized the Christian conscience as a person's guide, rather than a hierarchy of priests, but that also applies today to a whole bevy of self-interested political parties, candidates and factions who want to appropriate the "Christian vote" (as if there was only one) for their own cynical aim.

As we have seen, Luther's anger against the Jews, and his rather casual approval of robbing them of property and burning their synagogues, was a disastrous failure of humanity, not to mention Christian charity, and was enthusiastically employed by the Nazis as justification for their genocide against Jews. Through his fear of the threat of anarchy in the Peasant's Revolt, Luther want off the deep end in enthusiastically recommending their slaughter.

All of this proves that Luther was, as he would admit, a sinner in need of God's grace. Through his sincere devotion to a life of Christian integrity, his brave stand against the Catholic hierarchy, and translation of the Bible into everyday speech, he not only made the Reformation possible, but made an important contribution to the idea of the worth of the individual conscience, the separation of church and state, and the democratization of republican government, all of which we as Americans benefit from.

Martin Luther's prophetic example was lived out by a father and son pair who were also ministers. In 1934, Michael King, an African American preacher at the Ebenezer Baptist Church in Atlanta, visited Germany and was so inspired with the example of Martin Luther that he changed his and his son's first names from Michael to Martin Luther. That son, Martin Luther King, Jr. would become the spiritual leader of the Civil Rights Movement which, through the Civil Rights Act, abolished racial discrimination as legally permissible. At the time of his assassination in 1968, King was planning a Poor People's Campaign for the American poor of all races.

While Luther was the first, many other clergy were moved by the Spirit to continue to contribute to the Reformation; John Calvin in Geneva and later the Puritans and Presbyterian denominations, Zwingli in Switzerland and later the Mennonites in America, the Society of Friends (Quakers) in England and America, John Wesley and the Methodist denomination, Roger Williams and the Baptist denomination, and the leaders of the African American churches, segregated from their White brethren, who upheld both the Gospel and the prophetic tradition of challenging social injustice, and many others.

This inclusion of other Protestant denominations does not mean I reject the Roman Catholic Church. Indeed, there has been a doctrinal reconciliation between the Catholic Church and major Protestant denominations, in a group known by the acronym LARCUM; Lutherans, Anglicans, Roman Catholics and United Methodists, that seeks ongoing ecumenical communion between them.

The idea of focusing on Luther was to take us back to the beginning of the Reformation so we could learn from the clarity of Luther's faith and teachings to practice Christianity that is honest, has integrity, and free from the control of today's secular culture or political agendas.

As we will see, Luther was far from perfect, but his antisemitism was not part of his Reformation teachings. Since Christianity in the United States is largely Protestant, it's appropriate to consider how it all began, in order to see if and how we've wandered from the original genius of the Reformation.

Concluding Prayer for This Chapter

Heavenly Father, we thank you for the witness of your prophets through the ages, especially for Martin Luther, and his courage in witnessing to the truth that we are "saved by grace through faith," not by our efforts or through human intercessors. As Americans we thank you that our Founding Fathers had the wisdom to separate church and state so that each could, as Luther said, be free to have authority in their own realms, and that we are not bound to any particular church or religion as Americans. We also thank you for Luther's emphasis on the importance of Christian conscience, and for those Americans who affirmed this in the Abolitionist movement, the struggle for women's' right to vote, and the Civil Rights Movement to ensure equal opportunity and dignity for all citizens.

Chapter Two

Is the United States a "Christian" Nation?

We need to understand the difference between a nation that is full of individual Christians and their churches, and a nation where any specific religion has official government sanction. The First Amendment to the U.S. Constitution (also first in the Bill of Rights) prohibits the making of any law respecting an "establishment of religion," as well as prohibiting infringements on free speech and a free press, the right for peaceable assembly, and the right to petition the government.

The first part is known as the Establishment Clause, ensuring that there is no prohibition on the free exercise of religion. This has been understood to mean that our federal government abstains from recognizing as "true", or even official, any particular religion, so that all religions may be practiced in private (so long as they don't involve human sacrifice or other such abuses), as well as in public.

Some evangelicals have claimed that "since the Founding Fathers were Christian, the Constitution is a Christian document, and we are a Christian nation." This overlooks several things, and is an illogical syllogism.

The Founding Fathers were more motivated by the ideals of the Enlightenment than by Christian dogma. As Benjamin Franklin noted, "How many observe Christ's birthday! How few, his precepts." Thomas Jefferson was a Deist who edited the Gospels with a scissors, removing what he felt were superstitious, non-rational parts such as miracles.

The Establishment Clause of the Constitution, specifically repudiating a favored place for any particular religion, also repudiates the notion that it is a "Christian" document. Just because many Americans are Christian, it does not logically (or legally) follow that the national government is, or should be, "Christian", and how would that even be defined, and by whom?

Finally, while it is true that Christianity has thrived in America, a blessing for both the nation and the religion, a nation that is filled with practicing Christians, influencing the country for good, is not the same as one where Christianity is the "official" religion, despite the Rev. Jerry Falwell's declaring (without bothering to offer any evidence) in 1976 that "There's no question about it, this nation was intended to be a Christian nation by our founding fathers."[112]

To settle the matter, the Treaty of Tripoli in 1796, between the United States and the "Bey and subjects of Tripoli of Barbary", contains a clause in Article 11 stating that "the Government of the United States of America is not, in any sense, founded on the Christian religion."[113]

In considering our religious heritage as Americans, we should also consider recent history at the time the Constitution was designed. Religious dissenters like the Puritans left Britain for America to be free to worship as they felt directed by their consciences. Ironically, Roger Williams, the founder of the first Baptist Church in America, had been a Puritan but had been exiled by the Massachusetts Bay Colony where the (Puritan) church and secular state were entwined, for spreading "new and dangerous ideas."

The 17th century Wars of Religion in Europe joined church and state in "holy" wars, supposedly to fight "heretics", but really to advance the influence of one state over another. To show you how little this had to do with matters of faith, Cardinal Richelieu of France supported Protestant forces fighting fellow Catholic Hapsburgs in Germany. Richelieu's first loyalty was to France, despite his being not only a Catholic, but a Cardinal!

In the British Isles, this played out as a very long-running insurrection by the Scots and Irish to depose Protestant monarchs and replace them with Catholic Stuarts.

Having a Protestant monarch did not secure the religious liberties of the Scots or Irish, or even the English if they belonged to a non-Church of England Protestant sect. This is why the Puritans sailed to Plymouth Bay in what became Massachusetts, and also why other Dissenter denominations like the Quakers (Society of Friends) and Presbyterians came to colonial America from England and Scotland, and why the Amish came from Germany.

Roger Williams was a century ahead of his time in how he thought of private religion and the state. When exiled from the Massachusetts Bay Colony by intolerant Puritans, he had to wander the nearby estuarine wilderness west of the Seekonk River. Due to his respect for Native Americans, he in turn was respected by them and was allowed to bring fellow refugees like Ann Hutchison to his Providence Plantation, for which he later obtained a royal charter as the new colony of Rhode Island. This began a tradition of religious tolerance in Rhode Island, where the first synagogue in the English colonies was established.

Williams was an enlightened, godly man of integrity. He was a firm advocate for religious freedom, or "liberty of conscience," separation of church and state, and fair dealings with American Indians. He was one of the first abolitionists, and wrote an influential book, *A Key into the Language of America* (1643), in which he also wrote some observations about the natives' behavior and urged toleration for them:

> Boast not proud English, of thy birth & blood;
> Thy brother Indian is by birth as Good.
> Of one blood God made Him, and Thee and All,
> As wise, as fair, as strong, as personal.[114]

I mention Williams here because he was the first to use the metaphor of a "wall of separation" between church and state, which was later used by Thomas Jefferson in his *Letter to Danbury Baptists* (1801).[115]

American Baptists today should remember that they were once a persecuted religious minority, and that Williams, though he could have followed the example of the Massachusetts Puritans in creating a Baptist theocracy in Rhode Island, decided against it. Williams considered it "forced worship" if the state attempted to promote any particular religious idea or practice, and he declared, "Forced worship stinks in God's nostrils."[116]

As educated persons, the Founding Fathers were well aware of the recent history of religion, war and politics in Europe, and of what they considered the evil of favoring any religion or sect above another. At the same time, the English colonies in America all had established religions. This means that not only were the colonial churches "official" in the legal sense, but citizens of other, or no faith, were compelled to pay taxes to support the churches and their clergy.

In *Notes on the State of Virginia,* Thomas Jefferson observed that "It does me no injury for my neighbor to say there are twenty gods, or no god. It neither picks my pocket nor breaks my leg." Why should it be another person's business, or more importantly, the government's, to judge or censor a person's private beliefs?

Jefferson's Enlightenment ideals and commonsense pragmatism led him to draft, and submit to Virginia's General Assembly, the Statutes for Religious Freedom in Virginia which they approved in 1786. This disestablished the Episcopal church, and not only in Virginia, but was used as a model for all other new American states. Importantly, it did not only level the field for all Christian denominations, but also legalized any other religious tradition including Judaism, Islam, and Hinduism.

This was remarkable when you consider the legacy of the Puritan church in Massachusetts, the Catholic church in Maryland (specifically founded by Lord Baltimore for English Catholics), or the Episcopal Church in most of the 13 colonies. It was a brilliant way to leave the nastiness of church and state collusion that had had such a sordid history in Europe behind, and helped the young American nation demonstrate to the world that in the world of faith and ideals, the "worshiping field" was level.

In his argument for the necessity of the Statutes, Jefferson echoed Martin Luther in explaining that "That to compel a man to furnish contributions of money for the propagation of opinions, which he disbelieves is sinful and tyrannical." Jefferson himself considered the Statutes such an important achievement that he had it listed as one of his three major achievement on his tombstone, along with being the author of the Declaration of Independence and the founder of the University of

Virginia (which was the first university in the Western world to be founded without an affiliation with a church).

Jefferson's dis-establishment of the Episcopal church was welcomed by Baptists of his day, who were being persecuted because they did not belong to the Congregationalist establishment in Connecticut. In a letter by the Danbury Baptist Association to Jefferson in 1802, they affirmed the beliefs of Roger Williams for the liberty of conscience: "Our sentiments are uniformly on the side of religious liberty--that religion is at all times and places a matter between God and individuals--that no man ought to suffer in name, person, or effects on account of his religious opinions--that the legitimate power of civil government extends no further than to punish the man who works ill to his neighbors..."[117]

Jefferson's response ("Letter to the Baptists of Danbury") is summarized as follows:

Believing with you that religion is a matter which lies solely between Man & his God, that he owes account to none other for his faith or his worship, that the legitimate powers of government reach actions only, & not opinions, I contemplate with sovereign reverence that act of the whole American people which declared that their legislature should "make no law respecting an establishment of religion, or prohibiting the free exercise thereof," thus building a wall of separation between Church and State.[118]

The Virginia Statutes for Religious Freedom paved the way for the inclusion of the Establishment Clause in the First Amendment to the Constitution and in the Bill of Rights. It was his affirmation of Williams' "wall of separation" between church and state and "liberty of conscience" that he meant in his letter to Benjamin Rush of September 23, 1800 when he wrote, "For I have sworn upon the altar of God eternal hostility against every form of tyranny over the mind of man;" this is his epitaph on the national Thomas Jefferson Memorial at the tidal basin in Washington, D.C.

When Jefferson's home Monticello was sold to pay his debts after his death, it was acquired by Uriah Levy, the first Jewish Commodore (admiral) in the U.S. Navy. Levy was inspired by Jefferson's work with the Statutes, and in appreciation for Jefferson's contribution to religious freedom in America, he used his own funds to repair and restore the house which otherwise would have fallen into ruin. Ironically, at the outbreak of the Civil War, the Confederate Government seized Monticello as enemy property, but Levy's estate recovered it after the war, and his nephew Jefferson Monroe Levy took control of it in 1879, continuing to maintain and repair the premises; together the Levy's preserved Monticello for future generations over a century.

After many years of fundraising and restoration, Monticello has been painstakingly restored, with many of Jefferson's personal effects added to the estate, and his gardens and grounds having been restored based on his garden book, including a vineyard planted to classic European varieties (now grafted on American rootstock). Today, Monticello hosts a naturalization ceremony for new citizens every Fourth of July (also the day on which both Jefferson and John Adams died in 1826).

While it's a fact that our national government does not, and should not, favor a particular religion, persons of (any) faith should engage in our political process so that their convictions can contribute to the greater good. In fact, since colonial times, the United States has seen successive waves of (Protestant) religious revival which began in the religious community but expanded beyond, to influence national politics for the better.

This began with the Puritan Awakening which brought the Pilgrims to settle Massachusetts, through the Great Awakening which influenced the American Revolution, to the Second Great Awakening from the mid-1880s to 1908 which attacked the social and economic ills of laissez-faire Capitalism, to the Civil Rights Movement for African American equality.

In each of these "Awakenings", we see the dynamic of religious revival and secular reformers whose coincidental efforts bring forth a new and improved America. While Christians of all kinds were prominent in advocating for social justice in these Awakenings, Jews and those from other religious communities as well as persons of conscience from non-faith communities, have all made their contributions towards improving America with pressure for social justice. Because faith was separate from government, it was free to encourage people of faith and their religious communities to pressure the government on issues of social justice without being pressured by the government to knuckle under.

We've touched on the unfortunate consequences for those who ended up on the losing side of the struggle for secular power between religious sects in the British Isles in the 17th and 16th centuries. In places like Northern Ireland, this entwined political and religious struggle had deadly, recurring consequences until 1994. With the awful example of ISIS, we see how the combination of totalitarian control of the state by religious leaders leads to tyranny and fanaticism with no space for the individual conscience to be heard or even respected.

However, our own American history demonstrates that even a "godly" Protestant community, if it combines both civic and temporal authority, can by tyrannical. From February 1692 to May 1693, mass hysteria led to accusations of witchcraft against 200 people in the Puritan villages of Massachusetts, most infamously, Salem. Nineteen of these were found guilty and hanged (fourteen women and five men), while a man who refused to testify was pressed to death with rocks.

As a bad example for American government, the witch trials cast a long shadow over our history. The historian George Lincoln Burr states "the Salem witchcraft was the rock on which theocracy shattered."[119] As early as 1695, the Quaker Thomas Maule criticized the handling of the Salem (and related) trials by the Puritan leaders in chapter of his book *Truth Held Forth and Maintained,* stating that "It were better that one hundred witches should live, then that one person be put to death for a witch, which is not a witch."[120]

Maule's articulation that it is better for those who may be guilty to go free than for the innocent to be punished has been (at least, until very recently) a foundational American value. Lenin, for example, believed the opposite was necessary for the success of the Bolshevik Revolution, which is now on the ash heap of history, with millions of innocent victims.

Unfortunately, Maule had to pay a price for his stand of conscience. For his public criticism of Puritan leadership, he was imprisoned for a year before being tried and then found not guilty.

The Founding Fathers were well aware of the dangers of established (state-funded and supported) religion, and were able to save the integrity of both through the Establishment Clause of the First Amendment. As we have seen, throughout American history churches (and other communities of faith) have responded as witnesses to God in the face of social injustice, from slavery to child labor to objectification of women.

Concluding Prayer for This Chapter

Lord, we thank you for the wisdom of our Founding Fathers in keeping church and state separated, to keep both in integrity from coercing or corrupting the other. Let us celebrate the freedom we have as Americans to worship as the Spirit guides us, and let us use that freedom not only to find spiritual sanctuary but to advocate local and national government on behalf of the needy, and to enact responsible policies to prevent people from becoming disadvantaged.

Chapter Three

It's Not Just <u>What</u> You Believe,
But <u>How</u> You Believe That Matters

Are Christians "Better" than other people? Recalling what we learned in chapter one, we should affirm as Martin Luther did, that "We are saved by grace through faith, and this is not your own doing; it is the gift of God— not the result of works, so that no one may boast."[121]

Humility is an interesting virtue, in that we prefer to see it practiced by others than to practice it ourselves. When it comes to Christian identity however, it does matter that we are clear on the order in which our salvation happens. God may guide us to Him through Christian parents, a special person like a minister or friend, or through the Word. It is up to us to affirm Christ as our Lord, as an act of faith, which is made possible through grace.

It's important to then consider the next verse (10) of Ephesians 2, following "For by grace you have been saved through faith, and this is not your own doing; it is the gift of God— not the result of works, so that no one may boast." It is, "For we are what he has made us, created in Christ Jesus for good works, which God prepared beforehand to be our way of life."[122] So with affirmation of faith and salvation by grace, should come a willingness to live out this faith in good works, since God intended this for us as "our way of life."

While the performing of good works (by anyone of any or no faith) is a better way to live than mere self-indulgence, and was intended by God to be our way of life, how can we think that we, or other Christians, are "better" than non-Christians, since we did not and indeed cannot earn our own salvation? As Paul said in Romans 3, "For there is no distinction, since all have sinned and fall short of the glory of God; they are now justified by his grace as a gift, through the redemption that is in Christ Jesus, whom God put forward as a sacrifice of atonement by his blood, effective through faith."[123]

Anyone who feels superior at being a Christian should remember what John the Baptist said in Luke 3:8: "Bear fruits worthy of repentance. Do not begin to say to yourselves, 'We have Abraham as our ancestor'; for I tell you, God is able from these stones to raise up children to Abraham."[124]

We are called to live lives that inspire others, and draw them to Christ. As He said in the Sermon on the Mount, "You are the light of the world. A city built on a hill cannot be hid. No one after lighting a lamp puts it under the bushel basket, but on the lampstand, and it gives light to all in the house. In the same way, let your light shine before others, so that they may see your good works and give glory to your Father in heaven."[125]

Are we living our lives faithfully enough to give others cause to glorify our Father in heaven on account of our good works? And is it our place to dismiss or criticize the works of non-Christians, merely because they follow another (or no) faith? We should celebrate all the people of goodwill who are working in their own ways and traditions to contribute to the common good, globally and locally, and try to work with them and appreciate them; after all, this world can't have too many people of goodwill these days.

We can't celebrate the importance of the individual conscience in the tradition of the Reformation, without acknowledging that it applies to all people. And we are all works in progress, so you have no way of seeing someone today and concluding that God is finished with them. Consider this parable Jesus told in the Gospel of Matthew:

"What do you think? A man had two sons; he went to the first and said, 'Son, go and work in the vineyard today.' He answered, 'I will not'; but later he changed his mind and went. The father went to the second and said the same; and he answered, 'I go, sir'; but he did not go. Which of the two did the will of his father?" They said, "The first."[126]

Getting into debates about whether Christians are "better" than other people brings up the title of this chapter. In exploring "how you believe matters as much as what you believe," we should note that our motives matter. Why would you want to position yourself (and your religious brethren) as being "better than others", since we can't save ourselves or boast of our works?

Remember how the disciples James and John, sons of Zebedee, had the nerve to ask Jesus if each of them could sit at his left and right hands. When the other ten disciples heard of it, they were angry.

So Jesus called them and said to them, "You know that among the Gentiles those whom they recognize as their ruler's lord it over them, and their great ones are tyrants over them. But it is not so among you; but whoever wishes to become great among you must be your servant, and whoever wishes to be first among you must be slave of all. For the Son of Man came not to be served but to serve, and to give his life a ransom for many."[127]

Perhaps the most inspiring exhortation on Christian humility came from the Apostle Paul in his letter to the Philippians:

Do nothing from selfish ambition or conceit, but in humility regard others as better than yourselves. Let each of you look not to your own interests, but to the interests of others. Let the same mind be in you that was in Christ Jesus, who, though he was in the form of God, did not regard equality with God as something to be exploited, but emptied himself, taking the form of a slave, being born in human likeness. And being found in human form, he humbled himself and became obedient to the point of death— even death on a cross.[128]

Why focus on motives mattering? Because the Gospel contrasts the way Jesus lived with his disciples and how he performed his ministry, with the correctly legalistic but spiritually empty way that the Pharisees and scribes of His day lived. In Matthew chapter six, Jesus warns his disciples against putting on a show of piety that is not sincere.

"Beware of practicing your piety before others in order to be seen by them; for then you have no reward from your Father in heaven." He then gives them several examples: giving alms, fasting and praying ostentatiously and conspicuously, "so that they may be praised by others."

Instead he tells them to pray and fast in secret, and when giving alms, "do not let your left hand know what your right hand is doing."

Why is this important? Because doing something good for an impure motive means one can't expect a reward for it from the Lord, since the motive corrupted the doing of the deed. When Jesus gives several examples of ostentatious (and corrupt) piety, he tells the disciples repeatedly, "Truly I tell you, they have received their reward," meaning the public attention they got is all they will get for their trouble.[129] How many of our prayers and good deeds are free from selfish motives?

In his writing "Letter from the Recording Angel", Mark Twain assumes the voice of an angel in heaven responding to weekly prayers made by a miserly coal merchant in Buffalo. The angel alludes to the role of motives in prayer, and the distinction between "public prayers" made with earnest ostentation before multitudes, and "secret supplications of the heart", which no one else but God hears, which "always receive our first and special attention."

The angel points out that there are only two classes of Christians; "professing Christians," and "professional Christians," and explains "By a rigid rule of this office, certain Public Prayers by Professional Christians are forbidden to take precedence over Secret Supplications of the Heart."

For example, the recording angel pointed out that the merchant's prayer for God to "be mercifully inclined toward all who would do us offense in our persons or property," was a public "Family Prayer," contradicted by the merchant's Secret Supplication of the Heart "for application of some form of violent death to the neighbor who threw a brick at the family cat, whilst same was serenading."[130] Does this hypocrite think he can fool God as well as his neighbors?

Luther was unsentimental about human nature and knew how easily people can fool themselves. He even argued that every good work designed to attract God's favor is a sin.[131] All humans are sinners by nature, he explained, and God's grace (which cannot be earned) alone can make them just. On 1 August 1521, Luther wrote to his theologian friend Melanchthon on the same theme: "Be a sinner, and let your sins be strong, but let your trust in Christ be stronger, and rejoice in Christ who is the victor over sin, death, and the world. We will commit sins while we are here, for this life is not a place where justice resides."[132]

Luther also said that all the people who were so sentimental about the birth of Christ, saying they all would have been at the manger in Bethlehem, were fooling themselves; they would not have welcomed the Holy Family, he wrote.

Today we have seen millions of Christians blithely unconcerned about separating children from immigrant parents at our borders, because they have been told that these aren't people equal to them. President Trump has described them as "rapists" and even "animals", to justify inhumane treatment under his administration. Would these Christians have left their comfortable homes to trek to a stable in Bethlehem, to visit immigrant parents, when the mother wasn't even married?

In Jesus, we see one who obeyed, and taught others to obey the Law (the Ten Commandments and the many ritual practices of Judaism), but whose motive--love so great as the salvation of mankind--made his ministry and teachings transformational. There are many worthwhile examples in the Gospels to learn how motives matter. One of the Pharisees asked Jesus to eat with him, and he went into the Pharisee's house and took his place at the table.

And a woman in the city, who was a sinner, having learned that he was eating in the Pharisee's house, brought an alabaster jar of ointment. She stood behind him at his feet, weeping, and began to bathe his feet with her tears and to dry them with her hair. Then she continued kissing his feet and anointing them with the ointment. Now when the Pharisee who had invited him saw it, he said to himself, "If this man were a prophet, he would have known who and what kind of woman this is who is touching him—that she is a sinner." Jesus spoke up and said to him, "Simon, I have something to say to you." "Teacher," he replied, "speak." "A certain creditor had two debtors; one owed five hundred denarii, and the other fifty. When they could not pay, he canceled the debts for both of them. Now which of them will love him more?" Simon answered, "I suppose the one for whom he canceled the greater debt." And Jesus said to him, "You have judged rightly."

Then turning toward the woman, he said to Simon, "Do you see this woman? I entered your house; you gave me no water for my feet, but she has bathed my feet with her tears and dried them with her hair. You gave me no kiss, but from the time I came in she has not stopped kissing my feet. You did not anoint my head with oil, but she has anointed my feet with ointment. Therefore, I tell you, her sins, which were many, have been forgiven; hence she has shown great love. But the one to whom little is forgiven, loves little." Then he said to her, "Your sins are forgiven." But those who were at the table with him began to say among themselves, "Who is this who even forgives sins?" And he said to the woman, "Your faith has saved you; go in peace.[133]

There's a lot going on in this story, but it's a good passage for illustrating why motives matter. The Pharisee invites Jesus to dinner at his house, but shows a disappointing lack of hospitality and respect, neglecting the common courtesy shown to guests, not to mention an honored prophet. Why then, did he invite Jesus to dinner at his house? From what we know of his attitude, it could have been to show Jesus off to his other guests; "The Teacher came to *my* house for dinner."

It was clear that affection for Jesus was not his motive. Jesus could tell that Simon judged him for letting a "sinner" touch him (likely a euphemism for her being a prostitute).

This story shows a dramatic difference in the attitude of two people judged very differently by society; a respectable Pharisee, and a female "sinner" (women were already considered the inferiors of men). It is the female sinner who knows who Jesus is and treats him with reverence and respect, in an intensely touching way, from the heart. All that Simon can think of is that Jesus can't really be a prophet for letting a woman like that touch him.

In Matthew chapter five, Jesus begins a lesson by affirming his reverence for the Law:

> Do not think that I have come to abolish the law or the prophets; I
> have come not to abolish but to fulfill. For truly I tell you, until heaven
> and earth pass away, not one letter, not one stroke of a letter, will pass
> from the law until all is accomplished. Therefore, whoever breaks one
> of the least of these commandments, and teaches others to do the
> same, will be called least in the kingdom of heaven; but whoever does
> them and teaches them will be called great in the kingdom of heaven.
> For I tell you, unless your righteousness exceeds that of the scribes
> and Pharisees, you will never enter the kingdom of heaven.[134]

Jesus' audience were his Jewish disciples, so the specific language about
"not one stroke of a letter will pass from the law" would be powerfully
meaningful to them. But to their ears, the last verse must have been
astonishing. How could anyone's righteousness exceed that of the scribes
and Pharisees? These people lived righteousness, as far as fulfilling the
letter of the law went.

Jesus then goes on to explain with many examples what he meant by
this. If keeping the law allows you to look good publicly, but you don't live
a sincere inner life, then it's just phony righteousness, for show.

> You have heard that it was said to those of ancient times, 'You shall not
> murder'; and 'whoever murders shall be liable to judgment.' But I say to
> you that if you are angry with a brother or sister, you will be liable to
> judgment; and if you insult a brother or sister, you will be liable to the
> council; and if you say, 'You fool,' you will be liable to the hell of fire."
> "You have heard that it was said, 'You shall not commit adultery.' But I
> say to you that everyone who looks at a woman with lust has already
> committed adultery with her in his heart." "It was also said, 'Whoever
> divorces his wife, let him give her a certificate of divorce.' But I say to
> you that anyone who divorces his wife, except on the ground of
> unchastity, causes her to commit adultery; and whoever marries a
> divorced woman commits adultery.[135]

Motives matter, says Jesus. You can fool other people by looking respectable but none of that matters to God if it's all just a front. Jesus is demanding! Who can pass this kind of test? No one—on their own merits or efforts. It's only grace that gives us the faith to ask Jesus to make us His and guide us, and to forgive our shortcomings. But remember, we are still bound to forgive others; it's so important that it's part of the Lord's prayer.

"Then Peter came and said to him, "Lord, if another member of the church sins against me, how often should I forgive? As many as seven times?" Jesus said to him, "Not seven times, but, I tell you, seventy-seven times."[136] Jesus then tells them the parable of the servant who owed a great sum who managed to beg forgiveness from his master, only to throw a fellow servant in jail who owed him a very small amount and who begged him to let him repay, but the servant refused.

When his fellow slaves saw what had happened, they were greatly distressed, and they went and reported to their lord all that had taken place. Then his lord summoned him and said to him, 'You wicked slave! I forgave you all that debt because you pleaded with me. Should you not have had mercy on your fellow slave, as I had mercy on you?' And in anger his lord handed him over to be tortured until he would pay his entire debt. So, my heavenly Father will also do to every one of you, if you do not forgive your brother or sister from your heart.[137]

There are several examples of Jesus technically breaking the Law by doing something on the sabbath. In Mark chapter two, he and his disciples are walking through a grain field, and they plucked heads of grain for food. The Pharisees complained to Jesus, asking "Why are they doing what is not lawful on the sabbath?"[138] Jesus points out first, that King David ate the bread at the altar, which only priests were allowed to eat, and shared it with his companions, so there was a precedent. "Then he said to them, 'The sabbath was made for humankind, and not humankind for the sabbath; so, the Son of Man is lord even of the sabbath.'[139]

Next, Jesus cures a man with a withered hand on the sabbath.

Again, he entered the synagogue, and a man was there who had a withered hand. They watched him to see whether he would cure him on the sabbath, so that they might accuse him. And he said to the man who had the withered hand, "Come forward." Then he said to them, "Is it lawful to do good or to do harm on the sabbath, to save life or to kill?" But they were silent. He looked around at them with anger; he was grieved at their hardness of heart and said to the man, "Stretch out your hand." He stretched it out, and his hand was restored. The Pharisees went out and immediately conspired with the Herodians against him, how to destroy him.[140]

Notice that before he healed the man with the withered hand, Jesus knew the Pharisees were waiting for him to break the law of the sabbath (Jews kept the sabbath by doing no work on that day). I like how he challenged them by asking them "Is it lawful to do good or to do harm on the sabbath, to save life or to kill?" They did not answer, and were only waiting to judge him for a technicality, instead of praising God for this miracle and the difference it would make in the life of this man.

They were proud keepers of the Law, but their motives were not pure because they would condemn Jesus for healing a man with the power God had given him, just because it was on the sabbath. Jesus had said at the end of chapter two, that "The sabbath was made for humankind, not humankind for the sabbath."

It's about having the courage to see where God's priorities would be, even if they seem to conflict with the Law, and while Jesus follows the Law, He knows that there can be times when the priorities of God, showing love and mercy, are worth affirming even if they happen to break a technicality of the Law.

If we worship the Law but leave no place in our hearts for love, we are not living godly lives, because our priorities are misplaced.

Concluding Prayer for This Chapter

Lord Jesus, thank you for the many ways you show us that sincere Christianity requires obedience, humility and action that helps others and comes from the heart. Help us always to remember that our motives matter in whatever we do, but that we don't have to earn your favor since we accept it by grace through faith. Teach us to love others more than ourselves or our own comfort. "Create in me a clean heart O God, and put a new and right spirit within me. Cast me not away from your presence, and take not your holy spirit from me. Restore to me the joy of thy salvation and sustain me in a willing spirit."[141]

Chapter Four

The Church in The World

Christian Integrity

Although the church is an intentional religious community that consciously sets itself apart from society, it is influenced by society, and all its members are influenced by it. There examples of communities that attempt to resist this tendency, more or less. The "religious" in holy orders in the Catholic or Greek Orthodox churches live very obviously and intentionally separate from the world; to a lesser extent, so do the Amish (a Swiss anabaptist sect most prominent in Pennsylvania). A common and recurring question for Christians over the centuries is to what extent one can practice honest Christianity in the society of the day.

In the United States, there are Christians of all denominations who self-identify with secular political labels or sensibilities, as well as with some cultural values or trends. This has always been the case, and the danger of turning our backs on the world is to forget our duty to be God's ministers in the, and to the world.

In the Evangelical Lutheran Church in America (the majority organization for Lutheran churches in the U.S.) we call it "God's work, our hands." How can we pray that God help the miserable, homeless and hungry, if we do not provide for it with our own hands, donations and the work of relief organizations?

In the first letter of James, the apostle writes "Religion that is pure and undefiled before God, the Father, is this: to care for orphans and widows in their distress, and to keep oneself unstained by the world." [142]

I know a retired pastor who once preached a very insightful sermon at my church, on the topic of "The Good Shepherd," from the tenth chapter of the Gospel of John:

Very truly, I tell you, anyone who does not enter the sheepfold by the gate but climbs in by another way is a thief and a bandit. The one who enters by the gate is the shepherd of the sheep. The gatekeeper opens the gate for him, and the sheep hear his voice. He calls his own sheep by name and leads them out. When he has brought out all his own, he goes ahead of them, and the sheep follow him because they know his voice. They will not follow a stranger, but they will run from him because they do not know the voice of strangers."

Naturally, this parable is a metaphor, and Christians are very comfortable in the metaphor of Jesus as the Good Shepherd. Rev. Larry Closter pointed out that the sheepfold, or stone enclosure, was meant to keep the sheep safe at night, but they could not survive for long in the sheepfold. Jesus is the gatekeeper, and is the one who opens the gate "and leads them out."

Where does he lead them? "I am the gate. Whoever enters by me will be saved, and will come in and go out and find pasture. The thief comes only to steal and kill and destroy. I came that they may have life, and have it abundantly." [143] The sheep can only have abundant life by going, through Jesus, to the pasture where their food is, and to the sheepfold, where they can rest at night.

The pasture is in the world. The sheepfold is separate from the world, but there is no nourishment there for the sheep, only temporary shelter. Here Jesus shows us that he is the safe passage between haven and our daily toil to find nourishment in the world. And as we are in the world, that is where we witness to Him, in our lives and in our Christian works to help others and our church (what we Lutherans call time, treasure and talent).

There is a dilemma in the U.S. for any congregation of any faith: how to attract members without compromising on the core tenants of that faith? As we've seen, the U.S. has no official religion, which is meant to keep both the state and churches honest.

One down side to freedom of worship without state oversight, is the competition for members in the marketplace of the faithful. Let's face it, being a Christian and participating in a church community are both commitments that fly in the face of entertainment and the self-indulgent culture of the world.

But what if churches are tempted to become clubs, just another attraction in the marketplace that puts self-indulgence (spending revenues on church movie theaters or bowling lanes and such), or indulging its members in imagining that they are somehow better than others, ahead of ministering to the needy at home and abroad?

I have seen this trend and there are many examples, especially among the mega-churches where the head count of parishioners might be valued above actual ministry beyond the congregation. This isn't as much about dogma, as it is integrity of purpose.

This is one problem of a free church in a free marketplace: how can you attract and retain members (and their donations) while remaining true to the Gospel? There's always a temptation for a church to latch onto a popular cultural trend and hope to attract more members and become more "relevant" that way. These trends can be political (either liberal or conservative), or cultural, and the temptation may not always be a conscious one, as we all live and breathe in the culture of our times as do fish in the water.

This is generally not as much of an issue for Catholics as for Protestants in the U.S. Since a Catholic diocese takes a top-down management approach to its faithful and assigns them to parishes, "shopping around" for a parish that fits one's sensibilities is frowned on.

For American Protestants, however, there is a great temptation to "shop" for a church that fits one's tastes and sensibilities, whether or not these are true to the Gospel. In the competition for parishioners, churches can find themselves pandering to the tastes of the marketplace instead of providing an honest presentation of the Gospel. This should always remind parishioners that they are in constant need of God's grace, but that salvation frees us to live as agents of God's love in this world.

Richard G. Leahy

One temptation is to foster the idea that a church can offer its parishioners a safe refuge from "the world", which can become a cocoon where there is little or no ministry to the needy in the community or the world. This can lead to a slippery slope where a church puts all its resources into recruiting new members, and spending revenues on essentially entertainment facilities for its own members. Is this really ministry? I still remember an article from *Newsweek* in the 1980s talking about the mega-church phenomenon, in which one such church built a bowling alley for its members.

In the next issue's letters section, I'll always remember the brief but powerful letter of a Catholic nun, who pointed out that "On the last day, the Lord Jesus will tell the faithful, 'I was hungry and you fed me, naked and you clothed me, in prison and you visited me, thirsty and you gave me to drink.' I hardly expect him to add, 'I was bored, and you took me bowling.'" Imagine if Jesus had told someone "Follow me", and they replied "Yes Lord, but first let me go bowling with my friends."

It's about priorities. Indulging ourselves while retreating from the Lord's work is hard to justify, especially if you spend church money for the entertainment of its members that could be used for the needy.

Another problem of finding a church based on your sensibilities is the problem of what a minister friend of mine calls PLU, or "people like us." Protestant churches are notorious for factionalism and splits in the congregation, with one faction often storming out in a huff to start a new congregation, leaving the "problem people" behind, but there's no guarantee the same thing won't keep happening. This started with the Puritans leaving Britain for Massachusetts Bay, but continued in America.

Roger Williams, co-founder of the first Baptist church in the New World, began as a devout Puritan member of the Bay Colony, but was evicted because his faith led him beyond blind obedience to that church's dictates. He crossed into what is now Rhode Island, which became a haven for religious freedom in early colonial America.

We all feel comfortable in a church where others are like us, but the

Church does not exist to please your sensibilities. The honest mission of the church is to witness to God to and through its members, and to reach out to those in need. If you feel you have to leave your church because you don't like the minister, there could be good reasons for this, but if you feel you have to leave because the people aren't enough like you, you should ask yourself what your own priorities are in attending church in the first place. Is it to find a comfortable social club, a mutual admiration society (who always seem to need a group of people they can mutually dislike as well), or because it's the respectable thing to do? As Mark Twain once wrote, "Virtue has never been as respectable as money."[144]

Churches can also become political clubs with a religious affiliation. Lutherans have been called one of the "purple tribes" of America because they can be either politically liberal or conservative. Also, we Lutherans don't consider it good form to inquire of a fellow parishioner person what their political affiliation is, because worshipping together isn't about being in a political club. I like worshipping with people who may or may not agree with me on politics, because our common bond is our faith, which should transcend politics.

In the Lutheran church, you may see the American flag in the narthex (or space just outside the sanctuary), but you will not find it in the sanctuary, because this is holy space, and symbolizes the kingdom of God, not the kingdom of this world. I think this is a respectful and appropriate separation of church from state, even church from country or nation. Of course, you love America, but as Jesus said, "Give to the emperor the things that are the emperor's, and give to God the things that are God's,"[145] and "My kingdom is not from this world."[146]

For if you place the American flag in the sanctuary, how are you sure you won't confuse who is the God you're worshipping; Jesus, or "America?" Have you ever considered that they are not the same? Could not the church be corrupted by the idea of America being greater than other countries, especially if the symbolism of the nation is in the place of worship?

If you attend a church where you're pretty sure you know how everyone else votes (the same way), what's your real priority; adding religious certification to a political club, or worshipping and serving the Lord? Why would He not also belong to others who may disagree with you politically? I like the bumper sticker I have seen that says "God bless everyone. No exceptions." That is His way.

I feel uncomfortable in a church where the God seems to be, not Jesus, but respectability, with everyone always dressed in their Sunday best and the children all told to behave and not embarrass their parents, and the minister is always so smiling and upbeat and cheerful.

It's not that this is bad, but if it's all there is, then it doesn't really speak to people about how God can be there for them in dark and painful times in their lives. It may even give people the impression that their pain and sorrow have no place in the church, which can seem to only exist to encourage people to show how happy they are that Jesus has saved them. That's pretty superficial and insubstantial, sort of the religious equivalent of cheery television programming. After all, "He was despised and rejected by others; a man of suffering and acquainted with infirmity."[147]

I respect pastors who can speak to their congregations about their own brokenness; it allows me to acknowledge my own brokenness as a constant state of my humanity, while reminding me we are all saved by God's grace.

However, the opposite of superficial cheerfulness is no better. As an example, I can think of nothing worse than the "sermon" of Amos Starkadder, leader of the Quiverers, a sect that makes Calvinism look down downright jolly by contrast. Starkadder was a character in *Cold Comfort Farm*, a novel by the British author Stella Gibbons.

Starkadder explains to his niece Flora Poste, the protagonist, that his followers are called Quiverers because "They quiver from the visions of damnation that are set before them," and launches into the following tirade by way of a sermon:

Ye miserable, crawlin' worms. Are ye here again then? Have ye come like Nimshi, son of Rehoboam, secretly out of your doomed houses, to hear what's comin' to ye? Have ye come, old and young, sick and well, matrons and virgins, if there be any virgins amongst you, which is not likely, the world being in the wicked state that it is. Have ye come to hear me tell you of the great, crimson, licking flames of hell fire? Aye! You've come, dozens of ye. Like rats to the granary, like field mice when it's harvest home. And what good will it do ye? You're all damned! Damned! Do you ever stop to think what that word means? No, you don't. It means endless, horrifying torment! It means your poor, sinful bodies stretched out on red-hot gridirons, in the nethermost, fiery pit of hell and those demons mocking ye while they waves cooling jellies in front of ye. You know what it's like when you burn your hand, taking a cake out of the oven, or lighting one of them godless cigarettes? And it stings with a fearful pain, aye? And you run to clap a bit of butter on it to take the pain away, aye? Well, I'll tell ye, there'll be no butter in hell![148]

We tend to prefer to be in a church that operates in a lot of our comfort zones: doctrinally, socially, behaviorally, and esthetically, but the point of worshipping God isn't about catering to our sensibilities. I still remember some 20 years ago I was worshipping with my brother and his wife in their Harrisburg, PA Catholic church. Well after the service was underway, I was startled by the sound of someone rushing down the aisle and noisily into the pew behind me. I turned to look, and it was a woman who was now kneeling and praying rapidly (in silence).

At first, my orderly Lutheran sensibilities were offended, as we tend to revere punctuality and quiet comportment as next to godliness, and she also had put speed above silence in settling herself. Then, I suddenly realized that her behavior was completely appropriate. What did it matter to God if this woman was late? She had come to the place where she knew she would be accepted and forgiven by the One who mattered.

We're often in a hurry, but seldom for a reason like this. That's a church where people can be genuine and trust that God can accept them in whatever state they are, whether it pleases others' sensibilities or not. And, by the way, nobody else seemed to notice or care.

If you choose to commit to attending a church, you should expect to be asked to serve and make a contribution (of time, talent and treasure) for the ministry of the church, both internally and externally. If all this seems a burden, maybe you should stay out of the church until you feel a genuine commitment to join with others in service.

Christian Obligation in the World

Luther returned to Wittenburg in March of 1522 from the Wartburg castle, where he had been translating the bible. He traveled around Saxony and was dismayed at the ignorance of both the laity and the clergy on basic Christian doctrines.

> Dear God, what misery I beheld! The ordinary person, especially in the villages, knows absolutely nothing about the Christian faith, and unfortunately many pastors are completely unskilled and incompetent teachers. Yet they all supposedly bear the name Christian, are baptized and receive the holy Sacrament, even though they do not know the Lord's Prayer, the Creed, or the Ten Commandments. As a result, they live like simple cattle or irrational pigs and, despite the fact that the gospel has returned, have mastered the fine art of mis-using all their freedom.[149]

Accordingly, Luther codified the core principles of Christianity in his two catechisms of 1529 (the Large for the clergy and the Small for the laity) such as the Ten Commandments, the Apostle's Creed, the Lord's Prayer, and the sacraments of baptism and the Lord's Supper. The Small *Catechism* has earned a reputation as a model of clear religious teaching, and was effective as a tool for families to teach core aspects of the faith to their children. [150]

In Luther's Small Catechism on the Ten Commandments, he frames our response to the Commandments beginning with "We should fear and love God so that...", with an appropriately respectful and loving attitude to the party whom the commandment refers to.

For example, with the fifth commandment, "Thou Shalt Not Kill", Luther's interpretation is framed by respect and care for the neighbor: "We should fear and love God, so that we do no bodily harm to our neighbor, but help and befriend him in every need." Here, we not only see the negative that we avoid doing (killing), but it's opposite, to "help and befriend him in every need." We see this attitude of Christian care in his interpretation of other commandments.

In the seventh and eighth commandments against stealing and bearing false witness, Luther writes "We should fear and love God, so that we do not take our neighbor's money or goods, nor get them in any dishonest way, but help him to improve and protect his goods and means of making a living...We should fear and love God, so that we do not lie about, betray or slander our neighbor, but excuse him, speak well of him, and put the best construction on everything."

Here we see a deep, pro-active attitude of care and respect towards the neighbor rather than a mere legalistic avoidance of harm, which informed Luther's attitude of the Christian in the world, and should inspire all Christians of any denomination to follow suit.

For example, when Hurricane Florence devastated Robeson County, South Carolina in September 2018, still recovering from Hurricane Matthew, the local St. Mark Lutheran Church played an important role in the community distributing food and clothing vouchers, teaching mold remediation, handing out personal hygiene and cleaning supplies. It's important for Lutherans to remain involved, said Jean Horman, a visiting supply pastor at St. Mark. "Acting in God's love is the essence of what our faith is about," she said.[151]

Luther's Doctrine of "Two Kingdoms"

Luther actually called this idea "Two Governments", and his thinking was influenced by the writings of St. Augustine and Thomas Aquinas as well as by scripture. Luther saw that the Catholic Church and its princes had combined both spiritual and temporal powers. Luther stated that the church should not attempt to exercise temporal power, and that state governments should not attempt to exercise power over the church.

As we've seen, Luther believed God's kingdom could be divided into two parts, governed by gospel and law, respectively. First, was the church, the laity and clergy of faithful believers who made up the Body of Christ, which Luther also called God's "right hand" on earth. Second was the rest of creation, from the natural world in all its levels, to institutions of science, learning and reason, up to temporal government, which was the "left hand" on earth.

"God's left-hand governing extends then into establishing our most basic human relationships and enduring social life and institutions (family, work, citizenship and other institutional arrangements for creating and preserving human and environmental well-being)."[152]

Far from recommending that Christians retreat from the world, Luther urged the faithful to use their Christian values in contributing to the care of the world in all its aspects. "We are called and sent in our various vocations to be God's "masks" in the world, as he liked to say, through which God's left-hand governing happens. As God's co-creative creatures, we serve our neighbors in solidarity and love, seeking justice, peace and well-being."[153]

Luther anticipated the separation of church and state promoted by Thomas Jefferson and other Enlightenment philosophers, so that both might exist in their proper realm with integrity and without infringing on the realm of the other. At the same time, he urged active Christian engagement in the world; urging them to "'put on' our neighbors" as Christ has "put on" us. In this way, Christian faith enlists the capacities of the faithful in order to serve our neighbors.

Citing Psalm 82, Luther urged citizens and political authorities to promote social justice with special attention to the most vulnerable among us: "Give justice to the weak and the orphan; maintain the right of the lowly and the destitute." Doing so, citizens become 'partakers of Divine majesty.'"[154]

Earlier we read of Luther's doctrine of "two worlds", and of his framing of the Small Catechism's teaching on the Ten Commandments. In both, we saw Luther's deep concern for the neighbor's welfare, and of Christian responsibility to actively care for it.

Jerry Falwell, Sr. and his son Jerry Falwell, Jr. show contrasting philosophies of Christians in the world and the role of faith in our national government.

A long litany of warnings about what would happen to America if it continued down a godless path, goes back to the Puritans. The most infamous of these diatribes came from a conversation between Jerry Falwell, Sr. and televangelist Pat Robertson on the "700 club" television show, shortly after the terrorist attacks of 9/11.

Falwell, talking two days after the attack to host Robertson, said "What we saw on Tuesday, as terrible as it is, could be minuscule if, in fact, God continues to lift the curtain and allow the enemies of America to give us probably what we deserve."

Mr. Robertson responded: "Jerry, that's my feeling. I think we've just seen the antechamber to terror. We haven't even begun to see what they can do to the major population."

A few moments later Mr. Falwell said: "The abortionists have got to bear some burden for this because God will not be mocked. And when we destroy 40 million little innocent babies, we make God mad. I really believe that the pagans, and the abortionists, and the feminists, and the gays and the lesbians who are actively trying to make that an alternative lifestyle, the ACLU, People for the American Way, all of them who have tried to secularize America, I point the finger in their face and say, 'You helped this happen.' "

To which Mr. Robertson said: "I totally concur, and the problem is we have adopted that agenda at the highest levels of our government."[155]

This opportunistic and tasteless finger-pointing, which Falwell later tried to claim was "taken out of context", shows a certain logic. Evangelicals have believed that America is supposed to be a "Christian" nation, and when things happen which offend their sensibilities, they could claim that any national calamity was "God's judgment" for the nation's failure to be a

Richard G. Leahy

theocracy (of their choosing).

Now, Jerry Falwell Jr. has somehow gone to the other extreme. In an interview with Joe Heim of *The Washington Post*, Falwell took the idea of the Two Kingdoms and divorced Christian ethics completely from his view of the state and its role.

It's such a distortion of the teachings of Jesus to say that what he taught us to do personally — to love our neighbors as ourselves, help the poor — can somehow be imputed on a nation. Jesus never told Caesar how to run Rome. He went out of his way to say that's the earthly kingdom, I'm about the heavenly kingdom and I'm here to teach you how to treat others, how to help others, but when it comes to serving your country, you render unto Caesar that which is Caesar's. It's a distortion of the teaching of Christ to say Jesus taught love and forgiveness and therefore the United States as a nation should be loving and forgiving, and just hand over everything we have to every other part of the world. That's not what Jesus taught. You almost have to believe that this is a theocracy to think that way, to think that public policy should be dictated by the teachings of Jesus." [156]

After centuries of evangelicals calling America to be faithful to its alleged Christian destiny, now all of a sudden Jerry Jr. throws that out the window and puts us all in the position of Christians in the pagan Roman empire. Let us "render unto Caesar" when serving the country, and support him in a Roman-style reign of terror (they crucified people guilty of theft) to teach punks a lesson, and so other nations will fear us, and this will protect us righteous Christian citizens. This is an ethically as well as scripturally unsound position.

To be sure, we must have prisons, laws, punishments, safe borders, and ways of protecting our national interests, including the deterrent of powerful armaments. Luther agreed with the need for these things to ensure the peace and public safety, as did the Founding Fathers.

As Christians, we are responsible for the "talents" each of us was given, which include our obligation to support or agitate for justice and for

75

sensible policies for spending our taxes in government programs. Most people agree that we need a more sensible, less emotionally driven policy for immigration and border security, and that an actual physical wall along the 1,954 miles of our southern border is both unnecessary and not a substitute for dealing with the complex issues of immigration and illegal drug smuggling.

But the idea that we should support Homeland Security separating children from their parents, putting the children in detention where several have already died, and pursuing other draconian policies to scare people away from even approaching our southern border, is not only bad policy but is completely un-Christian.

Jesus told us "You are the light of the world." He told us that the actions of the good Samaritan were how you acted as a neighbor to someone in need. He also announced the start of his ministry by reading from Isaiah in the Nazareth synagogue, "The Spirit of the Lord is upon me, because he has anointed me to bring good news to the poor. He has sent me to proclaim release to the captives and recovery of sight to the blind, to let the oppressed go free, to proclaim the year of the Lord's favor."[157] Does this sound like Jesus would support unjust and cruel government policies, for the earthly benefit of His people? How could that be?

It's true that Jesus didn't teach that governments should "just hand over everything we have to every other part of the world", but who is suggesting that we as a nation should do this?

While it's true that we don't (and shouldn't) have an officially "Christian" government, why shouldn't our laws and policies reflect our Judeo-Christian values, and the decency of the Enlightenment? And while Jesus told us to "render unto Caesar the things that are Caesar's" (the subject here was paying taxes), he also told us right after that to "render unto God the things that are God's."[158]

Christian's can't absolve themselves from their responsibility to pressure legislators for laws that are even-handed and just, and for taxes that put social well-being on a plane at least as much of a priority as national defense. And for that matter, what kind of "national defense" policy is it to let anyone purchase a gun without sensible background checks, or to allow semi-automatic weapons to be covered under Second Amendment rights?

> There's two kingdoms. There's the earthly kingdom and the heavenly kingdom. In the heavenly kingdom the responsibility is to treat others as you'd like to be treated. In the earthly kingdom, the responsibility is to choose leaders who will do what's best for your country. Think about it. Why have Americans been able to do more to help people in need around the world than any other country in history? It's because of free enterprise, freedom, ingenuity, entrepreneurism and wealth. A poor person never gave anyone a job. A poor person never gave anybody charity, not of any real volume. It's just common sense to me."[159]

Here, Jerry Falwell Jr. is making a number of errors. First, he's describing Luther's "two kingdoms" as being different realms, the "heavenly" and the "earthly." For Luther, the two kingdoms were both in our earthly experience, only one was our mystical experience as the body of Christ in the church, while the other was a collection of earthly institutions, from the state to universities, schools, all the way down to nature itself. Falwell implies that the "kingdom" of the church is only in heaven, and by extension, the "heavenly" way we treat people won't happen on this earth.

This also reduces Christian responsibility for humane and responsible governance of God's creation and society, from active personal engagement, to outsourcing decisions to some strongman whose fierce love of country (and strong distrust of "outsiders") means we assume he has our best interests at heart, and we no longer are obliged to consider the consequences.

The question of what is best for our country is the dynamic of politics, and should be actively engaged in by all citizens as voters. But it's absurd to assume that a man like Donald Trump, who professes love of country but acts in irresponsible and dangerous ways, should be taken at his word without looking at the consequences of his policies, even if you do want what's best for the country.

Falwell seems unaware of how dangerously close his vision of the "two kingdoms" is to what was promulgated by the Nazis to the Germans. Using the false gospel of fear, Hitler convinced Germans that they had been betrayed in the First World War by the Jews, and that the Jews were after their property and livelihood. In this context, it's understandable why the Germans would want a strong national leader without mercy, to act in "the best national interest", namely frightening other nations and peoples away (sound familiar?)

Hitler may have been sincere, in his twisted thinking. He projected his own ego on the German people, then swore that he would defend them and in eerily familiar language, restore their nation to greatness. We know the answer. The Second World War not only set the world on fire, killing an estimated 70-85 million people, it destroyed Germany, killing millions and reducing the survivors to near-starvation amongst bombed and ruined cities.

For over 40 years, a third of the country was occupied by the hostile Russians presiding over a sham "Democratic Republic" of puppets and stooges, where any independent thinker was treated as a traitor to the state. When the nation was finally re-united in 1989, Germans in the east found that they had become very different people, due to Russian propaganda and the socialist economy, then their West German brethren. Instead of uniting the German people and making them "great again," Hitler inspired them to self-destruction; even after re-unification, they're arguably two different kinds of Germans.

Let's remember the wise words of Edmund Burke, quoted by Reinhold Niebuhr in the 1930s; "All that is necessary for the triumph of evil in the world is for good people to do nothing."[160]

"Why have Americans been able to do more to help people in need around the world than any other country in history? It's because of free enterprise, freedom, ingenuity, entrepreneurism and wealth. A poor person never gave anyone a job. A poor person never gave anybody charity, not of any real volume. It's just common sense to me."

Falwell's dismissive contempt for the poor is typical of those who believe that the poor have gotten what they deserve, something I never read that Jesus believed. Like his father, Falwell has an expansive and uncritical view of capitalism as having no down side.

To be sure, free enterprise, ingenuity, entrepreneurism and our collective national wealth have been blessings to us individually and collectively, but like all human things, they have a down sides with a human impact. The economic fallout of the Great Recession of 2008 left millions of hard-working, decent Americans of all backgrounds without jobs or even homes they thought were theirs, through no fault of their own.

As the movie "The Great Short" illustrated, massive, unregulated greed by financial institutions, and the huge financial bailout they got from Congress based on the belief that bad players were "too big to fail", left average Americans instead of the bad actors holding the bag, and paying the price. And that doesn't even address the "original sin" of American capitalism: the "peculiar institution" of slavery.

Institutional racism is still with us, most awfully in long-established and repeated police brutality against minorities and especially Black men, most notoriously in the choking death of George Floyd by officer Derek Chauvin on Memorial Day 2020.

Sadly, the people who voted for Donald Trump in justifiable anger at a political system that had ignored them and their plight, still have a child-like faith that if we could magically return to the 1950s (when straight, White, Christian men were in charge and everyone else knew their place), everything would return to their idea of "normal".

But aside from the fact that magical thinking is fantasy, the truth is that it's not the primary function of corporations to give people jobs, at least not high-paying middle-class jobs with benefits that have rapidly disappeared over the past two decades (and especially since the pandemic began). The nature of today's capitalism is to cut costs, seek new opportunities for growth, and to generate dividends for shareholders while enhancing stock value. This has nothing to do with keeping employees happy or well-paid, or refraining from laying them off, and in fact has much to do with the very opposite.

Everywhere we look, automation is eliminating jobs; a few wealthy officers, inventors or shareholders at the top make a lot of money, and most of society just struggles to stay even with the pay they had made in the past. No amount of blind optimism or lectures on self-reliance can change the grim way that the deck is still stacked against most Americans by the widest gap in wealth since the Gilded Age a century ago.

As I write this, in September 2020, a million acres of forest have burned in the states on the Pacific coast; it has been well-documented by credible scientists that climate extremes (including the melting of the polar ice caps and rising sea levels) are being driven by greenhouse gases caused by human activity such as coal-fired power plants, the internal combustion engine, industrial farming, and many other things.

Unregulated capitalism, concentrating wealth at the very tiny top of society, is also destroying the earth. As has been pointed out, "There is no planet B." Thankfully, the young today is demanding change, but will enough governments see the imperative to change before we pass the point of no return?

To Jerry Falwell Jr., private wealth and the free-enterprise capitalist system are the treasure of America, where the "poor", who today could include formerly middle-class people fallen on hard times as much as illegal immigrants, are the problem, because he thinks they have nothing of value to given anyone. This is a non-Christian way of looking at both money and people. Jesus never said "Blessed are the rich, for they will be admired and emulated," but that's what too many American Christians seem to think.

Four hundred years ago, Thomas Morton, an Englishman and Anglican Christian, visited the early Plymouth Bay colony in today's Massachusetts. He wrote a classic, wide-ranging book in three volumes in 1637 called *The*

New English Canaan documenting what he observed there, from the local flora and fauna to the native tribes and their interactions with the Puritan settlers. He was thrown into jail by the Puritans who also burnt down his house, for daring to question their theocracy. He returned to England, concluding that the Puritans were a people who "made a great show of Religion, but no humanity."

How far have we really come from this in 400 years, when the poor are blamed for their own condition? When innocent children die in U.S. custody for the crime of accompanying their parents (as your ancestors did) to the "shining city built on a hill", or when unarmed Black men are killed by the police on a nearly monthly rate since Trevon Martin was fatally shot by George Zimmerman in 2012? The real question is, what can we do to change it (and by "we", I mean you and the rest of us)? That brings us back to the church in the world, and the idea of doing "God's work with our hands."

Towards the end of his work advocating for civil rights for all Americans, Dr. Martin Luther King, Jr. came to believe that poverty and hunger in such a (largely) wealthy society showed that our national priorities were wrong. In a speech he gave to Newcastle University in the U.K. in November 1967, where he was awarded an honorary degree, he declared "There are three urgent and indeed great problems that we face not only in the United States of America but all over the world today. That is the problem of racism, the problem of poverty and the problem of war."[161]

That same month, he began work on The Poor People's campaign, an idea suggested to him by Marion Wright, director of the National Association for the Advancement of Colored People's Legal Defense and Educational Fund in Jackson, Mississippi. King believed that African Americans and other minorities would never enter full citizenship until they had economic security.

Through nonviolent direct action, King and the Southern Christian Leadership Conference hoped to focus the nation's attention on economic inequality and poverty. King described the campaign as "the beginning of a new co-operation, understanding, and a determination by poor people of all colors and backgrounds to assert and win their right to a decent life and respect for their culture and dignity". Many leaders of American Indian, Puerto Rican, Mexican American, and poor White communities pledged themselves to the Poor People's Campaign. [162]

King was assassinated in April 1968, and Ralph Abernathy, the new president of the SCLC, decided to proceed with the event. Starting on Mother's Day 1968, thousands of women, led by Coretta Scott King, formed the first wave of demonstrators. The following day, Resurrection City, a temporary settlement of tents and shacks, was built on the Mall in Washington, D.C. Braving rain, mud, and summer heat, protesters stayed for over a month. Demonstrators made daily pilgrimages to various federal agencies to protest and demand economic justice.

During this month, presidential candidate Robert F. Kennedy was assassinated. While the campaign was able to qualify 200 counties for free surplus food distribution and secured promises from several federal agencies to hire poor people to help run programs for the poor, it was disbanded when their park permit expired.[163]

Rev. Dr. William Barber II points out that despite its short six weeks, the original Poor People's Campaign had a lasting impact, with additional spending for Head Start, subsidized school lunches and food programs in poverty-stricken counties, and the creation of the Children's Defense Fund, which has pushed legislation to help poor children and families for the past half century.

"Still, we have never completed the Reconstruction that our federal government admitted was necessary after the Civil War. Just as the Poor People's Campaign proposed, the Reconstruction we need now must arise from the efforts of people harmed directly by racism, poverty, environmental degradation, and the war economy," wrote Barber in *The Atlantic* in February, 2018. [164]

In the article, Barber announced a new Poor People's Campaign: A National Call for Moral Revival, coordinating direct actions across the country that began in May 2018, to mark the 50th anniversary of the original campaign. "Only by joining together and asserting our authority as children of God can we shift the moral narrative in this nation and create a movement that will challenge those in power to form the "more perfect union" to which we aspire."[165]

I'm encouraged to say that what began in 2018 continues. According to the organization,

> What ensued was the most expansive wave of nonviolent civil disobedience in the 21st century United States. More than a series of rallies and actions, a new organism of state-based movements was born. Now, in over 40 states, the groundwork for a mass poor people's movement is emerging.

> In June 2019, we convened over 1,000 community leaders in Washington, D.C. for the Poor People's Moral Action Congress, which included the largest presidential candidates' forum of the pre-debate season, the release of our Poor People's Moral Budget, and a hearing before the House Budget Committee on the issues facing the 140 million poor and low-income people in the nation. Over the next nine months, we embarked on a 25+ state We Must Do M.O.R.E. Tour (Mobilize, Organize, Register, and Educate), which led toward an unprecedented Digital Mass Poor People's Assembly and Moral March on Washington on June 20, 2020.[166]

To learn more about the new Poor People's Campaign, visit their website, www.poorpeoplescampaign.org.

Concluding Prayer for This Chapter

Lord Jesus, help us avoid the temptation to turn worship, and church membership, into a club of sensibilities or anything not guided by your priorities for us to grow spiritually, in communion with others and in service to the church and the world. Help us remember that, while resolving to live an upright life, love is our primary aim, and that without it, we are nothing. Help us to be active examples of your love, remembering that we are "created in Christ Jesus for good works, which God prepared beforehand to be our way of life," and remind us that you love all humanity and we should not discard or disregard other people if they are different from us and especially if they are in need.[167]

Chapter Five

Christian Living in a Time of Pandemic

It's appropriate to follow a chapter on Christian obligation in the world and considering the idea of "Two Kingdoms" with asking ourselves how Christians should live in a time of pandemic.

At this writing in October 2020, the curve of coronavirus cases has not flattened, but has jumped alarmingly, as alluded to in the preface. The seven-day average for daily new cases nationwide, considered a more reliable indicator of the virus's impact rose almost 165 percent from July, from 20,594 in the second week of June to 54,499 by July 12, according to tracking by *The Washington Post*.[168]

Only five days later, the national tally of new COVID-19 infections rose another 50% higher to 77,255 by July 17.[169] The country's daily death toll also increased last week after months of decline,[170] as of this writing it is 215,000 with 7,850,000 documented COVID-19 cases.[171] The *Journal of the American Medical Association* published an article on October 12, 2020 that compared American COVID-19 infection rates per 100,000 persons with those of other Western nations.

The US COVID-19 mortality rate is 60.3 per 100,000 people. Canada's rate is 24.6 per 100,000, and Australia's was 3.3 deaths per 100,000. If we had had the same rate as Canada, we would have lost 117,000 fewer people, and 188,000 Americans would have been saved if we had the same death rate as Australia.[172]

First, let's be honest with ourselves and admit that this is a very scary time to be living anywhere, and that we can't deny this deadly pandemic away. Not only is this the worst public health crisis in a century but it has given a body blow to our economy. The second quarter of 2020 had the worst economic performance in our recorded history, even worse than the Great Depression, contracting by 32.9%.[173]

Second, even though life looks very scary right now, let's affirm our faith in God, remembering His promise that "I am with you always, to the end of the age."[174] We can pray for reassurance, for strength, for thanksgiving that he is faithful and will always be with us, and for our safety. We should pray for all those here and around the world in suffering and need because of this pandemic and economic loss.

This is a good time to make Psalm 46 a regular prayer mantra: "GOD is our refuge and strength, a very present help in trouble. Therefore, we will not fear, though the earth should change, though the mountains shake in the heart of the sea; though its waters roar and foam, though the mountains tremble with its tumult."[175] It was this psalm that inspired Martin Luther to write his famous hymn, "A mighty fortress is our God."

Third, we know there is much wisdom in the Serenity Prayer; "God, grant me the serenity to accept the things I cannot change; the courage to change the things I can; and the wisdom to know the difference."[176]

Let's admit that there is very little that we can do to change the economic outlook, but thankfully we know that we can keep ourselves and our families safe through responsible behavior that public health experts have outlined: wearing masks or face coverings in public, especially indoors; maintaining social distancing of at least six feet, and washing our hands frequently.

The coronavirus does not take vacations or care about who catches it and dies. Where there is a group of careless, carefree people gathered together, at a party or a bar, it's very likely that the coronavirus will be in the midst of them.

While we are assured of God's presence with us, we also have a Christian responsibility to ourselves, our families, and the wider community to respect the danger of the coronavirus by following the simple protocols mentioned above, being diligent and mindful of them, for as with driving a car, the care you take on the road not only protects you and your car but others and their cars as well.

It's understandable, to an extent, that in the early weeks of the shutdown in March and April, some people were skeptical of the whole thing or of the need to take precautions against something they couldn't' see. Now, with some seven million documented COVID-19 cases in the US and over 200,000 deaths, there's no excuse for complacency, carelessness or denial.

In recent decades, we Americans have become used to the idea of outsourcing the solution to our national security problems to the military-industrial complex and our all-volunteer armed forces, so we can continue carrying on our lives without any inconvenience, but containing this pandemic, an invisible and deadly enemy, is not that easy. It requires personal sacrifice to the greater good, which has become an alien, even sinister concept for too many Americans.

Today, too many interpret the Declaration of Independence's famous phrase that "All men are created equal, and are endowed by God with unalienable rights to life, liberty and the pursuit of happiness," as meaning "The road goes on forever, and the party never ends:"[177] they feel entitled to do whatever they feel like, anytime, anywhere. "You always hear Americans say, 'I know my rights,' but you never hear an American say, 'I know my responsibilities and obligations,'" says Stanford University public-opinion specialist Morris Fiorina.[178]

Part of the problem leading to such a bad outcome in the US for containing the spread of the coronavirus is a sense of personal entitlement combined with a lack of an ethic for sacrificing even a little bit for the common good. You see this even when people are too lazy to flick their wrists to put on their turn signals. How much trouble is that?

Let's recall Luther's catechism on the Ten Commandments, which shows that the attitude behind them is a responsibility to consider and treat the neighbor so as to avoid doing him or her any harm. For example, concerning the Fifth Commandment, "Thou shalt not kill", Luther answers the question "What does this mean?" by explaining, "We should fear and love God that we may not hurt nor harm our neighbor in his body, but help and befriend him in every bodily need [in every need and danger of life and body]."[179]

If we can accept the need to limit our individual freedom for the sake of our own safety by wearing seat belts, how can we refuse to wear masks during a pandemic, when we know that it is a simple, easy thing we can do that will greatly reduce our own risk of contracting the virus as well as protecting others? Remember, many people mysteriously carry the virus but don't know they have it, and researchers believe that if they don't wear masks or social distance, they can (and are) spreading the virus everywhere they go.

In the coal country of southwest Virginia, where "Trump digs coal" signs can be seen, there was resistance to Governor Northam's call for people to wear masks while in public, partly because the pandemic had been politicized and downplayed by President Trump (Northam is a Democrat).

"Once you lose your rights, you don't get them back," read one local Facebook post; "The people I see being the biggest advocates of this are women and effeminate men."[180] Naturally, women, who tend to be the caregivers in their families, will tend to do whatever they can to protect them, which doesn't rate this dismissive sexism. Who knows how many "manly" men caught the coronavirus, and even died, because they feared being seen as "effeminate" more than catching a deadly virus?

The situation is made worse by President Trump's reaction to having caught the virus himself, thanks to his disdain for wearing facial masks and social distancing. I hoped the experience would make him more empathetic with others suffering from the disease. He received the kind of care very few other mortals have available to them, and instead went out and told the world that he was feeling great, and that he had beaten the virus.

"Don't let it dominate your life," he tweeted when he was discharged from Walter Reed Medical Center.[181] This only reinforces the idea that fighting the virus is just a matter of manly willpower, and allows the economic shutdown to be blamed, as Miranda Devine of the *New York Post* said on Fox News, on "older people or neurotic people who are timid and afraid and won't come out of their basements."[182]

Meanwhile, with ten million coronavirus infections in this country, the (current) death toll is over 227,000. Jared Kushner, the president's son-in-law, has said it is "hysterical" to be alarmed by the pandemic.[183] During the first presidential debate on September 30th—the date the president arguably became infected with the coronavirus—he bragged that he didn't wear face masks, and ridiculed Joe Biden for doing so; "Every time you see him, he's got a mask. He could be speaking 200 feet away...and he shows up with the biggest mask I've ever seen."[184]

Lori Wagoner is a retail clerk in a store on the North Carolina Intercoastal Waterway that caters to boaters. In North Carolina, it's required to wear a mask in public, but many store customers weren't doing it. Employees decided to post signs politely asking customers to wear masks.

"We'd have 20 or 30 people walk by the sign and come in without a mask. I'd try to get their attention and point to the sign. It was a lot of: 'You're infringing on my rights. This is a free country, and I'm here to shop, so who's going to stop me?' Then the local sheriff went on Facebook and said he wasn't going to enforce the state requirement because he didn't want to be the 'mask police.' So now what? I have customers who are breaking the law and putting my life at risk, and what am I supposed to do?"[185]

In June 2020, Lenin Gutierrez, a Starbucks barista, refused to serve customer Lynn Gilles because Gilles did not have a face covering on, despite California law requiring people wear masks in public. Gilles went on to shame Gutierrez on social media, posting a photo of him on Facebook and writing, "Meet lenen [sic] from Starbucks who refused to serve me 'cause I'm not wearing a mask. Next time I will wait for cops and bring a medical exemption" (note: it's a myth that there's a "medical exemption" from being required to wear a facial covering in public).

In response, Gutierrez received an outpour of support, and a GoFundMe campaign acting as a virtual tip jar for the barista has gone on to raise over $100,000. However, Gilles is now demanding that half that money belongs to her for "discrimination."[186]

Christian responsibility is more important than "individual freedom" which is being worshipped as a false god to such an extent that it is now threatening to destroy both our economy and millions of American lives. A fine example of Christian (and even secular respect for fellow human beings) is seen in the attitude of Albert Cook, a retired coal miner who was interviewed in Grundy, VA while shopping at the Wal-Mart and wearing a mask, saying he did it out of respect for the store workers, saying "If they've got to wear it for 12 hours, I can wear it for 20 minutes."[187]

Pastor Todd Bell of Calvary Baptist Church in Sanford, ME officiated at a wedding in Millinocket that has been linked to Maine's largest coronavirus outbreak to date (as of 9/7/20); 144 cases, two deaths, an outbreak at a nursing home in Madison and another at the York County Jail.[188]

"I love liberty!" declared Bell in an interview on NPR.[189] If Pastor Bell had Luther's attitude towards care and concern towards one's neighbors so as to avoid doing them any harm in any way, the wedding COVID-19 outbreak could have been avoided. Despite CDC guidelines, as of early September, 2020 Bell continued to have in-person church services with singing by choir members standing shoulder-to-shoulder. Singing indoors is considered a dangerous activity since it extends the range of a person's breath.

In November 2020, Chief Rabbi Jonathan Sacks died, but his last work, *Morality: Restoring the Common Good in Divided Times,* had already been completed and is now published (Basic Books). Rabbi Sacks pointed out that "A society in which everyone feels free to do what they want is not a free society. It is not society at all. It is anarchy."[190]

I think Bell should prayerfully ponder St. Paul's words on freedom: "For you were called to freedom, brothers and sisters; only do not use your freedom as an opportunity for self-indulgence, but through love become slaves to one another. For the whole law is summed up in a single commandment, 'You shall love your neighbor as yourself.'"[191]

Bell's church also has a school, Sanford Christian Academy, that started September 8 with in-person classes. The more than 70 students enrolled, said Bell, will attend five days a week, and all sports are still on. Sanford City Councilor Maura Herlihy is concerned: "The school is located in a very dense part of our community," she said. "The students come from different towns; they don't just come from Sanford. And that with school starting, and the fact that the pastor doesn't seem to want to work with the state of Maine and the CDC to keep things safe, what's the potential impact of an outbreak at the school should it occur?"[192]

Pastors, Christian leaders and national leaders should be in the forefront of demonstrating safety protocols for showing others how to keep safe during the pandemic.

President Trump sets a very poor example. Once he wore a mask and told others to do the same, but has not done it during his rallies or indeed much of anywhere else, and Vice President Pence follows suit. During his rally on June 20th in Tulsa, OK, President Trump's staff removed the "Do Not Sit Here" stickers the venue management had placed on every other seat, for social distancing, because he wanted to enjoy the sight of a packed house.

On July 30th, Herman Cain, a onetime Republican presidential candidate and former CEO of Godfather's Pizza, died from coronavirus; he had attended President Trump's Tulsa rally two weeks earlier.[193]

Why was President Trump so unconcerned about the spread of the coronavirus during his rallies? On Sunday September 13th, he held an indoor campaign rally in Nevada even though the state still has a ban on gatherings of more than 50 people. Photos and videos of the rally showed mask-less Trump supporters standing shoulder-to-shoulder, drawing rebukes from his political opponents.

"The President appears to have forgotten that this country is still in the middle of a global pandemic," said Nevada Gov. Steve Sisolak (D). Trump defended the rally in an interview with the Las Vegas Review-Journal by saying that he is "very far away" from the crowd while he's onstage, "and so I'm not at all concerned." [194] Oh, now I get it. He encourages crowding at his rallies because he enjoys the optics, and since *he's* protected, that's all that matters to him. On the week of that rally, the U.S. was expected to exceed 200,000 killed by the coronavirus.

Even after he caught the coronavirus, President Trump was back campaigning when medical professionals said it was "reckless." Dozens of supporters stood closely in line for the chance of attending his first post-diagnosis campaign rally on the South Lawn of the White House, and the president made a point of removing his mask and smiling before beginning his speech.

How should we behave as Christians in the world at a time like this, when we can't even attend our own churches or if we do, we all have to social distance, wear masks and can't even sing hymns (because the volume of exhaled air is too dangerous)? Certainly, it is a sad thing to be separated from our brothers and sisters in Christ, but thankfully with Zoom and other online tools, churches can arrange virtual worship service; I've even seen some that offer "drive-through" communion.

Certainly, we should not deny science or put ourselves or others at risk by refusing to wear masks, socially distance and follow other commonsense ways of avoiding COVID-19 -19. We should also do whatever we (safely) can to help the vulnerable and needy; between the pandemic and the economic shutdown, there is need wherever we look.

Martin Luther gave us specific, practical and godly advice on this subject. In 1527, Wittenburg suffered an outbreak of the bubonic plague, or the Black Death, which was as infectious as COVID-19 today.

He published a pamphlet titled "Whether One May Flee from a Deadly Plague;" his thoughts are eerily relevant to America today. He noted that some people "are much too rash and reckless, tempting God and disregarding everything which might counteract death and the plague. They disdain the use of medicines; they do not avoid places and persons infected by the plague, but lightheartedly make sport of it and wish to prove how independent they are... This is not trusting God but tempting him. God has created medicines and provided us with intelligence to guard and take good care of the body so that we can live in good health."[195]

We recently read of Luther's preface on the Fifth Commandment (against murder) being based in a brotherly love and concern for the neighbor's well-being. Luther then admonished his readers in his pamphlet to resolve: "I shall avoid places and persons where my presence is not needed in order not to become contaminated and thus perchance infect and pollute others, and so cause their death as a result of my negligence."[196]

I found it depressing that when I tried to donate blood, the center was closed from COVID-19 concerns, and it's risky even to work in a church soup kitchen. Aside from the personal contact we need and crave in our faith walk, we want to still be of service and we can be if we make it a priority.

Although there is a natural psychological temptation to want to retreat from the world entirely, we can keep a safe physical distance and still be engaged and involved doing God's work by donating online (or by mail).

Those of us fortunate enough to still be working or to have some savings can support our churches and their social ministries either near to home, nationally or internationally, or to any number of NGOs and charitable organizations from the Salvation Army to Doctors Without Borders to the Red Cross, and more.

While it still can feel lonely just sitting in front of a computer instead of interacting with people, giving money, especially at a time like this, is an affirmation that we trust God cares about us, and trusting that He will continue to do so, while we can do His work in a world which so badly needs it. I once heard that "Money is a transferrable form of love;" when was the last time you heard that? This pandemic is an opportunity to act on this.

My church, St. Mark Lutheran ELCA of Charlottesville, volunteers to host the homeless for two weeks through the PACEM ministry. Even though we can no longer host during the pandemic, we decided to provide meals for them twice recently, along with a beverage and dessert which volunteers will drive from the church to the hotel where they are staying. By necessity, much of life today has changed in ways we cannot control, so let us do what we can to be God's hands doing His work in the world however we can. Of course, we must also remember to continue to support our churches financially even if we're not physically attending at this time.

When I got my stimulus check, I gave most of it away to a range of charities both in my community and abroad. I felt a sense of joy being able to help so many people, even though I would never see them, trusting that the money would enable others to physically care for people I could not. Those who are out of work can still do God's work by volunteering at a food bank, delivering meals, or other things that they can do while keeping safe COVID-19 protocols.

Government During the Pandemic and its Moral Obligation to Society

At the time of this writing, we have seen how a variety of governments around the world, from authoritarian China to a range of democracies, have dealt with the pandemic, and which were the most and the least effective.

The governments with the most effective programs to reduce and contain the spread of the coronavirus combined a focused plan for testing, contact tracing, and enforcement, with clear, unambiguous public messaging based on science that communicated the deadly, serious nature of the virus and the need for public cooperation.

On April 13, a month after President Trump declared the pandemic a national emergency, *Forbes* published a piece showing that many of the countries with the best results for flattening the curve of coronavirus infections and containing its spread, were countries with female leaders. These include: Denmark, Iceland, Finland, Germany, New Zealand, Norway and Taiwan.[197]

The tactics they employed to achieve this success included: being honest, telling the truth clearly and emphasizing the seriousness of the pandemic; taking decisive action; a bold commitment to free testing as widely as possible and robust use of contact tracing, such as done in

Iceland.

Jacinda Ardern in New Zealand banned all foreigners from visiting and enforced a 14-day quarantine on all New Zealanders. By April 13th, these two tactics had kept that country from having to shut down while identifying and isolating as many cases as could be found. Use of social media by national leaders as a tool for the common good, instead of for schoolyard taunts shouted to the world, made a big impact in Finland, where Sanna Marin, a Millennial, invited social media influencers of any age to spread fact-based information on managing the pandemic.

An especially touching and effective tactic of love and compassion in action was employed by Norway's prime minister Erna Solberg to communicate directly to the country's children. Solberg held a dedicated press conference where no adults were allowed. She responded to kids' questions from across the country, taking time to explain why it was OK to feel scared.

"Generally, the empathy and care which all of these female leaders have communicated seems to come from an alternate universe than the one we have gotten used to. It's like their arms are coming out of their videos to hold you close in a heart-felt and loving embrace. Who knew leaders could sound like this? Now we do," says the writer of the article, Avivah Wittenberg-Cox.[198]

By contrast, for an advanced, industrialized nation, on a per capita basis, the US has the seventh-highest death rate of any country in the *world*, and that with an advanced health care system. This is measured in COVID-19 deaths per million, currently at over 473.[199]

The U.S. only has five percent of the world's population, but so far has 21% of the world's total deaths from COVID-19 19, with a current national daily death toll from the disease of over 1,200.[200] Let's look at how we have failed so badly, and what the moral obligation of governments are facing the pandemic.

Before a vaccine becomes widely available, diagnostic testing is critical for identifying those infected with the coronavirus, especially those who feel fine and are not showing any symptoms, to keep them from spreading it to others.

A national average of 634,000 people were being tested in the second week of July in the US, but that is about one million short of daily tests needed for the mitigation of the virus, and far below what would be necessary to suppress it, according to a methodology developed by the Harvard Global Health Institute.[201] In some states like California and Nebraska, testing sites had to close because of a shortage of testing kits, chemical reagents and related supplies. [202]

As we know, humans have no immunity to the novel coronavirus and it is easily transmittable between people breathing the same air within six feet of each other. The fact that it has infected twelve and a half million and killed over a million worldwide,[203] and the fact the U.S. has the fastest-growing rate of infection, make the pandemic the single most serious danger to national security the United States has faced in a lifetime, since the bombing of Pearl Harbor in 1941, and the largest public health crisis since the Spanish flu pandemic of 1918.

Normally in such an unprecedented crisis, national leadership in both the White House and Congress could be relied upon to put partisan concerns aside, rise to the challenge and build robust and bold plans of action with a united front that gives everyone clear, unambiguous instructions on how citizens can protect themselves, avoid risky behavior, and stay healthy.

Unfortunately, that did not happen. President Trump first ignored the pandemic, then downplayed its danger, then politicized it by criticizing any medical information that implied it was not already under control. On January 21st, the first COVID-19 case was reported in the Seattle area. The next day, a reporter asked the president if there were worries about a pandemic. The president responded, "No. Not at all. And we have it totally under control. It's one person coming in from China, and we have it under control. It's — going to be just fine."

Richard G. Leahy

On February 20th, the World Health Organization (WHO) reports nearly 77,000 cases worldwide in 27 countries. On February 24th, the stock market plummeted as the Dow Jones Industrials fell more than 1,000 points. The same day, Trump asks for $1.25 billion in emergency aid. It grew to $8.3 billion in Congress. He tweeted that the virus "is very much under control" and the stock market "starting to look very good to me!"

On March 6th, the president said "Anybody that wants a test can get a test." The Poynter Institute, which helps facilitate professional development for journalists and also calls out falsehoods in the news on its Politifact "truth-o-meter", noted that at the time of this statement, testing kits were in short supply nationwide and rated this statement a "pants on fire" falsehood.[204]

The next day, in an opinion piece in the *New York Times*, Jeremy Konyndyk, principal investigator for the Center for Global Development, said that initially "federal officials responded in a way that fit the narrative Trump preferred."

"It is no coincidence that the coronavirus has broken out across the country as the president continues to brag about keeping the disease off the United States border," he wrote. "Pretending that we could eliminate the virus not only gave the public a false sense of security, but it also left the United States unprepared for the threat it now faces."[205] This assessment turned out to be a prophecy of how the lack of a strong, coordinated national strategy for fighting the virus put the whole country at risk.

Trump seemed to have lost the seriousness of the moment at the start of the outbreak, according to Aaron David Miller, a senior member of the Carnegie Endowment for International Peace.

"This is the deepest crisis that Americans have faced in terms of how it impacts their daily lives," Miller, author of the *End of Greatness: Why America Can't Have (and Doesn't Want) Another Great President,* told Al Jazeera. However, Trump "failed at responsibility number one," which is "leveling out with the American public about the nature and severity of this crisis."[206]

We know President Trump was influenced by the mid-century preacher Norman Vincent Peale, who emphasized the power of positive thinking. In the case of the pandemic however, Trump has taken this attitude to an extreme of denial of a national emergency, repeating the fantasy that "someday, it will just go away", while refusing to take responsibility for dealing with it. On March 13th at a news conference, when asked about the national lack of testing kits, he responded churlishly "I am not responsible at all," then promised the shortage had already been resolved (it had not, and continues so.)[207]

"I am not responsible at all," seems to be President Trump's attitude when it comes to having to deal with actual, real problems. In the case of the worst national threat since the attack on Pearl Harbor, he washed his hands of responsibility and instead gave it to state governors, and continues to repeat that the virus will someday "just disappear." Even on July 21st when he said in a press conference "It will probably, unfortunately, get worse before it gets better. Something I don't like saying about things, but that's the way it is",[208] he concluded by saying he hoped it would disappear.

We now know from Bob Woodward's book *Rage* that President Trump admitted that he knew the novel coronavirus causing COVID-19 was much deadlier than the normal flu as early as February 2020, telling Woodward "this is deadly stuff", but that he chose to downplay its seriousness to "avoid causing a panic." When the book was published and he was asked why he downplayed the danger, he said "I'm a cheerleader for this country."[209] Not only has he continued to reassure people throughout 2020 that it COVID-19 was not so bad, but kept saying it would someday disappear, even as infections soared.

He also refused to use the power of the federal government to fight the pandemic by using his executive powers to authorize the mass production of PPE, testing kits or ventilators, forcing state governors to compete with each other for increasingly scarce private sector supplies. As early as March 20th, a week after declaring the pandemic a national emergency, he rebuked state governors for expecting the federal government to supply testing kits, saying in a coronavirus press briefing that "we are not a shipping clerk."[210]

On April 6th, he outsourced the responsibility for testing and other public health actions to state governors, washing his hands of any coordinated federal response. According to Maryland governor Larry Hogan, the president said "States can do their own testing. We're the federal government. We're not supposed to stand on street corners doing testing."[211]

President Trump has falsely claimed that "99 percent" of COVID-19 cases "are totally harmless"[212], but being hospitalized for COVID-19 is a serious strain on the metabolism, generally resulting in a national fatality average of 5.5%.[213] The data show that a range of long-term complications may manifest even after patients recover, which can include heart damage from inflammation and scarring of the heart muscle, blood clotting, stroke and embolisms, lung damage and neurologic damage.[214]

In a new CDC report, researchers show that 35 percent of people who had COVID-19 and were able to self-treat were still not at their usual level of health two to three weeks after testing. For people ages 18 to 34 with no underlying health issues, 1 in 5 were still feeling ill weeks later, and that's a young, healthy population sample.[215] Besides, being bed-ridden or hospitalized and in isolation prevents you from doing important things like working and paying the bills. On August 18, Dr. Anthony Fauci said the long-term effects COVID-19 can have on survivors, especially younger people, are "really troublesome.[216]

President Trump and leading Republicans have also politicized the pandemic, with disastrous consequences for the nation. This created two very different narratives; one which was clear about the dangers of the coronavirus and the need for isolation, social distancing, and (after some time) the effectiveness of wearing face masks to both prevent the virus' spread and protect oneself from it. The other circulated by the president and many Republican state governors not only downplayed the seriousness of the pandemic, but ultimately, and repeatedly, chose to prioritize restoring the economy over saving human lives.

This narrative implied that since the first major outbreaks that occurred in the U.S. were in the largest Democratic strongholds of New York and California, that the virus was a "Democrat" problem most common amongst immigrants, the urban poor and others (like liberals) who were scarce in God-fearing Republican states like Texas, Florida and Arizona (all now suffering high rates of coronavirus infection).

On July 12, 2020, Florida broke a national, not state, record for reporting the highest number of new daily cases of infection, at 15,300.[217] By late October, the US had reported a record half-million new COVID-19 cases within the past week; states with the fastest-growing rates of COVID-19 cases included the Dakotas, Wyoming, Utah, Montana, all deep red states with sparse population densities and limited hospital facilities. [218,219]

President Trump and his advisors would criticize Drs. Anthony Fauci and Donna Birx if they stressed the danger of the pandemic, or the numbers of infection rising. Someone sent Trump a hashtag on Twitter of "#firefauci"; Trump re-tweeted it. He also encouraged populist rebellion by residents of states with Democratic governors, such as Michigan and Virginia, by tweeting that they "should liberate" their states from executive orders to wear masks and shuttering public businesses.

This encouraged men from the Michigan Liberty Militia, dressed in camouflage or flak jackets, to storm the state capitol in Lansing, with thousands of others somehow convinced masking or the pandemic itself were a nefarious plot to stifle "liberty". The president did nothing to discourage this,[220] and this pandering to self-appointed "freedom fighters" probably encouraged members of the Wolverine Watchmen in Michigan to plot to kidnap Governor Gretchen Whitmer (a Democrat) over coronavirus restrictions she put in place.

According to CBS news, 13 men were charged in the plot; six for plotting to kidnap Governor Whitmer and put her on trial for treason before the November election, and seven others for attempting to find the home addresses of law enforcement officers to target them, making threats of violence intended to "instigate a civil war" and engaging in planning and training to attack the Michigan capitol building and kidnap government officials, including Whitmer.[221]

In a press conference, Whitmer accused President Trump of encouraging extremism: "Just last week [during the first presidential debate], the president of the United States stood before the American people and refused to condemn white supremacists and hate groups like these two Michigan militia groups," the governor said. Whitmer said the president's response at last week's debate to questions about whether he would denounce white supremacy — "Stand back, and stand by" — served as a "rallying cry, as a call to action."[222]

Republican governors in Tennessee, Alabama, Arkansas, Louisiana, Montana, South Carolina, South Dakota and Utah have resisted calls for mandating the wearing of masks in public spaces, stressing "personal responsibility" instead. "You shouldn't have to order somebody to do what is just in your own best interest and that of your family, friends and neighbors," Alabama Gov. Kay Ivey, a Republican, said in early July as she urged people to wear masks and take other precautions but downplayed the effectiveness of statewide orders.[223]

On July 14, four former directors of the Centers for Disease Control published an opinion piece in the *Washington Post* warning that no other president had ever politicized science the way Trump was doing, and that his administration was undermining public health. "Through last week, and into Monday, the administration continued to cast public doubt on the agency's recommendations and role in informing and guiding the nation's pandemic response."

"That Sunday, Education Secretary Betsy DeVos characterized the CDC guidelines as an impediment to reopening schools quickly rather than what they are: the path to doing so safely. The only valid reason to change released guidelines is new information and new science — not politics."[224]

Why would anyone put the lives of children and their teachers in jeopardy just to keep a (false) façade of optimism?

On July 16, Georgia Governor Brian Kemp (a Republican) announced he was suing Atlanta mayor Keisha Lance Bottoms over the city's mask mandate, claiming the measure violates his emergency orders. "This lawsuit is on behalf of the Atlanta business owners and their hardworking employees who are struggling to survive during these difficult times," Kemp tweeted. "These men and women are doing their very best to put food on the table for their families while local elected officials shutter businesses and undermine economic growth."

Bottoms fired back moments later, tweeting "3104 Georgians have died and I and my family are amongst the 106k who have tested positive for COVID-19 -19. Meanwhile, I have been sued by @GovKemp for a mask mandate. A better use of tax payer money would be to expand testing and contact tracing." (#ATLStrong)[225] Mayor Bottoms is a Democrat.

Even Texas Governor Greg Abbott, one of the first governors to re-open his state and one of the most skeptical about imposing any restrictions on the operations of business, decided to reverse course and close the state's bars on June 27th when new coronavirus cases in the state had spiked dangerously; when he did, he found himself sued in federal court by a group of Texas bar owners for some $10 million.

The bar owners say in the lawsuit that Abbott's order violates their constitutional rights and "may very well leave long-term scarring on the republican form of government if left unchecked."[226] A second group of some 30 bars in Travis County had filed a separate suit for the same reason, earlier that week.[227]

Why the dangerous (and ultimately deadly) push to politicize the pandemic, and urge businesses to re-open, people to return to work, and students to return to schools, when conditions were not safe?

This goes beyond a blind optimism. President Trump kept repeating in the early days of the shutdown in the spring that "We cannot let the cure be worse than the problem itself."[228] Stop and think about that for a minute. The problem is the coronavirus. The cure is fighting a deadly and invisible pandemic, by taking any and all measures necessary to protect American lives. At the time of this tweet, the nation was in a shutdown, allegedly in a bid to buy time for the government to prepare and implement a national public health plan, which never happened. How can taking the necessary steps to save American lives be "worse than the problem itself?"

What President Trump revealed is that he viewed the economic consequences of the shutdown to be more of a threat (to Republican interests and his own re-election prospects) than the impact of the deadly coronavirus on millions of innocent Americans. This attitude was shared by most Republican governors. They went along with Trump in downplaying the seriousness of the pandemic, pushed for early re-opening, and resisted putting executive orders in place to wear masks in public; some like Georgia's Governor Kemp suing Atlanta Mayor Bottoms to overturn the public masking order she put in place.

Until now, it's been assumed that robust economic growth is good for both the nation and individual Americans. With the pandemic, we've seen that, given a choice between prioritizing and protecting human lives or prioritizing the economy by encouraging everyone to return to work and businesses to re-open, despite the risk to human lives, Republican leaders have clearly chosen to prioritize economics over human lives. Perhaps it's because they are personally somewhat insulated from the danger; they can pay others to shop and do errands for them while they stay safely at home, a luxury most Americans can't afford.

Consider "essential" workers, who are expected to work through the pandemic but often are not given the proper PPE (personal protective equipment) or are expected to use it repeatedly beyond recommended use, or whose general work environments are high risk but where the needed safeguards are not in place. It seems like "essential" has come to mean "expendable" in the pandemic. Economic output itself is considered "essential" by the President and his allies, but the people whose health is at risk every day when they go to work, are considered expendable. If not, why are they asked to put their lives on the line without proper protection?

The Centers for Disease Control and Prevention says about 130,000 health care workers have been diagnosed with COVID-19 and more than 600 have died, but adds that, because of incomplete data collection, those numbers are probably low (the death of 600 health care workers was first reported in June; this statement from the CDC came in August). Also, no government agency thoroughly tracks the deaths of health care workers or holds their employers accountable for safety lapses.[229]

Grocery store checkout clerks are visible "front line" examples of "essential workers," but the sense of purpose and being appreciated they felt back in April is reportedly gone. "We lost our hazard pay, and people are quitting every day," says Angel Manners, who processes vendor deliveries at a Meijer store in Kentucky. "Those of us who are left are really stretched thin—working so much harder for $11.50 an hour."[230]

A report on grocery workers across the country in the *Washington Post* says that morale is "crushingly low as the pandemic wears on with no end in sight. Overwhelmed employees are quitting mid-shift. Those who remain say they are overworked, taking on extra hours, enforcing mask requirements and dealing with hostile customers. Most retailers have done away with hazard pay even as workers remain vulnerable to infection, or worse. The mounting despair is heightened by the lack of other job options; the retail sector has shed 913,000 jobs and chalked up more than a dozen bankruptcies during the pandemic."[231]

Public health crises of national, pandemic proportions should never be politicized. We have a large federal government in part to do things the private sector can't do on a scale or cost-efficient or timely way. It was only on July 21st that President Trump re-instated the press coronavirus briefings that had been discontinued in May after he gave bogus medical advice about fighting the coronavirus by ingesting disinfectants. "It will probably, unfortunately, get worse before it gets better," Trump said on that date in prepared remarks. "Something I don't like saying about things, but that's the way it is."

In a reversal of past comments, Trump advocated for Americans to wear masks. Trump, who for many weeks refused to encourage Americans to wear masks, now called it patriotic to wear a face covering, and offered to work with China (who he had been criticizing for months) if they develop a vaccine first.[232]

By giving masking lip service but refusing to make it mandatory, saying it's an issue of "personal responsibility", some Republican governors are sending the message that people can essentially do whatever they feel like, and face no penalty for behavior that threatens public health. They are also shifting responsibility from themselves as public executives to individuals, outsourcing the consequences.

Remember the statement given by the group of Texas bar owners suing Governor Abbott for closing state bars because they were identified as hot spots for spreading the pandemic? They said Abbott's executive action (for the sake of saving lives and health) "may very well leave long-term scarring on the republican form of government if left unchecked."[233]

It's quite a stretch to claim that our republican form of government (in which the people elect others to represent their interests) is being threatened by a rare but urgently necessary executive order to close businesses known to be hot spots for spreading a pandemic. It's also instructive in demonstrating that for too many business owners, they prioritize making a buck no matter who else pays the price for their staying open, by catching a deadly disease.

This argument, and the dereliction of duty shown by Republican politicians who urge "personal responsibility" but avoid taking any executive responsibility, shows the complete lack of any duty to the greater good of society, and idolizing money and money-making above all else. This is not an abstraction; with seven million COVID-19 cases nationally and a death toll approaching 225,000, we've seen the terrible price ordinary people are paying for Republican leaders' dereliction of duty.

If a government refuses to act to help save lives, because it's more convenient for the wealthy few if everyone pretends life is still normal, no matter who dies, how does that government have any moral legitimacy? This pandemic has been a test for America and its leaders, to choose the public good over private gain, and so far, we have failed miserably, and become an object of pity for the other nations of the world. We had the resources; what leadership failed at was the moral courage to do the right thing.

It's clear that we don't have government in any meaningful sense unless it prioritizes the common good over private gain, in the face of an invisible, deadly pandemic.

Marcus Licinius Crassus was a wealthy Roman in the first century BC who owned an interesting fire company. When a fire broke out, the company would rush to the burning house, only to offer to buy it before putting it out. The longer it took the owner to agree, (and the more the house burned), the lower the price became.[234]

That was laissez-faire "government" under pagans with no morals beyond greed and personal gain. How is America substantially different today, especially for an allegedly "Christian" nation?

Concluding Prayer for This Chapter

Dear Lord, these are indeed scary times for us. Help us to remember, and repeat as often as we need to, "In You, O Lord, I take refuge; let me never be put to shame. In your righteousness deliver me and rescue me; incline your ear to me and save me. Be to me a rock of refuge, to save me, for you are my rock and my fortress." Give us the strength to trust you despite the scariness of living during the pandemic, and also give us the courage and empathy not to shut ourselves off from those in need but to help where and how we can while remembering to keep ourselves safe. Inspire our leaders to prioritize the safety of Americans above profit.

Chapter Six

God's Word is "Our Great Heritage" (Don't Abuse It)

God's Word is our great heritage
And shall be ours forever;
To spread its light from age to age
Shall be our chief endeavor.
Through life it guides our way,
In death it is our stay.
Lord, grant, while worlds endure,
We keep its teachings pure.
Throughout all generations.[235]

Aside from Luther's doctrine of justification by grace through faith, his greatest contribution to the Protestant legacy was his translation of the Bible into vernacular German, and the way in which he did it. Unlike the now-archaic King James Bible (some 400 years old), Luther struggled to make his translation easy for ordinary Germans of his day to understand.

The publication of the Bible in turn led to a movement of education in Lutheran lands in Germany (notably, which included girls) and a broader movement of literacy, which encouraged the printing of more books, which encouraged more literacy.

Luther realized that his ability to challenge Catholic Church authorities was based on his ability to read the Bible (in original Hebrew and koine Greek). In a way, Luther could be called the original fundamentalist, since his view was that anything that claimed authority over a Christian which was not found in the Bible, was either phony or irrelevant.

If the faithful could read the Bible in their own, everyday language, then they would have access to a deeper practice of faith in the ability to read it whenever they wished. Interestingly, Luther's was not the first translation—or the first printing—of the Bible in German. In total, there were at least eighteen complete German Bible editions, ninety editions of the Gospels in the German vernacular by the time Luther first published his own New Testament translation.[236]

Three things made Luther's translation a publication hit. First, his translation used the variant of German spoken at the Saxon chancellery, intelligible to both northern and southern Germans.[237] Second, it was published at a time of rising demand for German-language publications. Third, with the name of the Reformer as editor, his version quickly became a popular and influential Bible translation, and went on to become a major influence in the standardization of the German language and in German literature. It also helped that Luther worked with his publisher to incorporate many quality woodcut illustrations.[238]

To understand the attitude of the Catholic Church on this topic, consider the fate of William Tyndale. He was an English scholar who was inspired by Luther's translation of the Bible into German. He attempted to make an English translation but was denied permission by the Cuthbert Tunstall, the Bishop of London, who described the project as "heretical."

Tyndale went to the Continent, where he published a partial edition in 1525, but was betrayed to the Catholic authorities and fled to Worms in Germany (where Martin Luther had been declared a heretic a few years earlier), and a complete translation was published there in 1526.

Despite the publication of his English translation of the Bible, Tyndale himself had been captured by Holy Roman Empire authorities in Antwerp (in the Spanish Netherlands) and was imprisoned in 1535. The following year he was tried as a heretic for his translation of the Bible and was burned at the stake (after first kindly being strangled).

Interestingly, it was not the invention of the printing press or Luther's translation of the Bible that started this "readable" Bible-as-heresy reaction by the Catholic Church. As Bernard Starr writes in *Jesus Uncensored: Restoring the Authentic Jew*[239], rulings by various church authorities in the Middle Ages had all agreed on a strict prohibition on the laity from possessing Bibles translated into the vernacular.

One of these, the "Ruling of the Council of Tarragona of 1234" (in Spain) read: "No one may possess the books of the Old and New Testaments in the Romance language, and if anyone possesses them, he must turn them over to the local bishop within eight days after promulgation of this decree, so that they may be burned..."[240]

Tyndale is a martyr of the Reformation and his translation of the Bible was a key part of the success of the new, Protestant Church of England. Despite Martin Luther's narrow escape and Tyndale's martyrdom, the cat was out of the bag and the translating and publication of the Bible in the European languages of the day could not be stopped.

Unfortunately, there is a down side, or a dark side, to having the entire Bible available to anyone in the common language. People may be tempted to use a passage from the Bible to justify criticizing, judging, or even condemning and sentencing others to death. Since we can affirm that "God is love,"[241] using His word as a weapon should be discouraged, especially if the motive is to put others down and raise up ourselves in contrast.

Luther felt it was important enough to risk his life, to point out that the sale of indulgences invalidated Christ's sacrifice on the cross, and he had the texts and experience to stand up to the Catholic Church during his testimony at the Diet of Worms.

For the rest of us who all have the Bible available in our native languages, our first impulse should always be to turn to it for guidance and reassurance in God's love for us, for all people, and of His presence with us; "I am with you always, to the end of the age."[242] Remember, "For God did not send his son into the world to condemn the world, but that the world through Him might be saved."[243] If Jesus was willing to be humbled in becoming a man, so that all might be saved, why should we turn to scripture with an aim to judge others?

Luther and his contemporary scholars could read the Bible in the original texts, and understood that, having been written and passed down over thousands of years, it was necessary to interpret the words from the perspective of the writer, his historical context, and the meaning behind the words, to make as authentic of a translation as possible. This approach, known as the "historical-critical" method of Biblical interpretation, is used by ministers in mainstream Judaism and mainline Protestant churches, which is why part of getting a doctorate of divinity involves learning Hebrew and *koine* Greek (the version of that language used at the time of Christ).

You may be surprised to learn that Methodist, Baptist, Lutheran, Presbyterian and Episcopalian ministers are expected to research their sermons on scripture lessons by studying the passages in the original languages and then interpreting them in today's American English vernacular.

Even Luther and his early Protestant co-reformers ran into disagreements on biblical interpretation, most notably on the meaning of Holy Communion. Was Christ literally or only figuratively present in the bread and wine? Luther insisted on the <u>Real Presence</u> of the body and blood of Christ in the consecrated bread and wine, while his opponents believed God to be only spiritually or symbolically present.

With two alpha males invested in their own interpretations, the debate sometimes became confrontational. Citing Jesus' words "The flesh profiteth nothing" (John 6.63), Zwingli said, "This passage breaks your neck". "Don't be too proud," Luther retorted, "German necks don't break that easily. This is Hesse, not Switzerland."[244] On a tablet Luther wrote the words "*Hoc est corpus meum*" ("This is my body") in chalk, to continually indicate his firm stance based on Christ's words.[245]

The Lutheran Church continues to affirm the mysterious, but real presence of Christ in the Eucharist for the faithful who partake of it. Unfortunately, the debate over the nature of Christ's presence in the Eucharist continues to divide some Christians and even prohibit some from partaking of it, if they don't agree with a church's own belief. For example, the Catholic Church believes in transubstantiation, meaning that (when an ordained priest) proclaims the bread and wine to be transformed, they become the *literal* body and blood of Christ.

Luther's belief (accepted by mainline Protestant churches) is described as "sacramental union": "For the reason why, in addition to the expressions of Christ and St. Paul (the bread in the Supper is the body of Christ or the communion of the body of Christ), also the forms: under the bread, with the bread, in the bread [the body of Christ is present and offered]."[246]

At my own father's funeral, I sadly declined the Eucharist, because I knew that would have been his wish.

Father Ronald D. Witherup, S.S., is provincial of the American Province of Sulpician Fathers. He speaks and writes frequently on biblical topics. He is the author of *The Bible Companion: A Handbook for Beginners*. He presents a thoughtful and enlightened summary of how to read and interpret the Bible in an appropriate way, and how to avoid mis-using the Bible, because "sadly, in many instances the Bible is not being used properly. In fact, it is being abused." [247]

During the 1970s, some suggested that the Watergate affair during the Nixon presidency was predicted in the Bible on the basis of the mention of the "water gate" (see Nehemiah 3:26; 8:1). "Such a reading is not only inaccurate; it trivializes the Bible into some sort of Ouija board or crystal ball. The Bible's authority stems from the Church's belief that while we do not know how biblical inspiration works, the Bible, under the guidance of the Holy Spirit, can guide our lives in areas of faith and morals."[248]

Witherup warns that "in biblical interpretation, the biggest danger is ignoring the context of a passage." The responsible interpretative method, he says, is to relate any given verse to the verses immediately in front and after it, to create a narrow context, then to consider the meaning in the context of the particular book you're studying, then to consider that meaning in relation to what we know of the entire Bible.

Paying attention to this larger context helps us avoid misreading the Bible. The most damaging way to interpret a biblical passage is to rip it from its context. Taking a passage literally and cutting it out of its natural "home" almost always leads to abusing the Scriptures. The late

Father Raymond E. Brown, S.S., one of the greatest Catholic biblical scholars of the 20th century, used to say, "A biblical passage is only biblical when it is in the Bible." You can't go wrong looking carefully at the context.[249]

Witherup mentions the temptation, indulged in by many, to search the Bible for things that can be interpreted in light of the Last Days, about to happen in our own time. But he reminds us that Jesus himself did not know when God's ultimate justice would occur. In Mark 13:32 He says "But of that day or hour, no one knows, neither the angels in heaven, nor the Son, but only the Father. Be watchful! Be alert! You do not know when the time will come."

As Witherup points out, if Jesus does not know, but only God his Father, how can some claim today that they know? "Some may wish to flee into a mysterious apocalyptic world in order to escape from their daily troubles, but using the Bible to justify arcane theories about exactly how, when and where God will choose to act to bring the kingdom to its fullness is a waste of time and an abuse of the sacred word."[250]

Witherup summarizes with ten points for Christians to follow in interpreting the Bible:

1) The Bible is God's word in human words. Calling the Bible God's inspired text does not alter the human dimension of that word. Remember that culture, historical setting and means of expression all influenced how the Bible came to be and needs to be read.

2) Not every passage is equally applicable in every age. The Bible contains apparent contradictions (compare, for example, Isaiah 2:4 and Joel 3:10 which give opposite advice). God's word in a given circumstance may not apply in exactly the same way at another time in history.

3) The literal meaning is not the *only* meaning. The meaning of any given biblical passage is multilayered. The literal meaning cannot legitimately be ignored or contradicted, but to get to the deeper spiritual meaning of some passages requires a more thorough understanding of the historical and cultural background.

4) There is no one foolproof method of biblical interpretation. Each passage must be handled on its own in its various contexts.

5) Your personal interpretation is not *the* interpretation.

6) The Bible does not contain every detail for living an ethical life. Many modern ethical dilemmas (nuclear arms, genetic engineering, cloning, etc.) are not specifically addressed in the Bible, even if it contains basic principles from which we can deduce proper ethical directions.

7) The Bible concerns as much what happens in this life as what takes place in the next.

8) Some biblical passages reflect an earlier moral perspective no longer acceptable. The acceptance of slavery or the total annihilation of an enemy, essentially genocide, is not part of our moral fabric today even if the Bible assumes or condones such practices in some passages. As the faith has grown, so has our moral perspective.

9) **Nothing in the Bible justifies hatred of others** (my emphasis). Nor can the Bible be used to justify the superiority of one race over another, such as some hate groups have asserted. Controversial passages, such as those on homosexuality (like Romans 1:27), also do not justify intolerance and persecution. Jesus' command is to judge not, lest we be judged (Matthew 7:1)

10) Some parts of the Bible remain a mystery. Even for scholars, the wording of some passages is so ambiguous, or the background so obscure, that no one can be said to have the final word on interpretation.[251]

In our time, a tragic abuse of the Bible has been to use it to exclude and condemn the LGBTQ community (a spectrum of gay, lesbian, and transexual and bisexual orientation), whether from the Church, or refusing to cater to gay customers who are planning a wedding, or opposing their marriages, or even killing them.

Witherup gives us an awful example: "In the wake of the terrible torture and killing of a gay college student in Wyoming in October 1998, religious anti-homosexual protesters were seen with signs such as 'God hates fags—Rom 9:13.'[252] Ironically, the passage has nothing to do with homosexuality!" (The verse actually reads "As it is written, 'I have loved

Jacob, but I have hated Esau.' "253 Not even close!)

Biblical justification for homophobia is sometimes given by those who point to the book of Leviticus, part of the Pentateuch (the original five books of Moses in the Old Testament). Leviticus 19:22 reads "You shall not lie with a male as with a woman; it is an abomination."254 The book of Leviticus carries an exhaustive list of specific details for the people of Israel, most of which involve ritual cleansing rites.

Leviticus also prohibits the eating of pigs and shellfish, and a bewildering number of other animals (including alligator, birds of prey, and insects with specific segmented legs, as follows: "All winged insects that walk upon all fours are detestable to you. But among the winged insects that walk on all fours you may eat those that have jointed legs above their feet, with which to leap on the ground." 255

Leviticus also tells men "You shall not round off the hair on your temples or mar the edges of your beard," which some orthodox Jews have interpreted to mean that they let their forelocks grow long on both sides from the edges of their foreheads, and grow such long beards that they could be mistaken for members of the rock band ZZ Top (as once happened on an episode of "The Simpsons").

Now, if you just want to pull one verse out of Leviticus and hold it up like it should have our reverent attention, but you ignore all the other detailed ritual commandments in that book, then you really don't have a pure motive about interpreting scripture. Do you want to judge gay people, but you freely eat pork and shrimp, don't keep a kosher kitchen, and cut your hair and trim your beard like a normal person? Then you have no business holding up one thing in Leviticus and ignoring the rest of that book. And that doesn't even address Jesus' admonishment not to judge "lest you be judged."

If you're still big on that "Old Time Religion", the most famous commandment from Leviticus is "You shall love your neighbor as yourself,"256 which pretty much rules out condemning people due to their sexual orientation.

In the introduction to this book I mentioned that then-Attorney General Jeff Sessions had quoted St. Paul's letter to the Romans to urge Christians to support the Trump administration's disgraceful policy of forcibly separating migrant children from their parents at the southern border. Romans 13:1-2 reads, "Let every person be subject to the governing authorities; for there is no authority except from God, and those authorities that exist have been instituted by God. Therefore, whoever resists authority resists what God has appointed, and those who resist will incur judgment."[257]

I don't think either President Trump or then-Attorney General Jeff Sessions were aware of the fateful perversion of this scripture by the Nazis (unfortunately with the active help of the German Lutheran clergy). As Thomas Webber explained on CNN's website[258], that in March 1933 shortly after the Nazis had come to power, "Protestant theologian Otto Dibelius invoked the biblical passage Romans 13 to urge Germans to support Hitler. As the nation looked upon him that day, in his sermon in front of the newly elected members of the Reichstag (parliament), Dibelius told Germans that they had learned from Martin Luther that Christians may not fail to support the state, "even not when [the state] acts hard and ruthlessly."

Luther and St. Paul both shared the view that (in normal times) the state served an important function, to discourage anarchy with consequences for lawbreakers. Both the people of God and unbelievers benefitted from whatever established authority was in place to enforce the law and punish lawbreakers.

However, this narrow reading of St. Paul does not account for a government built on idolatry and destruction of any opposition to its complete authority, including the Christian conscience and the collective Christian church. Luther used this verse to justify repression of the Peasant's Revolt in Germany because he realized that when secular authorities were overthrown and revolution followed, the anarchy was even worse than harsh rule, but he could not have foreseen the rise of the 20th century totalitarian state and would certainly have opposed the Nazis if he had been aware of their ultimate crimes.

Unfortunately, many Germans, including most of the clergy, took the Nazis for people who would uphold "law and order", especially against communist agitators and did not think through the consequences of supporting violent thugs as a government.

The point is that Christians have a moral obligation to challenge secular authority when they enact ungodly and inhumane policies, most especially when they invoke scripture as a justification for them.

For example, in 1561 John Calvin had published his *Readings on the Prophet Daniel*, in which he had argued that when kings disobey God, they automatically abdicated their worldly power. This was new thinking for Calvin, who had argued earlier with St. Paul and Luther that even unrighteous kings should be obeyed. This gave Calvin and his followers moral justification to challenge the position of established power, most of which happened to be Catholic monarchs at the time.

Huguenot (French Protestant) writers began to promote the idea of the "sovereignty of the people", which became a cornerstone of Enlightenment thinking in the next two centuries. This principle, which should be familiar to all Americans, is that the authority of a state and its government is created and sustained by the consent of its people, through their elected representatives.

"Sovereignty of the people" became synonymous with the Enlightenment idea of the Social Contract, laid out a century later by English philosophers Thomas Hobbes and John Locke, then a century after that Jean-Jacques Rousseau and Montesquieu, whose writings influenced both the American and French Revolutions.

For Christians however, the "sovereignty of the people" must be that of the people of God. In this country, unlike during the Roman Empire, citizens have the right to hold the government accountable for its policies. Christians have an obligation not to take anything a politician says regarding what is "Christian" at face value but to carefully consider it, and to (peacefully) protest when they are convicted by Christian conscience to oppose it. Remember what St. Peter and the apostles said. When the chips are down and we have to make a clear choice between the authorities and God, "We must obey God rather than any human authority."[259]

Re-writing God's Word to Suit Yourself

You may have heard of "cafeteria Catholics", so-called by their more pious brethren because they only "pick and choose" what they want to believe or practice, rather than accepting the entirety of Catholic teachings and guides for living.

I have noticed that many Protestants are doing the same thing, without even realizing it, by way of interpreting scripture to suit their own sensibilities, so as to make Christianity more convenient, though they may not be aware that's what they're doing.

For example, concerning the issue of refugees escaping violence and terrorism in Central America, trying to claim asylum in the U.S., I've heard people say that the biblical injunction to "love thy neighbor" "really means, your actual neighbors, the people who live near you." Such a convenient way to interpret scripture, so that you feel no obligation to anyone not already in your familiar circle.

There are three scriptural responses I have for this. The first is from the Gospel of Matthew chapter five, where we also find the Sermon on the Mount.

For if you love those who love you, what reward do you have? Do not even the tax collectors do the same? And if you greet only your brothers and sisters, what more are you doing than others? Do not even the Gentiles do the same? Be perfect, therefore, as your heavenly Father is perfect.[260]

The second is Jesus' parable of the Good Samaritan from the Gospel of Luke, chapter 10:

Just then a lawyer stood up to test Jesus. "Teacher," he said, "what must I do to inherit eternal life?" He said to him, "What is written in the law? What do you read there?" He answered, "You shall love the Lord your God with all your heart, and with all your soul, and with all your strength, and with all your mind; and your neighbor as yourself." And he said to him, "You have given the right answer; do this, and you will live." But wanting to justify himself, he asked Jesus, "And who is my neighbor?" Jesus replied, "A man was going down from Jerusalem to Jericho, and fell into the hands of robbers, who stripped him, beat him, and went away, leaving him half dead. Now by chance a priest was going down that road; and when he saw him, he passed by on the other side. So likewise, a Levite, when he came to the place and saw him, passed by on the other side. But a Samaritan while traveling came near him; and when he saw him, he was moved with pity. He went to him and bandaged his wounds, having poured oil and wine on them. Then he put him on his own animal, brought him to an inn, and took care of him. The next day he took out two denarii, gave them to the innkeeper, and said, 'Take care of him; and when I come back, I will repay you whatever more you spend.' Which of these three, do you think, was a neighbor to the man who fell into the hands of the robbers?" He said, "The one who showed him mercy." Jesus said to him, "Go and do likewise."[261]

It should be clear that Jesus is telling us today, to do the same. We know from the outset that this lawyer was only asking Jesus a question to test him.

Since the lawyer's motivation was not sincere, instead of thanking Jesus, "But wanting to justify himself, he asked Jesus, 'And who is my neighbor?'" In other words, "how can I limit what is required of me by the law to appear righteous before God," for that was his real motivation, along with putting Jesus on the spot, and if Jesus was so smart, let him define who is "my neighbor." People have been asking the same question for over 2,000 years, and for the same reasons.

Jesus responded with a famous and graphic parable, since it was clear that the lawyer's frame of mind was not really attuned to what the law required, which was an attitude, and actions, of love. First, we hear the graphic details of violence; the traveler was robbed, beaten, stripped and left half dead. In this state, nobody passing on the road could ignore him or his plight.

Then, we learn that a priest passed by man, but on the other side of the road, the better to ignore him and his plight. You would expect more practice of religion from a priest than just anyone on the road. Then, a Levite (a member of the tribe of Levi, who had hereditary religious duties in the Temple in Jerusalem), did the same thing. These establishment religious figures (somehow, like the lawyer) did nothing to demonstrate any of God's compassion.

The victim's fortunes change when he is seen by a Samaritan. Samaritans were the Jewish fundamentalists of Jesus' time. They had stayed in their ancestral lands of Samaria (the northern West Bank) when the southern Judeans were taken off to captivity in Babylon, when the First Temple in Jerusalem was destroyed in 586 BC.

Samaritans held that only the first five books of Moses in the Old Testament (the Pentateuch) were the Word of God and rejected all subsequent books (which Christians hold in common with modern Jews as scripture).

As we know from the story of Jesus and the Samaritan woman at the well in the Gospel of John chapter four, Samaritans and Jews avoided each other. In fact, the religious authorities slandered Jesus in John 5:48 by asking him, "Are we not right in saying that you are a Samaritan and have a demon?"[262]

So, it is a very deliberate point Jesus is making when he makes the Samaritan the hero of the story who saves the helpless victim, takes him to an inn, pays for it in advance, and admonishes the innkeeper to take care of the man, and would pay for any additional charges on his return.

In his inspired sermon on the subject, Dr. Martin Luther King, Jr. says that "a man of another race" (which is how the Jews and Samaritans considered each other) did God's will in acting as a neighbor to a man who was presumably a Jew, while the religious elite in Jewish society looked the other way and avoided the plight of their fellow Jew (and human being). This sermon would be his last.

Jesus doesn't have to say this, but the message is clear: if you want to earn eternal life (the original question of the conversation), you'll have to do better than look the other way when you see obvious and dire need. Even a godly Samaritan is being, and acting, more righteous than the uncaring priest and Levite.

It is action on behalf of the needy, and a sense of urgency and identifying with the victim and oppressed, that is "loving your neighbor." Just because they don't look like you or live in the same community doesn't get you off the hook for doing God's work with your own hands.

The other verse I'll cite about the dangers of interpreting scripture to suit your own sensibilities or comfort level, is in the conclusion of the Revelation to John, chapter 22: "I warn everyone who hears the words of the prophecy of this book: if anyone adds to them, God will add to that person the plagues described in this book; if anyone takes away from the words of the book of this prophecy, God will take away that person's share in the tree of life and in the holy city, which are described in this book."[263]

Now, you might object that the author John (or the angel dictating the story) was only speaking of that one individual book. If you think you have license to re-write the Word of God for your own justification and convenience, keeping in mind the parable of the Good Samaritan, think on this:

Therefore, whoever breaks one of the least of these commandments, and teaches others to do the same, will be called least in the kingdom of heaven; but whoever does them and teaches them will be called great in the kingdom of heaven. For I tell you, unless your righteousness exceeds that of the scribes and Pharisees, you will never enter the kingdom of heaven.[264]

Concluding Prayer for This Chapter

Lord, we give you thanks for the gift of your Word and for the work of your servants who diligently recorded it over the centuries and translated it into our language in a way that we can understand, so we could be inspired to live and believe as your people. Keep us reverent in our reading your Word, and keep us from the temptation to interpret it in ways that are not faithful to you, but rather let us be inspired by it to live lives worthy of your calling, and never to use your word to justify our prejudices or to judge others.

Chapter Seven

"Christian": Default Identity, or Active Commitment?

And he told them many things in parables, saying: "Listen! A sower went out to sow. And as he sowed, some seeds fell on the path, and the birds came and ate them up. Other seeds fell on rocky ground, where they did not have much soil, and they sprang up quickly, since they had no depth of soil. But when the sun rose, they were scorched; and since they had no root, they withered away. Other seeds fell among thorns, and the thorns grew up and choked them. Other seeds fell on good soil and brought forth grain, some a hundredfold, some sixty, some thirty. Let anyone with ears listen!"

"Hear then the parable of the sower. When anyone hears the word of the kingdom and does not understand it, the evil one comes and snatches away what is sown in the heart; this is what was sown on the path. As for what was sown on rocky ground, this is the one who hears the word and immediately receives it with joy; yet such a person has no root, but endures only for a while, and when trouble or persecution arises on account of the word, that person immediately falls away. As for what was sown among thorns, this is the one who hears the word, but the cares of the world and the lure of wealth choke the word, and it yields nothing. But as for what was sown on good soil, this is the one who hears the word and understands it, who indeed bears fruit and yields, in one case a hundredfold, in another sixty, and in another thirty."[265]

Jesus lays out in this parable how the Word is received by a variety of people; few who hear hold fast and bear fruit.

One problem in today's world are people who are culturally religious but not personally religious. They are born into a family and society faith tradition, like Christianity, Islam or Judaism, and this is their default religious identity. They could live their whole lives this way without making a personal commitment to God in their faith (or converting to another), and be buried with the religious symbol of their default religion on their tombstone, but it might have no personal significance for them.

First, we must distinguish between "cultural Christianity" and the life of Christian discipleship. "Cultural Christians" are members of a large international tribe who understand the divine as described by very general Christian concepts, but have no faith commitment beyond a loose cultural allegiance.

The reason this is a problem, is that people naturally have tribal emotions about the culture they are born and socialized into, but if they have no deep awareness of the ways of God, they could easily be manipulated into thinking of God, and their religion, as a kind of cosmic team, that they belong to, and use their cultural "religion" as an excuse to persecute those of different backgrounds, or to cheer their "team" without considering a deeper personal commitment.

We have seen this played out with horrible consequences, in Myanmar with the Rohingya Muslim minority being driven out of their country and murdered by cultural Buddhists; with the Palestinian-Israeli conflict of the last 50 years, and of course with ISIS in Syria.

But cultural Christianity has plenty of blood on its hands, from the slaughter of the Jewish and Muslim residents of Jerusalem by Crusader soldiers in 1099, to countless petty wars in Europe through the Thirty Year's War between Catholic and Protestant forces in the 17th century, and up through the Bosnian civil war in the 1990s, which was perpetrated by Serbian "Christians" against a Muslim minority, and of course, the Holocaust against the Jews.

Although the Holocaust was engineered by the Germans, plenty of people of other "Christian" countries were eager to help the Nazis get rid of their own Jewish populations particularly in France, Austria, Hungary and Poland.

In the Cold War, our government gave aid to right-wing thugs throughout Central and South America whose death squads killed thousands. In El Salvador in 1980, in response to criticism from the Catholic Church, these death squads first assassinated Óscar Romero, the Archbishop of San Salvador, on March 24, while he was performing mass; eight months later, they raped and murdered four Marianist missionary nuns (all Americans). With cultural "Christianity" like this, who needs pagans...or even Communists?

Such are the consequences of using religion as a tool for culture wars which become actual wars, and which are a sin against God for taking His name in vain, as well as sins against other people. But what are the consequences of "cultural Christianity" on the individual level?

A person may think being "culturally Christian" is all they need is to acknowledge Jesus as Lord with their lips, when asked what they believe, and then continue doing whatever they want to satisfy their selfish desires. "You believe that God is one; you do well. Even the demons believe—and shudder."[266]

A mere intellectual or cultural default belief in God does not deserve, or bring, salvation from sins or eternal life.

Then there are "casual Christians," often also known as "C&E Christians", because you seldom see them in church except for Christmas and Easter (at least they know where to go twice a year). In America today it's far too tempting to go one simple step beyond the cultural Christians and think that this is enough. This kind of "Christianity" could also be called "convenience Christianity", because it isn't about serving God or your neighbor, it's about having the superficial trappings of religion without any commitment or obligation.

I think it's too tempting in America today to fall into this superficiality, because there are churches (and manger creche scenes at Christmas) all over the country. Who will challenge you if you show up occasionally at a church in easy driving distance, or that looks pretty enough to suit your taste, and claim that you're a Christian? Maybe no other person, but then you don't answer to people on the Day of Judgment.

Interestingly, among conservative American voters who support Trump, their church attendance is substantially lower in frequency than those who supported Cruz, Carson, Kasich, Bush, Fiorina, Christie and Rubio in 2016, according to researcher Geoffrey Layman. "Trump does best among evangelicals with one key trait: They don't really go to church. In short, the evangelicals supporting Trump are not the same evangelicals who have traditionally comprised the Christian Right and supported cultural warriors such as Rick Santorum and Ted Cruz."[267]

The Lukewarm Christian is maybe more committed in church attendance than the Convenience Christian, but has grown comfortable and complacent. There's no more eloquent description of this Christian, and the dangers of complacency, than the words of Jesus to John in Revelation:

> "And to the angel of the church in Laodicea write: The words of the Amen, the faithful and true witness, the origin of God's creation: "I know your works; you are neither cold nor hot. I wish that you were either cold or hot. So, because you are lukewarm, and neither cold nor hot, I am about to spit you out of my mouth. For you say, 'I am rich, I have prospered, and I need nothing.' You do not realize that you are wretched, pitiable, poor, blind, and naked. Therefore, I counsel you to buy from me gold refined by fire so that you may be rich; and White robes to clothe you and to keep the shame of your nakedness from being seen; and salve to anoint your eyes so that you may see. I reprove and discipline those whom I love. Be earnest, therefore, and repent."[268]

Does this church sound familiar? It could be like thousands of churches in the United States today. An Anglican priest named Frederick Lewis Donaldson delivered a sermon in Westminster Abbey on March 20, 1925, titled "Seven Social Sins," but six months later a nearly identical list was published in *Young India* by Mohandas Karamchand Gandhi.[269] These Seven Social Sins were:

1. Wealth without work.
2. Pleasure without conscience.
3. Knowledge without character.

4. Commerce without morality.
5. Science without humanity.
6. Religion without sacrifice.
7. Politics without principle.

A century later, each and all of these seem especially relevant, and worthy of ongoing discussion and soul-searching. Here, I'd like to focus on number six, Religion without Sacrifice, because it seems so relevant to Jesus' letter to the church at Laodicea and, I believe, also to many American Protestant churches today.

It's only natural that if we have sincere and honest intentionality in our Christian journey, we will be moved by the Holy Spirit to want to give of what are called the three "T" s: our time, treasure and talent.

The time is not only showing up regularly to church but in how we serve the church and the wider community during other times of the week, by volunteering to serve on committees, assist with worship or be active in social ministry. The treasure of course is our financial offerings. During the COVID-19 quarantine and social distancing, we are not able to interact with others as personally as we would like, but we can offset that with increasing our giving.

The idea of "religion without sacrifice" is especially relevant for Protestant Christianity in America today. In his book *The Cost of Discipleship*, the Lutheran theologian Dietrich Bonhoeffer, writing to fellow German Lutherans under the Nazis, spoke of the problem of "cheap grace"; "Cheap grace is the deadly enemy of our Church. We are fighting today for costly grace."[270] What he meant was:

> Cheap grace means grace sold on the market like cheapjack wares. Grace without price, grace without cost! The essence of grace, we suppose, is that the account has been paid in advance; and, because it has been paid, everything can be had for nothing...Instead of following Christ, let the Christian enjoy the consolation of his grace! ...Cheap grace is grace without discipleship, grace without the cross, grace without Jesus Christ, living and incarnate.

Costly grace is the treasure hidden in the field; for the sake of it, a man will gladly go and sell all that he has...it is the call of Jesus Christ at which the disciple leaves his nets and follows him. Costly grace is the gospel which must be sought again and again, the gift which must be *asked* for, the door at which a man must *knock*. Such grace is costly because it calls us to follow, and it is grace because it calls us to follow Jesus Christ. It is costly because it costs a man his life, and it is grace because it gives a man the only true life. It is costly because it condemns sin, and it is grace because it justifies the sinner. Above all, it is *costly* because it cost God the life of his Son: "ye were bought at a price," and what has cost God much cannot be cheap for us.[271]

If our salvation was costly for Christ, then the appropriate sacrifice for us as Christians is to sacrifice our life of self-indulgence, pursuit of pleasure and pleasing of sensibilities, to become "dead" to that as being at the center of our lives, where Jesus should be.

Another false path for the Christian is the path of sentimental indulgence. There are both Catholic and Protestant versions of this. The emphasis of a church service in this environment is on how you *feel*, as if public worship were on the level of a movie or a Disney attraction, and this is played out in sappy hymns or sophisticated electronic acoustics to lift individual spirits and create a happy group experience.

As a Lutheran, I hesitate to criticize church music, but you learn a lot about the sensibilities of a church when you experience the music (both instrumental and vocal), and I've learned that churches that put a primary emphasis on ways of making you feel good, tend to avoid preaching the Word where sacrifice, and commitment from the parishioner, are mentioned or discussed in sermons.

The sentimental Christian may confuse intensity of emotional engagement (at least, during worship) for a sober commitment to actually doing and living a Christian life day by day. There can also be a rather sentimental idea that a person must have a dramatic (and often, public) personal crisis, to be seen in a wretched low point, and from which they "accept Christ as their personal savior", give up (fill in the blank), and they will be saved, as if a lifelong path of faith without melodrama is somehow insufficient in contrasting "before" and "after". What good is "accepting Christ as your personal savior" if your life afterwards doesn't reflect a deeper commitment to discipleship than conspicuously abstaining from alcohol or other things?

There may be other examples of shallow paths of Christian life, but we've covered enough here. The alternative to these, whatever your denomination, is the path of discipleship. It must start with an awareness of our own sinfulness that we know we cannot escape on our own. Whether in a public ceremony attended by 100 or in a sincere moment of prayer with God, it must also involve asking God's forgiveness and accepting His grace. But to keep grace from being cheap, it cannot end there; it must involve a commitment to live a Christian life.

So, what is the "Christian life?" Let's consider the preaching of John the Baptist, and the response from his audience in the third chapter of Luke.

As we know, John was fulfilling the prophecy from the book of Isaiah: "The voice of one crying out in the wilderness: 'Prepare the way of the Lord, make his paths straight. Every valley shall be filled, and every mountain and hill shall be made low, and the crooked shall be made straight, and the rough ways made smooth; and all flesh shall see the salvation of God.'"[272]

He did this to proclaim that, since Jesus was about to start his ministry, the kingdom of God was at hand. "He went into all the region around the Jordan, proclaiming a baptism of repentance for the forgiveness of sins."[273]

John said to the crowds that came out to be baptized by him, "You brood of vipers! Who warned you to flee from the wrath to come? Bear fruits worthy of repentance. Do not begin to say to yourselves, 'We have Abraham as our ancestor'; for I tell you, God is able from these stones to raise up children to Abraham. Even now the ax is lying at the root of the trees; every tree therefore that does not bear good fruit is cut down and thrown into the fire."

And the crowds asked him, "What then should we do?" In reply he said to them, "Whoever has two coats must share with anyone who has none; and whoever has food must do likewise." Even tax collectors came to be baptized, and they asked him, "Teacher, what should we do?" He said to them, "Collect no more than the amount prescribed for you." Soldiers also asked him, "And we, what should we do?" He said to them, "Do not extort money from anyone by threats or false accusation, and be satisfied with your wages."[274]

As John explains, after making a commitment to follow Jesus, "bearing fruits worthy of repentance" is an essential part of the authentic Christian life of discipleship. John warned against complacency by telling the crowds "Do not begin to say to yourselves, 'We have Abraham as our ancestor'; for I tell you, God is able from these stones to raise up children to Abraham." We could substitute "White American Protestant", or "correct conservative Catholic" for "children of Abraham" in John's warning for America today.

There is always danger in complacency, because John then warns "Even now the ax is lying at the root of the trees; every tree therefore that does not bear good fruit is cut down and thrown into the fire."

What I like about these verses is that they show that the grace and forgiveness of God should inspire "fruits worthy of repentance," and these are not difficult. Also, I like that we see some of the most despised people in Jewish society of the day, tax collectors and soldiers, also coming to be baptized, and taking John at his word by asking for specific instructions for demonstrating their repentance befitting their occupations.

Both tax collectors and soldiers were known to extort money; in fact, tax collectors weren't paid much, and were expected to shake down citizens to make up for the shortfall. Soldiers were the sword of foreign occupation, but in accepting John's call to repent, they became the spiritual equals of Jews receiving John's baptism. If these people can be allowed to be saved, so can anyone, but sincere repentance calls for sacrifice; producing "fruits worthy of repentance."

The path of Christian discipleship is difficult on the one hand, because it requires constantly remembering our commitment to bear fruit through our deeds, while remembering that we cannot take any credit for these personally, as they are the fruits of the Holy Spirit. One temptation for the Christian is false piety.

Remember, Luther's great inspiration was to realize he could not, and need not, do anything to earn God's favor; "For by grace you have been saved through faith, and this is not your own doing; it is the gift of God—not the result of works, so that no one may boast. For we are what he has made us, created in Christ Jesus for good works, which God prepared beforehand to be our way of life."[275]

The same was true for us as for those baptized by John; we have God's grace through faith, we cannot boast of it, and—last and most importantly— "For we are what he has made us, created in Christ Jesus for good works, which God prepared beforehand to be our way of life."

Concluding Prayer for This Chapter

Lord, move us to think the Christian life, not just as a cultural default, but that we are "created in Christ Jesus for good works, which God prepared beforehand to be our way of life," not as a means of boasting, but to demonstrate repentance and commitment to you. We ask you to help us desire a closer walk with you and to desire the "grace which costs", rather than "cheap grace" which asks nothing and grants nothing.

Richard G. Leahy

Chapter Eight

Discipleship: Commitment and Cost

And he called unto him the multitude with his disciples, and said unto them, "If any man would come after me, let him deny himself, and take up his cross, and follow me. For whosoever would save his life shall lose it; and whosoever shall lose his life for my sake and the gospel shall save it. For what doth it profit a man, to gain the whole world, and to forfeit his life? For what should a man give in exchange for his life? For whosoever shall be ashamed of me and of my words in this adulterous and sinful generation, the Son of man also shall be ashamed of him, when he cometh in the glory of his Father with the holy angels."[276]

We see the power of Jesus' call when he tells his chosen disciples, "Follow me;" they obeyed, literally dropping everything in order to do it. Note that Jesus didn't promise them anything at that moment; these men understood that Jesus was Lord, even though they didn't know how or why.

Then, we see what Jesus tells his disciples about the cost of discipleship. There are three basic, essential actions one must take: "let him deny himself, and take up his cross, and follow me." We can now include females in the pronouns here, so that "himself" and "his" also include "herself" and "her." Dietrich Bonhoeffer, the Lutheran theologian who bravely joined the resistance to the Nazis, and paid for it with his life, writes eloquently about discipleship in his book *The Cost of Discipleship:*

> Just as Christ is Christ only in virtue of his suffering and rejection, so the disciple is a disciple only in so far as he shares his Lord's suffering and rejection and crucifixion. Discipleship means adherence to the person of Jesus, and therefore submission to the law of Christ which is the law of the cross... Only when we have become completely oblivious of self, are we ready to bear the cross for his sake."[277]

Jesus is not reasonable. For God to sacrifice His only son for the sins of the world was not reasonable, and it follows that discipleship is also not reasonable or devoid of sacrifice. The disciple is not greater than the master. Jesus was without a home, "he was despised and rejected by others; a man of suffering and acquainted with infirmity, and as one from whom others hide their faces."[278]

As they were going along the road, someone said to him, "I will follow you wherever you go." And Jesus said to him, "Foxes have holes, and birds of the air have nests; but the Son of Man has nowhere to lay his head." To another he said, "Follow me." But he said, "Lord, first let me go and bury my father." But Jesus said to him, "Let the dead bury their own dead; but as for you, go and proclaim the kingdom of God." Another said, "I will follow you, Lord; but let me first say farewell to those at my home." Jesus said to him, "No one who puts a hand to the plow and looks back is fit for the kingdom of God."[279]

In case anyone was wondering, your "cross" is the sacrifice you make for the sake of following Jesus. As C.S. Lewis explained in "Mere Christianity", just putting up with people you don't like doesn't qualify as "carrying your cross", since that's the kind of thing everyone has to deal with and involves no specific Christian commitment.

Anything you give from your time, talent and treasure to God involves some sacrifice, and carrying your cross. Also, all the naughty things you'd like to spend your time doing, but refrain from doing, for the sake of a Christian life, is part of carrying your cross. Being a witness for Christ in the world, resisting social pressure and enduring ridicule, speaking up and out against social injustice, and working to heal the world, are all carrying one's cross.

If Jesus had not so graciously prepared us for this word, we should have found it unbearable. But by preparing us for it he has enabled us to receive even a word as hard as this as a word of grace. It comes to us in the joy of discipleship and confirms us in it... The cross means sharing the suffering of Christ to the last and to the fullest. Only a man thus totally committed in discipleship can experience the meaning of the cross. The cross is there, right from the beginning, he has only got to pick it up: there is no need for him to go out and look for a cross for himself, no need for him deliberately to run after suffering... When Christ calls a man, he bids him come and die. It may be a death like that of the first disciples who had to leave home and work to follow him, or it may be a death like Luther's, who had to leave the monastery and go out into the world. But it is the same death every time—death in Jesus Christ, the death of the old man at his call.[280]

But there is another aspect of carrying one's cross, says Bonhoeffer, which is to become the bearer of other men's burdens— "Bear ye one another's burdens, and so fulfil the law of Christ" (Gal. 6.2). "As Christ bears our burdens, so ought we to bear the burdens of our fellow-men... Thus, the call to follow Christ always means a call to share the work of forgiving men their sins. Forgiveness is the Christlike suffering which it is the Christian's duty to bear.[281]

If we refuse to take up our cross and submit to suffering and rejection at the hands of men, we forfeit our fellowship with Christ and have ceased to follow him. But if we lose our lives in his service and carry our cross, we shall find our lives again in the fellowship of the cross with Christ.[282]

As the old gospel song goes, "If you can't bear the cross, then you can't wear the crown."

Biblical Warnings on Spiritual Complacency

As we have seen from the letter to the angel of the church at Laodicea in the book of Revelation, complacency was a spiritual danger in the early church, and will ever be so, especially in societies like Protestant, White America where we are surrounded by creature comforts, don't face persecution for our faith, and thanks to cheap grace, aren't often called to account for ourselves.

There isn't a Christian anywhere today who shouldn't be asking themselves how much more faithful they could be in their walk with the Lord. As we learned from John the Baptist (and Paul in Ephesians), our new life in Christ is created for good works, but as we have also read, this is for the benefit of others, not for self-congratulation or for conspicuous show.

If you tell me, "I have been washed in the blood of the Lamb," I would answer "And what have you done for Him lately; where is your witness visible in the world around you?"

This chapter is meant to exhort anyone who thinks that because they're a Protestant American, that this alone means they will be saved. We'll spend some time on biblical verses here which should inspire you to have an honest dialog with yourself and with God. As Psalm 111 says, "The fear of the Lord is the beginning of wisdom."[283]

"Not everyone who says to me, 'Lord, Lord,' will enter the kingdom of heaven, but only the one who does the will of my Father in heaven."[284] Note that Jesus doesn't keep us in suspense but is clear that doing is even more important than talking. Once again, we see the necessary link between faith and appropriate action.

"For all of us must appear before the judgment seat of Christ, so that each may receive recompense for what has been done in the body, whether good or evil."[285]

The casual, cultural, convenience Christians should be worried by this last passage. It isn't about how many times you call Jesus "Lord, Lord"; faith is where you start, but when you appear before the judgment seat of Christ, you will receive "recompense for what has been done in the body, whether good or evil."

If non-believers must be judged for their deeds, how can Christians expect to be shown eternal life if they have nothing to show as a legacy for their lives on earth? "From everyone to whom much has been given, much will be required; and from the one to whom much has been entrusted, even more will be demanded."[286]

There's really no excuse for any Christian to not know the necessary link between their deeds in this life and their reward, since we have very specific and detailed explanation given by Jesus in the 25th chapter of Matthew:

"When the Son of Man comes in his glory, and all the angels with him, then he will sit on the throne of his glory. All the nations will be gathered before him, and he will separate people one from another as a shepherd separates the sheep from the goats, and he will put the sheep at his right hand and the goats at the left. Then the king will say to those at his right hand, 'Come, you that are blessed by my Father, inherit the kingdom prepared for you from the foundation of the world; for I was hungry and you gave me food, I was thirsty and you gave me something to drink, I was a stranger and you welcomed me, I was naked and you gave me clothing, I was sick and you took care of me, I was in prison and you visited me.' Then the righteous will answer him, 'Lord, when was it that we saw you hungry and gave you food, or thirsty and gave you something to drink? And when was it that we saw you a stranger and welcomed you, or naked and gave you clothing? And when was it that we saw you sick or in prison and visited you?' And the king will answer them, 'Truly I tell you, just as you did it to one of the least of these who are members of my family, you did it to me.'

Then he will say to those at his left hand, 'You that are accursed, depart from me into the eternal fire prepared for the devil and his angels; for I was hungry and you gave me no food, I was thirsty and you gave me nothing to drink, I was a stranger and you did not welcome me, naked and you did not give me clothing, sick and in prison and you did not visit me.' Then they also will answer, 'Lord, when was it that we saw you hungry or thirsty or a stranger or naked or sick or in prison, and did not take care of you?' Then he will answer them, 'Truly I tell you, just as you did not do it to one of the least of these, you did not do it to me.' And these will go away into eternal punishment, but the righteous into eternal life."[287]

This great parable illustrates one of Luther's great insights, the concept of sins of omission. The Catholic Church has always had a lurid list of Cardinal Sins, and ordinary sins, and it's all about avoiding doing bad things. Sins of omission are the good that you should do, that you don't; they are sins of non-action. Jesus tells us that the "real deal" with the Judgment is how you stack up on sins of omission. Especially for us

Christians, since this is one of our scriptures, how can we not know what's expected of us, and be accountable for it?

Luther gave us a real gift with making this distinction clear, but it was sadly ironic for Germany some 430 years later. The children of the devil were persecuting the weak, political enemies, gays, gypsies, and worst of all, the Jews, just for being who they were. Where were the children of God while this was happening? Sadly, mostly out to lunch, both in Catholic and Protestant parts of Germany. As Edmund Burke allegedly said, (without a source confirmation), "All that is necessary for the triumph of evil is for good men [people] to do nothing."

Even more startling is the fate that awaits some who were reckoned mighty in the Lord. "On that day many will say to me, 'Lord, Lord, did we not prophesy in your name, and cast out demons in your name, and do many deeds of power in your name?' Then I will declare to them, 'I never knew you; go away from me, you evildoers.'"[288] Clearly, there was a private life with these people that did not match their public piety and even great deeds, or their motives were not pure. Public acclaim, even from the faithful in this life, isn't enough without a sincere, faithful relationship with Christ.

The logical, and necessary, full circle of the Reformation is the union of faith and works. We know we cannot be justified before God by works, but by grace through faith, we have forgiveness of sins and the promise of salvation; therefore, we exist on this earth thereafter to do God's will in good works through our hands, to demonstrate our faith by understanding the cost of grace.

What good is it, my brothers and sisters, if you say you have faith but do not have works? Can faith save you? If a brother or sister is naked and lacks daily food, and one of you says to them, "Go in peace; keep warm and eat your fill," and yet you do not supply their bodily needs, what is the good of that? So, faith by itself, if it has no works, is dead. But someone will say, "You have faith and I have works." Show me your faith apart from your works, and I by my works will show you my faith. You believe that God is one; you do well. Even the demons believe—and shudder. Do you want to be shown, you senseless person, that faith apart from works is barren? Was not our ancestor Abraham justified by works when he offered his son Isaac on the altar? You see that faith was active along with his works, and faith was brought to completion by the works. Thus, the scripture was fulfilled that says, "Abraham believed God, and it was reckoned to him as righteousness," and he was called the friend of God. You see that a person is justified by works and not by faith alone... For just as the body without the spirit is dead, so faith without works is also dead.[289]

Concluding Prayer for This Chapter

Lord Jesus, keep us mindful of your sacrifice for us and all humanity. Since you bore the sins of the whole world though you were without sin, inspire us through your Spirit to take up our own cross and follow you, not only in avoiding sinful acts, but in doing acts of mercy and kindness to your children in need, so we may thus demonstrate our faith to you and the world.

Chapter Nine

Black Lives *Should* Matter

"I have a dream that my four little children will one day live in a nation where they will not be judged by the color of their skin but by the content of their character."—Dr. Martin Luther King, Jr. [290]

"Am I not a man, and a brother?"[291]

Events of 2020, most especially the killing of George Floyd by public suffocation under a policeman's knee on Memorial Day, have made the Black Lives Matter movement a rallying cry for American citizens of any race or ethnicity who are concerned with social justice and yearn to see this nation to live up to its ideals of equality before the law for all.

Some people who live fairly protected lives may ask "Don't all lives matter?" The point with affirming that "Black Lives Matter" is that "all lives *can't* matter unless Black lives matter, too."

After seemingly endless deadly police shootings of unarmed Black men, and earlier this year, the shooting death of Ahmaud Arbery in an Atlanta suburb by a couple of White men, apparently for the crime of jogging in a White neighborhood, seem to prove that, to much of White America, Black lives *don't* matter. The Black Lives Matter movement is affirming that Black lives *should* matter, as much as those of anyone else.

When President Trump and his (White) followers say "All lives matter," what they are really saying is that they deny the narrative that Whites owe anything to any other racial group, even acknowledging the consistent racism of American society for the last 300 years, since the Virginia slave code of 1705. If they did acknowledge it, they might then have to examine their role in participating in and perpetuating an unequal society based on racial hierarchy.

Many White Americans seem to have no understanding of the systemic racism Black Americans live under, from being the last to be hired and the first to be fired, to being excluded from middle-class neighborhoods through "redlining" by banks giving home mortgages, to little access to affordable health care, as well as violence and prejudice.

Bob Woodward's recently published book *Rage* is based on 18 hours of taped interviews that the author conducted with President Trump by telephone. Rosa Brooks, a law professor at Georgetown University, wrote a review of the book for the *Washington Post* on September 13, 2020.

Woodward urges Trump to display a tad more empathy towards racial justice protesters (the President, true to form, has been exulting in his ability to "send in the military" to deal with the protesters, whom he describes, variously, as "these poor radical lefts" and as "arsonists...thugs...anarchists" and "very bad people." Woodward, in response, attempts to explain "White privilege" to an incredulous Trump. "Do you have any sense that that privilege has isolated [you]?" the reporter asks. "And that [White, privileged people] have to work our way out of it to understand the anger and the pain, particularly, Black people feel?" But not even Bob Woodward can coax Trump into empathy. "No," Trump informs him. "You really drank the Kool-Aid, didn't you?" He goes on to boast about all he's done for "the Black people."[292]

In fact, President Trump is actively hostile to the idea that viewing American history through a lens informed by race, slavery and its impact on society. On September 17, 2020, President Trump called for "Patriotic education" in public schools while blasting progressive efforts at re-examining American history through a race-critical lens as "toxic propaganda."

He also called out a "twisted web of lies" he said is "left-wing indoctrination" in schools and curriculum, which he claimed "views every issue through the lens of race" in an effort to impose "tyranny" and "a new segregation." He specifically cited the 1619 Project, a series of essays in the *New York Times* re-examining America's legacy in view of slavery and its aftermath as "ideological poison" that will "dissolve the civic bonds" of

America."[293]

One good thing coming out of the dizzying sense that civil liberties, especially those of Black citizens, are under increasing attack, is the participation in demonstrations throughout the country after the death of George Floyd by White men and women, and those of other ethnicities, especially the young, and a visible commitment by younger Americans to be involved in effecting change.

For the benefit of my White brethren who may not be aware of the long and violent history of racism and its effects in America, I'll give some highlights. In 1619, the year the Jamestown Assembly became the first representative governing body to meet in North America, or anywhere in the Americas[294], a Portuguese ship, the São João Bautista, was captured by the English; aboard were 20 Africans who had been brought across the ocean to be traded into slavery.[295]

In the early seventeenth century, there were few settlers on the wild East Coast of what became the United States. Indentured servitude was a system by which colonists in Virginia would pay the passage of workers, in return for the use of their labor, unpaid, for a period of time, after which they would become free, and sometimes get a parcel of land to own.

Interestingly, the enslaved Africans brought to Virginia by accident were treated as indentured servants, not as sub-humans which would happen later. In part this might be because labor was scarce and a systemic slave-based agricultural economy had not yet developed.

In the seventeenth century, many Africans had earned their freedom, and they were each granted 50 acres of land when freed from their indentures, to raise their own crops. Anthony Johnson was an African who was freed soon after 1635; he settled on land on the Eastern Shore following the end of indenture, later buying his own African indentured servants as laborers.[296]

After the mid-seventeenth century we see a racist change in Virginia law. In 1661, Virginia passed its first law allowing any free person the right to own slaves. Additional laws detailing the status of Africans as slaves were passed in the later seventeenth century and codified into Virginia's first slave code in 1705.

One of these in 1662 said that children born in the colony would take the social status of their mothers, regardless of who their fathers were. Notably, this was in contrast to English common law of the time, and the result became generations of enslaved persons, including mixed-race children and adults, some of whom were majority White, such as Sally Hemmings, Thomas Jefferson's enslaved woman, who was a half-sister to his late wife, Martha.[297]

The burden of caring for these mixed-race children fell on their enslaved mothers. Interestingly, sexual relations between the races were not explicitly banned, just marriage which put husband and wife on an equal status before the law. This meant that White men who owned slaves (or who later employed Blacks in domestic labor) could have their way with these women, because they could, and get away with it, while leaving the women the burden of bringing up the children who would not have their father's status (or right of inheritance). This continued even into the mid-20th century.

The Virginia Slave Codes of 1705 show that in nearly a century, the Virginia colony had moved from considering Africans indentured servants, to putting systemic racism into law. The law achieved the following:

- Established new property rights for slave owners,
- Allowed for the legal, free trade of slaves with protections granted by the courts,
- Established separate courts of trial for Blacks,
- Prohibited Blacks, regardless of free status, from owning arms [weapons],
- Whites could not be employed by Blacks,
- Allowed for the apprehension of suspected runaways.[298]

This codification of systemic racist treatment of Americans of African descent was followed by the other Southern colonies. Interestingly, the era of "Jim Crow" laws following Reconstruction sought to bring back the same systemic inferiority of persons of African descent before the law, nearly

200 years after the Virginia Slave Codes. If federal law prevented owning slaves, the South could still find ways to institutionalize racism, to affect the legal inferiority of persons of African descent compared to Whites.

One interesting, recurring theme in the slave laws after 1705 was the attempt to keep the races separate, so they would not realize their common humanity and upset the rigged social system. One example was the prohibition on miscegenation, or intermarriage between the races. This continued in Virginia until the law was successfully challenged as unconstitutional in the Supreme Court case *Loving vs. Virginia*, where Richard Loving (a White Virginian) was ostracized and even jailed for marrying Mildred, a Black Virginian.

They had to leave the state and live in Washington, D.C. where interracial marriage was legal. The case was a landmark civil rights decision of the U.S. Supreme Court in which the Court ruled that laws banning interracial marriage violate the Equal Protection and Due Process Clauses of the Fourteenth Amendment to the U.S. Constitution.[299] This case led the way for dismantling these laws throughout the South.

Shockingly (to the author), the law prohibiting interracial marriage in Virginia was not thrown out in the Loving case, until *1967,* when I was eight! The case is touchingly memorialized in the Joel Edgerton movie "Loving", based on *The Loving Story* by Nancy Buirski. The 2016 film won the Producers of America award and the Stanley Kramer award.

We see another angle on intimate relations between the races with the late Senator Strom Thurmond of South Carolina. After his death, Thurmond, a long-time, staunch segregationist, was revealed by his mixed-race daughter Essie Mae Washington of having impregnated her mother, Carrie Butler, when Thurmond was 23 and Butler was 15; Washington was their daughter.

She was raised by her aunt, Mary Washington, Carrie's sister, in Pennsylvania. She only learned Butler was her mother when she came to visit when Essie Mae was 13, and met her father for the first time when she was 16. He agreed to provide for her and they met over the years. He put her through college and gave her over $100,000 over half a century, but never publicly acknowledged her as his daughter. [300]

Ironically, Thurmond's private life was at great odds with his public stance against civil rights for Black Americans. Thurmond was the candidate for president in 1948 for the Dixiecrat party, representing hardline Southern segregationists who objected to President Truman's integration of the armed forces and any other leveling of the field between the races.

He set a Senate filibuster record in 1957 for speaking for over 24 hours and 18 minutes against a civil rights bill. He then filibustered against the 1964 Civil Rights Act, and when it passed, he supported Barry Goldwater for president, who also opposed the Civil Rights Act.[301]

You wonder if Thurmond would have been held in such respect by his fellow White segregationists had they known he had fathered a mixed-race child, and that he was essentially leading a double life. All this only came to light after Thurmond died in 2003. But, in her own words, Washington said she was never "completely free" until she could stand before the world and say out loud that Strom Thurmond, the one-time segregationist South Carolina senator, was her father.[302]

Other parts of the New World like the Caribbean and much of South America also had slavery, but people were socially acknowledged who were racially mixed, as mulattos. As racism proceeded from post-Reconstruction into the 1920s, even areas of the South like New Orleans which had been racially mixed for centuries and where the mixed-race Creoles had a place of honor, saw a strict binary racial hierarchy put in place; you were either White, or "colored", and all coloreds were to be separated and segregated from Whites, with unequal and obviously inferior public facilities.

For Black Americans, the post-Reconstruction South, aided by the neglect of the federal government, imposed a comprehensive set of laws and restrictions to keep Blacks and mixed-race persons in economic bondage, prevent their education on the level of White students or employment as skilled workers, segregation from Whites, and most of all, intimidation and elaborate literacy tests or "grandfather" clauses to discourage them from voting.

Worst was the widespread (even outside the South) terrorist tactic of lynching. The Equal Justice Institute has documented 4,084 racial terror lynchings in twelve Southern states between the end of Reconstruction in 1877 and 1950, which is at least 800 more lynchings in these states than previously reported.[303]

The Equal Justice Institute has produced a detailed "Lynching Report", which explains that

Racial terror lynching was a tool used to enforce Jim Crow laws and racial segregation—a tactic for maintaining racial control by victimizing the entire African American community, not merely punishment of an alleged perpetrator for a crime. Our research confirms that many victims of terror lynchings were murdered without being accused of any crime; they were killed for minor social transgressions or for demanding basic rights and fair treatment."[304]

Six million Blacks fled the South in the Great Migration to the urban Northeast, Midwest, and West between 1916 and 1970 to escape the terror of random lynching and socially enforced poverty. It would be unfair, however, to suggest that only White Southerners were racist or violent against Blacks.

When Abraham Lincoln gave his immortal Gettysburg Address, he invoked a "new birth of freedom" for enslaved Americans by the sacrifice of blood by "those who gave the last full measure of devotion, that we here highly resolve these dead shall not have died in vain; that the nation, shall have a new birth of freedom, and that government of the people, by the people, for the people, shall not perish from the earth." However, the implications of the speech were not greeted with universal praise by Northerners.

An Ohio Democrat amended the party's slogan to proclaim, 'the

---
Constitution as it is, the Union as it was, the N_____S where they are.' "[305] This could have been the slogan of Whites throughout the segregated North from Boston to San Francisco, from the Reconstruction era until, well, judging by the 2016 presidential election results, the Republican Party today. As Randy Newman slyly pointed out in his 1974 song "Rednecks",

Now your Northern n_____r's a Negro.
See, he's got his dignity.
Down here we're too ignorant to realize,
That the North has set the n_____r free.

Yes, he's free to be put in a cage in Harlem in New York City,
And he's free to be put in a cage in the South Side of Chicago, and the West Side,
And he's free to be put in a cage in Hough in Cleveland,
And he's free to be put in a cage in East St. Louis,
And he's free to be put in a cage in Fillmore in San Francisco,
And he's free to be put in a cage in Roxbury in Boston,
They're gathering them up, from miles around,
Keeping the n_____rs down. [306]

Arriving in the North didn't guarantee a better life for Blacks, unfortunately. The 1950s and 60s brought federal government activism to help; *Brown vs. Board of Education* exposed the idea of "separate but equal" education for the races as a fraud, paving the way for school integration in the Civil Rights Act of 1964, which also prohibited discrimination in public places, provided for the integration of schools and other public facilities, and made employment discrimination illegal based on race.

Also necessary for removing racist preferences in public life was the Fair Housing Act of 1968, which prohibited discrimination concerning the sale, rental and financing of housing based on race, religion, national origin or sex.

Despite these gains, for a sad and sobering view of the history of violence against Blacks post-Reconstruction outside the South, the Equal Justice Institute has documented more than 300 racial terror lynchings during the period 1877-1950, and found these acts of violence were most common in eight states: Illinois, Indiana, Kansas, Maryland, Missouri, Ohio, Oklahoma, and West Virginia.[307] There was even lynching as far north as Duluth, MN, about as far north as you can go in the lower Continental U.S.

The landmark film *Birth of a Nation,* a silent epic film directed by D. W. Griffith and starring Lillian Gish, was released in 1915. It promoted the propaganda of the "Lost Cause", that the Confederacy was not defeated on the battlefield but lost due to overwhelming resources of the North, and that it was a noble endeavor that should be immortalized in monuments. *Birth of a Nation* portrays Black Americans (many of whom are played by White actors wearing Blackface) as unintelligent and sexually aggressive toward White women.

The film presents the Ku Klux Klan (KKK) as a heroic force necessary to preserve American values and a White supremacist social order. *The Birth of a Nation* was a huge commercial success and has been acknowledged as an inspiration for the rebirth of the Ku Klux Klan, which took place only a few months after its release.[308]

At this time, Tulsa, Oklahoma was a city where a thriving middle-class Black community had taken root outside the former Confederacy. Even though Oklahoma was not only not in the Confederacy but not organized as a U.S. territory during the Civil War, the newly created state legislature passed "Jim Crow" racial segregation laws as its first order of business. Voter registration rules effectively disenfranchised most Blacks, who were also barred from serving on juries or in local office.

These laws were enforced until after passage of the federal Voting Rights Act of 1965.[309] Also in the 1920s, lynchings were common in Oklahoma. [310] In 1921, an economic slump in that part of the state, the rise of the Klan inspired by *Birth of a Nation* and the "Red Summer" of 1919 which featured race riots of attacks by Whites on Black communities, combined to make a dangerous situation.[311]

The Greenwood neighborhood of Tulsa was settled by Blacks, and became so prosperous that it came to be known as "the Black Wall Street". Blacks had created their own businesses and services to cater to each other; Black professionals, including doctors, dentists, lawyers, and clergy, served their peers. During his trip to Tulsa in 1905, Booker T. Washington encouraged the co-operation, economic independence and excellence being demonstrated there.[312]

On Memorial Day, May 31st, 1921, in the late afternoon, a clerk in the Drexel building heard a woman scream, and saw Dick Rowland, a 19-year old Black shoe shiner, run from the elevator. When he investigated, he found Sarah Page, a 17-year old White elevator operator, in what he described as a "distraught" state. Assuming she had been assaulted, he called the authorities.

Page told the police that Rowland had grabbed her arm, but nothing more, and would not press charges, and the police concluded that what happened between the two teenagers was something less than an assault. Still, Rowland was arrested for assault, and Police Commissioner J. M. Adkison said he had received an anonymous telephone call threatening Rowland's life, and for his safety he ordered Rowland transferred to the more secure jail on the top floor of the Tulsa County Courthouse.[313]

The word had gotten out, helped by a brief but sensational story in the afternoon edition of the Tulsa *Tribune* with the headline: "Nab Negro for Attacking Girl in an Elevator", describing the alleged incident as a violent assault with graphic detail which the police had already determined was not the case. Page was described as an orphan working her way through business college, which may have fanned emotional flames.[314]

By early evening, several hundred White residents assembled outside the courthouse appeared to have the makings of a lynch mob to Sheriff McCullough, who took steps to protect Rowland. The sheriff went outside and tried to talk the crowd into going home, but they would not go.

Meanwhile, the Black residents of Greenwood had been discussing how they should protect Rowland from lynching. A number of them were World

War I veterans and they decided to arm themselves and offer their services to the sheriff on behalf of Rowland.

When approximately 50–60 Black men, armed with rifles and shotguns, arrived at the jail to offer their protective services to the sheriff, some of the more than 1,000 Whites who had been at the courthouse went home for their own guns. Groups of armed Black men venturing toward the courthouse in automobiles was interpreted by many Whites as a "Negro uprising." [315]

At the courthouse, a White man demanded that a Black man in the armed group surrender his gun. He refused; soon a shot was fired, and the Black and White forces fired on each other. Blacks then fell back to Greenwood, shooting and being shot at, pursued by the White mob. Some of the lynch mob were deputized by police and instructed to "get a gun and get a n____r". [316]

In the early hours of June 1st, White rioters began setting fires at the southern edge of the Greenwood district. Soon, the White mob began breaking into houses and buildings, looting; many set fires in the commercial district, then blocked the Tulsa fire department at gunpoint from putting them out.

By the time Adjutant General Charles Barrett of the Oklahoma National Guard arrived with 109 troops from Oklahoma City at 9:15 the morning of June 1st, thousands of Blacks had fled the city, and as many as 6,000 were held in city detention centers. Barrett declared martial law late that morning and by noon the rioting had been stopped.

In 2001, Oklahoma established a commission to establish facts about the rioting. Casualty estimates varied widely; one estimate was 100–300 (also stating right after that no one was prosecuted even though nearly a hundred were indicted).[317]

Greenwood's commercial section was destroyed. Losses included 191 businesses, a junior high school, several churches, and the only hospital in the district. The Red Cross reported that 1,256 houses were burned and another 215 were looted but not burned. The Tulsa Real Estate Exchange estimated property losses amounted to $1.5 million in real estate and $750,000 in personal property (equivalent to a total of $32 million in 2019). The Red Cross estimated that 10,000 people, mostly Black, were made homeless by the destruction. [318]

There were no convictions for any of the charges related to violence. There were decades of silence about the terror, violence, and losses of this event. The riot was largely omitted from local, state, and national histories, and was rarely mentioned in state history books, classrooms or even in private.[319]

In 1996, the state legislature authorized the Tulsa Race Massacre Commission to research the history of the event and produced a prepare a report detailing a historical account of it. the Commission delivered its final report on February 21, 2001, and recommended substantial restitution to the Black residents, listed below in order of priority:

1. Direct payment of reparations to survivors of the 1921 Tulsa race massacre,
2. Direct payment of reparations to descendants of the survivors of the Tulsa race massacre,
3. A scholarship fund available to students affected by the Tulsa race massacre,
4. Establishment of an economic development enterprise zone in the historic area of the Greenwood district, and
5. A memorial for the reburial of the remains of the victims of the Tulsa race massacre.

On June 1, 2001, Oklahoma Governor Keating signed the *1921 Tulsa Race Riot Reconciliation Act* into law. The act acknowledged that the event occurred, but failed to deliver any substantial reparations to the victims or their descendants.

Despite the Commission's recommendations, the state legislature did not agree that reparations were appropriate, and so did not include them in the reconciliation act.[320] The Act did however provide for more than 300 college scholarships for descendants of Greenwood residents; creation of the John Hope Franklin Reconciliation Park on October 27, 2010, named in honor of the notable African-American historian from Tulsa; and Economic development in Greenwood.

On May 29, 2020, the eve of the 99th anniversary of the event and the start of the George Floyd protests, Human Rights Watch released a report titled "The Case for Reparations in Tulsa, Oklahoma: A Human Rights Argument," demanding reparations for survivors and descendants of the violence because the economic impact of the massacre is still visible as illustrated by the high poverty rates and lower life expectancies in North Tulsa.[321]

Through an interesting coincidence, President Trump held a major campaign rally in Tulsa which was originally scheduled for June 19th, celebrated as "Juneteenth" by African Americans, the date when the last enslaved people in the South were notified of their freedom by Union forces in 1865. The choice of the city of Tulsa for his first live campaign rally in three months, being 99 years after the massacre and coinciding with Juneteenth, was criticized widely criticized as insensitive and even provocative.

Fox News host Harris Faulkner asked Trump whether he chose the location and date on purpose, to which the president said "no," although his campaign said the timing and location of the rally were deliberate, and his team views it as a chance to tout his "record of success for Black Americans."[322] Due to a major backlash, the rally was moved to June 20th instead.

As the killing of George Floyd by a Minneapolis policeman on Memorial Day, 2020, and the deaths of many other Black Americans in police custody, or even out on the street in daylight shows, even outside the old Confederacy, Black lives have not mattered enough to many White Americans to be treated with the same respect for human decency as White lives are considered to matter.

Escalating violence in Kenosha, WI following the shooting of a Black man at point blank range by a White police officer, prompted protests which led to Kyle Rittenhouse, a White 17-year old from Illinois, shooting three protesters, killing two and wounding a third. This demonstrates that the nation is on a knife's edge, in desperate need of national leadership showing compassion and calling for calm, instead of dismissing the protests and vandalism as "domestic terrorism" while refusing to address the shooting, as President Trump did.[323]

This book can't cover all the relevant issues, but I'll share one more example of people who actually say that Black lives *don't* matter, and the unconscious, societal racism of some White law enforcement members.

Leon McCray Sr., a Black American, was visiting an apartment he owns in Shenandoah County, VA on June 1st, when he noticed a man and a woman dragging a refrigerator from another property into his dumpster, and they became irate when he asked them to leave.

McCray said they threatened him and returned with three more people, attacking him physically, saying "they don't give a darn" about "my Black life and the Black Lives Matter stuff," and telling him they would "kill" him.

McCray said they backed up when he drew his legal concealed weapon to "save" his life, giving him enough time to call 911. Unfortunately for McCray, when deputies arrived and saw a Black man with a gun being opposed by a group of Whites, they took McCray's gun while talking with the five, who continued threatening him and yelling racist epithets at him.

The deputies wouldn't let McCray tell his side, he said; instead, he was "handcuffed in front of the mob," for brandishing the handgun, and driven away while the group stood with other deputies, waving at him as he went down the road.

McCray said the deputies rushed to judgment, "disarming a Black male brandishing a gun against five White individuals" despite his "second Amendment right to defend myself against five attackers that tried to take my life." The arrest "would not be tolerated if I was White," he added. The arresting deputy, who McCray had known for over 20 years, explained to him that he had to arrest him for brandishing the gun.

In a sermon to his church, McCray admitted "This was indeed the most humiliating, dehumanizing, damning and violating event of my life. I'm a pastor, a decorated 24-year Air Force master sergeant veteran, with no criminal record."

Fortunately, this story has a (somewhat) happy ending. Shenandoah County Sheriff Timothy Carter made the apology to McCray, not only dropping the charge for brandishing the gun, but announcing hate crime and assault charges against the five people involved, and two sheriff's office supervisors have been placed on unpaid administrative leave while the investigation continues, Carter said.

"I want the people of Shenandoah County to know that I and the sheriff's office staff appreciate and care about the minority communities, and especially our Black community," the sheriff said.[324]

It has been argued recently by Isabel Wilkerson in her book *America's Caste System* that in effect what America has is a caste system similar to that in India and Nazi Germany. In America, it is skin color that determines caste, and the racist laws going back to 1705 testify to this, as well as the binary nature of race; you're either White, or "other."

Barak Obama, technically, was half Black, half White, but American society would not let him identify as "mulatto", so since he was regarded as Black by Whites, he logically self-identified as Black. Interestingly, Wilkerson points out that Hitler used the racist arguments of the American writer Madison Grant as inspiration; he called Grant's 1916 book *The Passing of the Great Race* "my bible."

The book was responsible for the American eugenics movement (which Hitler admired and copied) and the passage of the Immigration Act of 1924, which hardened non-White immigration and eased White immigration from Western Europe. It also established the U.S. Border Patrol, the predecessor of Customs and Border Protection and ICE.[325]

Ironically, Grant's fears are coming true, a century later. Studies cite 2050 as the tipping point, when U.S. Whites will become a statistical minority, and most Americans will be people of color. "Whether in overtly racist language covertly racist immigration policies, fear of the 'great race' passing is used to win elections, cling to power, manipulate public opinion and grow organizational membership."[326] When White racists marched on the University of Virginia carrying tiki torches the night of August 11th, 2017, they shouted "Jews will not replace us!"

Diana Lesperance authors a blog titled "The Faithful Church" at www.thefaithfulchurch.com and has worked on the topic of racism to show the difference between a "faithful" (full, complete and non-biased reading of scripture), and the lies told by slavery apologists, Nazis and others.

Andrew McLeod, a Presbyterian minister, published what became a popular book (eleven editions were printed) titled *Negro Slavery Unjustifiable* in 1802. According to Lesperance, McLeod says he wrote his book to counter the "deceptive error" of the slave owners' biblical arguments. He didn't do this by appealing to "love" or to the spirit of the law, but by quoting a *direct commandment* of God:

"Anyone who kidnaps someone is to be put to death, whether the victim has been sold or is still in the kidnapper's possession." – Exodus 21:16, NIV

This means, if Southern slaveholders were obeying the whole counsel of God, anyone who kidnapped Africans and tried to sell them should have been arrested as soon as their ship came into port with its illegal cargo of human flesh. Since they defended their so-called "biblical" right to hold slaves, they should have also defended the biblical command to not kidnap someone against their will. If they were *actually* biblical literalists, Southern slavery would have been shut down immediately, but the Southern slaveholder "cherry-picked" the scriptures.

McCleod also pointed out this literal commandment from God:

If a slave has taken refuge with you, do not hand them over to their master. Let them live among you wherever they like and in whatever town they choose. Do not oppress them. – Deuteronomy 23:15-16, KJV

In fact, any slave who ran away from the surrounding nations was to be given *refuge* by the Israelites."[327]

As the "Unite the Right" rally tragically showed in Charlottesville August 11-12, 2017, there are many White supremacists across the country today, many in northern states, whose doctrine of hatred, violence and intimidation aptly echoes the legacy of both the Nazis and the Ku Klux Klan.

Following the violent Charlottesville rally in which Heather Heyer was killed by White supremacist James Alex Field who drove his car into her and fellow counter-protesters, about three dozen of whom were injured, Pastor Rob Pochek at the local Park Street Baptist Church proclaimed from the pulpit "Let me be clear. The white supremacy espoused by the like of David Duke, Richard Spencer and others is a lie straight from the pit of hell that cannot coexist with the gospel of Jesus Christ."[328]

Sadly, despite this witness, the (largely self-segregated White) churches throughout the U.S. have a long history of refusing to name, and confront, racism as a false and evil doctrine, possibly because it is largely ignored by general "White" culture as a whole, or considered to be a problem from the past.

On March 18th, 2019, *USA Today* ran a front-page story that only eight percent of American high school students know that slavery was the primary cause of the Civil War. But when we have young, unarmed Black men, on a monthly (or even more frequent basis) who are fatally shot by police, often while running away, and the general "White" population (including White Christians) don't feel impelled to get involved and demand an end to it, is it any wonder that there is a movement called "Black Lives Matter"? Why don't they matter to *all* Christians in America?

As we saw with Rev. Mike Huckabee and his evangelical supporters, they had more concern about gays being allowed to marry by the Supreme Court, than for the slaughter of 11 African Americans, in their own church, as an attempt to ignite a race war.

"And let the peace of Christ rule in your hearts, to which indeed you were called in the one body."[329] The one body Paul speaks of is the Body of Christ, which is His Church. All who acknowledge Him as Lord are part of His body. "As many of you as were baptized into Christ have clothed yourselves with Christ. There is no longer Jew or Greek, there is no longer slave or free, there is no longer male and female; for all of you are one in Christ Jesus."[330] Today we can add, "there is no Black or White."

Concluding Prayer for This Chapter

Dear heavenly father, please keep us from the sin of racism, or of judging anyone of a different culture or national origin as being inferior to us, since you made all humankind in your image. Help us resist messages of fear that tempt us not to trust others who are not like us. We pray you would guide us, individually and collectively, towards a society of peace and justice, turning from violence and fear. We pray for protesters, law enforcement, and all who meet in the streets over demonstrations for racial justice. Keep them from violence of any kind and help them see the humanity in the other. We ask for your Holy Spirit to give us the confidence to trust you and trust that letting go of fear and reaching out in love is our Christian calling, and guide us individually and as a nation to be able to affirm that all lives really do matter.

Chapter Ten

American and Christian Duty in Voting

As both Americans and Christians, we have the opportunity when we vote to advocate for government for the common good. As Alexander Hamilton explained in the Federalist Papers,

> The aim of every political constitution is, or ought to be, first to obtain for rulers men who possess most wisdom to discern, and most virtue to pursue, the common good of the society; and in the next place, to take the most effectual precautions for keeping them virtuous whilst they continue to hold their public trust.[331]

A republic, in the 18th century when the Founding Fathers established our Constitution, was understood to be a form of government in which (qualified) people (propertied White men over 25 who had lived in the state for some years), cast votes to elect representatives to a legislature. They called this state a "commonwealth", which is a traditional English term for a political community founded for the common good.[332] So we see that the rejection of the British monarchy by the Founding Fathers, was intended to be replaced by representative government to rule for the common good.

Likewise, in the early church, St. Paul explained:

> Now there are varieties of gifts, but the same Spirit; and there are varieties of services, but the same Lord; and there are varieties of activities, but it is the same God who activates all of them in everyone. To each is given the manifestation of the Spirit for the common good."[333]

And so, from our secular American roots of republican government, and from the bible, we have a common legacy of government for the common good, and that includes making provision for the lowliest and poorest among us. As Alexander Hamilton said in the *Federalist Papers,* "How is it possible that a government half supplied and always necessitous, can fulfill the purposes of its institution, can provide for the security, advance the prosperity, or support the reputation of the commonwealth?"[334]

Those Americans who dislike our secular society and even government, and who long for a return to that "old-time religion", might be surprised to learn what that actually was. If you search for the word "widow" in an e-book version of the bible, it occurs 117 times; the word "orphan" occurs 57 times, and usually together in this manner: "Do not oppress the widow, the orphan, the alien, or the poor."[335] Let's look at some detailed examples of this from the Old Testament: "Do no wrong or violence to the alien, the orphan, and the widow,"[336]

You shall not wrong or oppress a resident alien, for you were aliens in the land of Egypt. You shall not abuse any widow or orphan. If you do abuse them, when they cry out to me, I will surely heed their cry; my wrath will burn, and I will kill you with the sword, and your wives shall become widows and your children orphans. If you lend money to my people, to the poor among you, you shall not deal with them as a creditor; you shall not exact interest from them. If you take your neighbor's cloak in pawn, you shall restore it before the sun goes down; for it may be your neighbor's only clothing to use as cover; in what else shall that person sleep? And if your neighbor cries out to me, I will listen, for I am compassionate.[337]

For the LORD your God is God of gods and Lord of lords, the great God, mighty and awesome, who is not partial and takes no bribe, who executes justice for the orphan and the widow, and who loves the strangers, providing them food and clothing. You shall also love the stranger, for you were strangers in the land of Egypt.[338]

Cursed be anyone who deprives the alien, the orphan, and the widow of justice. All the people shall say, "Amen!"[339]

There is no end to your iniquities. For you have exacted pledges from your family for no reason, and stripped the naked of their clothing. You have given no water to the weary to drink, and you have withheld bread from the hungry. The powerful possess the land, and the favored live in it. You have sent widows away empty-handed, and the arms of the orphans you have crushed.[340]

God repeatedly reminds the Israelites that they should be kind to strangers because they were once strangers in the land of Egypt where their ancestors were badly mistreated. Isn't this the same situation that European-Americans find themselves in today?

Our ancestors suffered poverty and oppression in the Old World so they came here to find a better life, but instead of following God's exhortation to be kind to strangers, migrants and non-citizens, the federal government under the Trump administration has separated children from their parents; now 545 such children remain stranded here without a way to trace and notify their parents.

This excerpt from Exodus 22 sounds like a very timely warning for Americans today: "You shall not abuse any widow or orphan. If you do abuse them, when they cry out to me, I will surely heed their cry; my wrath will burn, and I will kill you with the sword, and your wives shall become widows and your children orphans."[341]

In order to have a government that provides for the common good, it needs to be funded accordingly. How does the United States, which has the largest, best funded and most powerful military in the world, tolerate its own citizens living in poverty?

A year ago (September 2019), the U.S. Census Bureau reported that one in eight families were living below the poverty line ($25,465 for a family with two adults and two children).[342] This was relatively good news at the time because it was the first time that poverty had declined to 2007 levels, before the Great Recession, but it's sad that one in eight families living below the poverty line was considered good news.

In addition, the bureau reported that the number of people in the U.S. who did not have health insurance rose from 25.6 million people in 2017 to 27.5 million in 2018, which included 4.3 million children. Health advocacy groups called the increase extremely troubling and blamed declines in Medicaid coverage, especially for Hispanic children and children under the age of six,[343] and Republican politicians have still not offered any alternative to the Affordable Care Act ("Obamacare").

The decade-plus economic blow of the Great Recession had hardly ended when the coronavirus arrived in the U.S. in February 2020, throwing millions of Americans out of work with a contraction of the gross national product by 32.9 percent (annualized).[344] The unemployment rate in August, 2020 was 8.4 percent, but the Bureau of Labor Statistics says it is likely somewhat higher due to misclassification of some workers like census workers.[345]

Despite passage of a $3 trillion stimulus and economic relief package by the Democratic-controlled House in May, to extend the relief that ran out in July, the Republican-controlled Senate refused to pass it before the November election, and both sides remain at an impasse as moratoriums on evictions expire and the economy officially continues into a recession, made official on June 8th.[346]

The physical and economic impacts of the coronavirus epidemic will be playing out for a long time. Researchers from the Institute for Health Metrics and Evaluation (IHME), which has been cited by the White House Coronavirus Task Force, said this week that deaths could skyrocket to 3,000 per day in December if current trends continue, and will top 400,000 by the end of the year, with 410,000 projected by January 1st.

The projections are based on data including cases, deaths, antibody prevalence, testing rates, mobility, social distancing mandates, mask use, population density, age and pneumonia seasonality. Deaths could be reduced by 30% if more Americans wear face masks, researchers said, adding that mask-wearing is actually on the decline among Americans.

"Looking at the staggering COVID-19 estimates, it's easy to get lost in the enormity of the numbers," said IHME Director Dr. Christopher Murray in a statement. "The number of deaths exceeds the capacity of the world's 50 largest stadiums, a sobering image of the people who have lost their lives and livelihoods."[347]

As a result, there is no ethical justification for our national government to avoid committing all available resources, including cuts to the defense budget (especially for expensive and redundant weapons systems) and increasing taxes on the wealthy, to give most Americans financial relief, and a fair (single-payer) health system so they don't have to pay the full cost of medical care or choose between that and paying the rent or buying food.

When you think about it, why don't we think of "national defense" in terms of what takes care of people, instead the weapons we use to kill other people? On the ethics of paying taxes to support the government, let us remember Jesus' words, "Give to the emperor the things that are the emperor's, and to God the things that are God's."[348]

As to the ethics of funding programs that help the needy, without blaming them for their poverty, "Religion that is pure and undefiled before God, the Father, is this: to care for orphans and widows in their distress, and to keep oneself unstained by the world."[349] As to the need for fair wages for fair work, Jesus said "The laborer deserves to be paid."[350]

We must remember that the destructive impact of climate change is an enormous ethical call to action; there can be no common good if there is no livable environment for humans and all other species. "The earth is the Lord's and all that is in it, the world, and those who live in it; 2 for he has founded it on the seas, and established it on the rivers."[351]

Considering a Candidate's Character

It's not being fully responsible either as a Christian or as an American citizen to vote for a candidate for public office merely on their stand on a divisive cultural issue like abortion or cutting taxes. It's every citizen's duty (especially if they're Christian) to look beyond the surface and consider a candidate's character from what we know of the public record. This is especially important in elections for President, because one person's character and judgment can have such a profound effect on the nation, and even the world.

Richard G. Leahy

When we consider candidates for public office, whether a person says they are a Christian is not enough, too many politicians cynically trade on Christianity, but how do we know they are sincere, or trustworthy? Some politicians will say anything if they think it will get them elected. Those who like to trade on Christianity (such as President Trump and Roy Moore) should be the first to invite public scrutiny of their personal lives, but when Roy Moore was accused by five women alleging that he sexually pressured them when he was in his 30s and married, and they were all underage, he not only responded with outrage but sued at least one of his accusers.

In the televised Presidential debates in 2004, someone asked President Bush if he could name a philosopher or moral teacher who had inspired him "What about Jesus?!" exclaimed Bush, offering no further comments. It would have been worthwhile if each candidate had spoken about the role of faith in their lives, instead of treating the name of Jesus like the winning card in a game of Texas hold 'em, with nothing more said.

When Pope Francis criticized President Trump's plan to build a wall on the border with Mexico by saying "A person who only thinks about building walls, wherever they may be, and not building bridges, is not Christian," Trump responded in typical fashion, calling the pontiff's remarks "disgraceful," and calling the Pope "a pawn" for the Mexican government. "No leader, especially a religious leader, should have the right to question another man's religion or faith," Trump said at a rally in Kiawah Island, South Carolina.[352]

If you're going to publicly disagree with (any) Pope, you'd better have at least as good of a hand to play as did Martin Luther in 1517, and President Trump falls pitifully short here. Besides his shameful comments which kind of prove the Pope's point, he's also wrong; *any* politician who claims to be a loyal member of *any* religion should expect that the devout members of that religion have the right to discuss, examine, comment on and challenge him or her, based on how that politician's words and actions do or don't uphold their claim of faith.

Jesus warned us against false prophets, and his words would apply to false Christians as well:

"Beware of false prophets, who come to you in sheep's clothing but inwardly are ravenous wolves. You will know them by their fruits. Are grapes gathered from thorns, or figs from thistles? In the same way, every good tree bears good fruit, but the bad tree bears bad fruit. A good tree cannot bear bad fruit, nor can a bad tree bear good fruit. Every tree that does not bear good fruit is cut down and thrown into the fire. Thus, you will know them by their fruits.[353]

Let us ponder how St. Paul compares the fruits of the Spirit with the works of the flesh:

Live by the Spirit, I say, and do not gratify the desires of the flesh. For what the flesh desires is opposed to the Spirit, and what the Spirit desires is opposed to the flesh; for these are opposed to each other, to prevent you from doing what you want. But if you are led by the Spirit, you are not subject to the law. Now the works of the flesh are obvious: fornication, impurity, licentiousness, idolatry, sorcery, enmities, strife, jealousy, anger, quarrels, dissensions, factions, envy, drunkenness, carousing, and things like these. I am warning you, as I warned you before: those who do such things will not inherit the kingdom of God. By contrast, the fruit of the Spirit is love, joy, peace, patience, kindness, generosity, faithfulness, gentleness, and self-control. There is no law against such things.[354]

Taking these verses together, we cannot trust politicians merely by their words, but by their actions, especially as concerns their attitude towards the common good.

Some Suggestions for Considering the Character of Candidates for Office

The men who debated and then established our Constitution and separation of powers were well aware of the lessons of history. Alexander Hamilton in the *Federalist Papers* examined the few republics of history and the reasons for their fall. The founders were careful to put limits on the power of any one branch or individual, being fully aware of the tendency towards authoritarianism, but they were creatures of the Age of Reason; it would be well over a century until Sigmund Freud's pioneering work *The Interpretation of Dreams* introduced the idea of the unconscious mind, and subsequently, the discipline of psychology, and the understanding that human decisions are not as rationally motivated as we would like to think that they are.

The upshot of this is that politics in republican democracies in the last century have become contests at evoking a range of emotions in the voter, from warm and fuzzy sentimentalism, to tribal loathing, to primal fear of losing what they value most, to create the largest emotional incentive to cast one's ballot. Any appeal to reason in making one's case is purely decorative window dressing, and not nearly as important as creating base emotional motivations; this may be depressing but as the 2016 and 2020 presidential campaigns demonstrated, is true nonetheless.

The reason I mention all this is for Christians to become aware of the many ways that politicians attempt to manipulate them, in every kind of medium, by subtle or in-your-face messages that attempt to transcend the boring and two-dimensional talk of policy options, and instead try to seize the fervor, and the vote, of the public.

All this doesn't mean that you can't trust anyone, but that it takes work and thoughtfulness to cut through the elaborate smokescreen that all candidates of all parties construct in order to make a decision you feel in your heart reflects consideration and conscience.

Scripture is an important moral guide but we have the responsibility to take the time to make ourselves as fully informed on the candidates and the issues as we can. We also should neither categorically trust, nor distrust "the media" as a whole, which includes *any* way that information (and not strictly "news") reaches us, and being especially cautious in trusting what we read on the Internet and social media.

Newspapers from accredited news organizations and their online websites, FM news radio, and broadcast television are generally more reliable than people or organizations with important sounding names with no ties to accredited news organizations (like the "Internet Research

Agency", a Russian company that undertakes online influence operations on behalf of Russian business and political interests.[355]) We know that the Russians, using Facebook and other online platforms, staged a massive campaign to influence the 2016 election in favor of Donald Trump and continued this in 2020,[356, 357] so we should be careful what or who we believe.

For example, if you hear on the Internet that Joe Biden is running a child pornography ring out of the basement of a Washington pizzeria, before you grab a gun, bust in and start shooting up the place, maybe you should call them first to see if they even *have* a basement.[358]

The League of Women Voters on How to Judge a Candidate

In 2020, we've reached a century of American women having the right to vote. Accordingly, I am including a guide to good citizenship voting that the League of Women Voters developed themselves, to help guide voters of any gender how to carefully make a well-considered decision on whom to vote for. This is condensed from their website and is found on https://www.lwv.org/blog/how-judge-candidate.

In summary, ask yourself these final questions:

- Which candidate's views on the issues do I agree with the most?

- Who ran the fairest campaign?

- Which candidate demonstrated the most knowledge on the issues?

- Which candidate has the leadership qualities I am looking for?

Is the choice clear? If so, pick a candidate.

See through distortion techniques

All candidates are trying to sell themselves to voters. Sometimes their language is so skillfully crafted that they distort the truth in ways that are difficult for even the most careful observer to detect. Here are examples of distortion techniques that you should watch for as you review candidates' campaign materials.

Common distortion techniques:

- *Name calling/Appeals to prejudice:* These are attacks on an opponent based on characteristics that will not affect performance in office. Accusations such as, "My opponent is arrogant and full of hot air," do not give any real information about the candidate. Reference to race, ethnicity or marital status can be subtly used to instill prejudice.

- *Rumor mongering:* These include statements such as, "Everyone says my opponent is a crook, but I have no personal knowledge of any wrongdoing," which imply (but do not state) that the opponent is guilty.

- *Guilt by associations:* These are statements such as, "We all know Candidate B is backed by big money interest," that attack candidates because of their supporters rather than because of their stands on the issues.

- *Catchwords:* These are phrases such as "Law and Order" or "un-American" designed to trigger a knee-jerk emotional reaction rather than to inform.

- *Passing the blame:* These are instances in which a candidate denies responsibility for an action or blames an opponent for things over which they had no control.

- *Promising the sky:* These are unrealistic promises that no elected official could fulfill.

- *Evading real issues:* These include instances in which candidates may avoid answering direct questions, offer only vague solutions, or talk about the benefits of proposed programs but never get specific about possible problems or costs. [359]

Note that thinking through these points requires some effort, and that the League understands that politicians are savvy in using rhetoric to trigger "knee-jerk emotional reactions" in people. If you feel yourself being manipulated by a politician, it's a good signal to beware of them and to spend some time looking into their record and character...using reputable sources on the record, not dubious "pizzeria conspiracies" spread online.

Unfortunately, as Jonathan Swift said, "A lie can travel around the world and back again while the truth is lacing up its boots," so the more outrageous something sounds the more suspicious you should be until you can verify it, through multiple, independent and accredited news sources.

I should point out that President Trump refers to any news media who won't fawningly praise him as "fake news", but that he has admitted this is a cynical ploy to discredit independent news media so his supporters would dismiss whatever negative things they said about him out of hand.[360]

In these very troubled times, it's more important to ask ourselves "Which candidate would Jesus approve of," than which candidate we happen to "like". Do you like every professional who does work for you? As someone has observed, in business, it's more important to be respected than liked, and in voting for the leader of the free world it is just as important.

Does the candidate try to unite Americans, or divide them? Do they brag constantly, or do they walk the walk of humility and public service? Do they inspire people with hope, or fear? Which candidate would you trust with your children?

Concluding Prayer for This Chapter

Dear Lord, we thank you for the gift of free elections in the United States and ask that you preserve that right for all Americans. We ask for your guidance as we ponder which candidates to vote for, considering the common good for all, not just for ourselves or those who look like us. Help us not to be distracted or mis-directed by fear, since you have encouraged us not to be afraid. Help us to vote for a future that is fair to all.

Chapter Eleven

Some False Gods, Doctrines and Prophets

From a scriptural perspective, there's not much more to say after the last chapter. However, we live in uniquely challenging times for Christians especially in the United States, where false gods, doctrines and prophets have crept in and have hardly been recognized, let alone called out and challenged.

In one sense we face the same temptations and demons' humans will always have in this world, but as members of a material and affluent society increasingly dominated by the Internet, we face new and insidious challenges. We need clarity to distinguish the false from the true and so stay faithfully on the path of discipleship.

False Gods

As Christians, we mostly face the eternal false gods of this world; things that we worship instead of the Lord. For the most part, they are the ancient and unholy trinity of money, sex and power.

Please realize that there is nothing inherently evil in any of these things, in their appropriate place. It is the taking of them out of that place and worshipping them as gods, that is idolatry and the road to addiction, abuse of others, injustice and misery for many.

When St. Paul spoke of the evils of money, he said "But those who want to be rich fall into temptation and are trapped by many senseless and harmful desires that plunge people into ruin and destruction. For the love of money is a root of all kinds of evil, and in their eagerness to be rich some have wandered away from the faith and pierced themselves with many pains."[361]

So is not money itself, but the lust after it that is the problem. I like how Paul points out that despite their wealth, "some have wandered away from the faith and pierced themselves with many pains." This is an interesting paradox of wealth that has been understood from ancient days but which we in today's America have somehow forgotten. We have been told that money is the natural reward of those who work hard, and that we can buy (almost) everything we could want with it. We are told that by commercial media constantly, every day.

In the United States, it has been said that our lives are out of balance, partly because we worship our work, work at our play, and play at our worship. The concentration camps of the Nazis had a cruel lie wrought in iron over their front gates: "Arbeit Macht Frei," or "Work Makes You Free." That could be the slogan for the United States today, since it's our attitude toward life. But it's a two-stage formula; work brings you the money, which then (you think) "sets you free", at least from poverty and social scorn.

Let's turn to the Bible for some guidance on poverty and God's attitude towards the poor. Consider the text of the Virgin Mary, in her response to her cousin Elizabeth who, filled with the Holy Spirit when the baby in her womb (who would be John the Baptist) leapt at the greeting of Mary when she entered Elizabeth's house, and cried "Blessed are you among women, and blessed is the fruit of your womb."[362] Mary responded,

My soul magnifies the Lord, and my spirit rejoices in God my Savior, for he has looked with favor on the lowliness of his servant. Surely, from now on all generations will call me blessed; for the Mighty One has done great things for me, and holy is his name. His mercy is for those who fear him from generation to generation. He has shown strength with his arm; he has scattered the proud in the thoughts of their hearts. He has brought down the powerful from their thrones, and lifted up the lowly; he has filled the hungry with good things, and sent the rich away empty. He has helped his servant Israel, in remembrance of his mercy, according to the promise he made to our ancestors, to Abraham and to his descendants forever."[363]

There are several parts to the Magnificat. The first part shows Mary's humility in her magnifying the Lord, and she acknowledges His holiness. While she declares that all generations shall call her blessed, she does not say that she will be called great; she acknowledges this is a gift from God, and her humility is further confirmed with her thanking God for having "looked with favor on the lowliness of his servant."

She then moves from the very personal and intimate to a general and historic witness of God's actions, saying "His mercy is for those who fear him from generation to generation," and then speaks words of judgment for the proud and wealthy of the world, "he has scattered the proud in the thoughts of their hearts. He has brought down the powerful from their thrones, and lifted up the lowly; he has filled the hungry with good things, and sent the rich away empty."

Mary is witnessing to God's power, but also to His specific mercy and concern for the poor, in lifting up the lowly, and filling the hungry with good things. In the space of many other things she could have said, she included these specific links to God and his desire for helping the lowly and needy. How can we ignore this witness? After all, the wealthy can, and do, take care of themselves. How can we claim to be a godly nation if we deny the poor and needy and instead give more tax breaks to the wealthiest few?

If you have any doubts on this, consider Jesus' reading from the book of Isaiah in the temple in Nazareth:

When he came to Nazareth, where he had been brought up, he went to the synagogue on the sabbath day, as was his custom. He stood up to read, and the scroll of the prophet Isaiah was given to him. He unrolled the scroll and found the place where it was written: "The Spirit of the Lord is upon me, because he has anointed me to bring good news to the poor. He has sent me to proclaim release to the captives and recovery of sight to the blind, to let the oppressed go free, to proclaim the year of the Lord's favor." And he rolled up the scroll, gave it back to the attendant, and sat down. The eyes of all in the synagogue were fixed on him. Then he began to say to them, "Today this scripture has been fulfilled in your hearing."[364]

"The Spirit of the Lord is upon me, because he has anointed me to bring good news to the poor." Consider how this scripture verse echoes what

Mary had said in the Magnificat. Jesus did not come for the sake of the wealthy, or the respectable, but to "bring good news to the poor," through his work and miracles, to show the world that God was among them.

If God shows his love through making a point of honoring the poor, how can we justify looking down on them? Let's listen to what St. James tells us:

Listen, my beloved brothers and sisters. Has not God chosen the poor in the world to be rich in faith and to be heirs of the kingdom that he has promised to those who love him? But you have dishonored the poor. Is it not the rich who oppress you? Is it not they who drag you into court? Is it not they who blaspheme the excellent name was invoked over you?[365]

Ensuring that our government puts budget priorities on preventing poverty, and mitigating it, instead of spending on more prisons and weapons, is a way we can help the poor on the state and national level; working with our faith communities, we can help the poor in many ways in our own communities, from volunteering at food banks to hosting the homeless in our churches, and with refugee re-settlement organizations to help those fleeing violence and persecution.

I'm sure many of you put up manger scenes on Christmas. The Holy Family were refugees, far from home and without even a room at the inn for Mary to give birth to Jesus. Then they had to flee to Egypt to avoid the murderous Herod.

If you have soft feelings for the Holy Family at Christmas, why are you not outraged when children who are fleeing violence in Central America are pulled from their parents and put in detention by our government? Two of them had died in U.S. custody by Christmas 2018, with President Trump falsely tweeting that it was the fault of the Democrats.

His shamelessness is a judgment on us as a nation, but what about those who elected him, and consider themselves Christians? What are they doing about this? On the day before the 2020 election, 545 such children remain separated from their parents, many too young to explain where they were from.

The Problem with Wealth

There is a body of spiritual wisdom across the centuries and cultures testifying to the spiritual risks of accumulating wealth for its own sake. Since the beginning of the English colonies in North America, there has been a tension between creating a just and godly society on the one hand, and with making a fortune on the other, with the contrast seen in legislation, administrations and Supreme Court decisions over the centuries.

In the Bible, we see godly examples of both the poor and the wealthy, with many admonitions on the corrupting influence of too much money on the soul.

As he was setting out on a journey, a man ran up and knelt before him, and asked him, "Good Teacher, what must I do to inherit eternal life?" Jesus said to him, "Why do you call me good? No one is good but God alone. You know the commandments: 'You shall not murder; You shall not commit adultery; You shall not steal; You shall not bear false witness; You shall not defraud; Honor your father and mother.'" He said to him, "Teacher, I have kept all these since my youth." Jesus, looking at him, loved him and said, "You lack one thing; go, sell what you own, and give the money to the poor, and you will have treasure in heaven; then come, follow me." When he heard this, he was shocked and went away grieving, for he had many possessions. Then Jesus looked around and said to his disciples, "How hard it will be for those who have wealth to enter the kingdom of God! It is easier for a camel to go through the eye of a needle than for someone who is rich to enter the kingdom of God."[366]

I like that the rich man in this parable is sincere; he really wants to do the right thing and has been faithfully following the commandments his whole life, and Jesus loves him for his sincerity and faithfulness. Jesus pointed out that he lacked empathy, and then gave him an invitation to follow him, but discipleship always has a cost, and the young man was unable to give up his wealth, even to follow Jesus.

It wasn't hard for Jesus to feel empathy for the poor, since he was one of them. He was born in a stable and shortly thereafter became a refugee, fleeing Herod into Egypt. He was an itinerant preacher and lived day by day, hand to mouth. His disciples were a motley group of humble, poor Jews. He suffered a criminal's death and didn't even have a grave to call his own. In fact, by the standards of the world, Jesus would be called by many a "loser," but Jesus' kingdom was "not from this world."[367]

On July 30th, 2017, the *Washington Post* published an editorial by Charles Mathewes and Evan Sandsmark of the University of Virginia's religious studies department about the psychological perils of wealth. They point to many sources, from the ancient Stoics to the Buddha and Aristotle, that warned against the dangers of excessive wealth.

"The point is not necessarily that wealth is intrinsically and everywhere evil, but that it is dangerous—that is should be eyed with suspicion, and definitely not pursued as an end in itself."

They move from ancient wisdom to recent studies from the behavioral sciences "that all say, more or less, 'Being rich is really bad for you.' Wealth, it turns out, leads to behavioral and psychological maladies. The rich think and act in misdirected ways."

They point out that "when it comes to a broad range of vices, the rich outperform everybody else. They are much more likely than the rest of humanity to shoplift or cheat, and they are more apt to be adulterers and to drink a great deal. They are even more likely to take candy meant for children." They are the worst tax evaders, and give proportionally less to charity than do others.

"They tend to believe that people have different financial destinies because of who they essentially are, so they believe that they deserve their wealth, thus dampening their capacity for gratitude, a quality that has been shown to significantly enhance our sense of well-being."

They conclude by saying "It's time to put the apologists for plutocracy back on the defensive, where they belong—not least for their own sakes. After all, the Buddha, Aristotle, Jesus, the Koran, Jimmy Stewart, Pope Francis and now science all agree: if you are wealthy and are reading this, it's time to give away your money as fast as you can."

They point out that Pope Francis continues in the faithful tradition of the Catholic Church as an institution that protects the poor. They say he has "proclaimed that unless wealth is used for the good of society, and above all for the good of the poor, it is an instrument of 'corruption and death.' And Francis practices what he preaches...when he entered the Jesuit order years ago, he took a vow of poverty, and he's kept it."[368]

Money tempts us by telling us that we'll be happy and powerful if we worship it, and we'll have everything we want. What money doesn't tell you, as the Beatles knew, is that it can't buy love.

Illustrating the lust for money's corrupting influence on the soul, I still remember when Paul Getty the oil magnate visited Vienna in the late 1970s. He paid cash for his hotel bill, and the concierge said that the change was only a few pennies, not wanting to insult Getty by taking the time to give him those few coins. Getty responded: "I'll wait." When asked how much money it would take to make him satisfied, he famously and devastatingly responded, "More." I don't know about you, but I want no part of that mindset corrupting my soul.

Dietrich Bonhoeffer condemned the corruption of sex in prostitution, but from a sense of opportunistic power. A person is trying to have absolute power over another person, in an ultimate and degrading way.

As members of the animal kingdom, we are burdened with sexuality which, although it provides pleasure, continually tempts us into thinking that if some is good, more is better, and not just "more" in frequency, but also in partners. Where does this end? In broken relationships, a callous and predatory attitude towards the opposite sex, unwanted pregnancies and STDs, including AIDS. There is a considerable emotional and spiritual toll on a person as well as a physical one.

Richard G. Leahy

Power, like sex and money, promises a kind of liberation that is actually slavery to a lust for itself. "Power corrupts, and absolute power corrupts absolutely. Great men are almost always bad men," wrote Lord Acton to Bishop Mandell Creighton in 1887.

Society has many layers of power, from world leaders of nuclear powers to legislatures to company executives down to political party officials, schoolteachers and principals, to heads of households. What a different place the world would be if each person in some authority over others, thought of it as a charge from God to model honesty and decency, instead of lording their petty, temporary power over others, which is our sinful, default nature.

Jesus himself was tempted by the devil in the wilderness over power.

Again, the devil took him to a very high mountain and showed him all the kingdoms of the world and their splendor; and he said to him, "All these I will give you, if you will fall down and worship me." Jesus said to him, "Away with you, Satan! for it is written, 'Worship the Lord your God, and serve only him.' "[369]

Of course, this was a false power, for Jesus would have transferred his allegiance to the devil from God, but you can appreciate that a vision of all the kingdoms of the world and their splendor could have been a temptation for a poor Jewish preacher.

Remember, whether it's power, sex, money or anything besides Jesus, "No one can serve two masters; for a slave will either hate the one and love the other, or be devoted to the one and despise the other. You cannot serve God and wealth,"[370] or indeed God and anything else. Something, or Someone, has to take priority. As Bob Dylan sang, "You gotta serve somebody. Well it may be the devil, or it may be the Lord, but you gotta serve somebody."[371]

The tenth commandment states "You shall not covet your neighbor's house; you shall not covet your neighbor's wife, or male or female slave, or ox, or donkey, or anything that belongs to your neighbor." [372]

In the United States, we tend *not* to be faithful followers of this commandment, but instead you could make an argument that the consumer economy (which is 75% of the national economy) is run by envy, or through "keeping up with the Jones'." And so it goes: envy prompts the greed for more money, which consumes more energy and time, all for superficial things as symbols of our social status.

Consumerism, or making the accumulation of possessions a god, can also include viewing sex as a recreational sport. In short, the pursuit or worship of a self-indulgent lifestyle, which many people seem to consider a right of American citizenship, is perhaps the most widespread and insidious of the false gods that we face today, in our country and culture, which encourages spending to keep the economy robust.

But for Christians, we must remember the words of Jesus; "Therefore do not worry, saying, 'What will we eat?' or 'What will we drink?' or 'What will we wear?' For it is the Gentiles who strive for all these things; and indeed, your heavenly Father knows that you need all these things. But strive first for the kingdom of God and his righteousness, and all these things will be given to you as well."373

Worship of youth and youthful sexuality not only objectifies human beings (of both genders) but de-humanizes mature and elderly persons because their surface beauty has diminished. Again, the consumer marketing forces tell men and women that they need the beauty or buff burnishing products or services companies offer, implying that if they don't buy these things, they won't be desirable or envied by others.

We also live in an age where technology, medicine and pharmaceutical industries have made the extension of youth more possible than ever before. Some people, worshipping youth, have even put their faith in cryogenics, believing that someone or something will bring them back to (youthful) life through culturing tissue from their frozen heads.

Today, aside from the timeless temptations that all Christians have faced in the past, we have the new god of the Internet. It is very much like the Tree of Life, the fruit of which God forbade Adam and Eve to eat, or else they would die. The serpent tempted Eve telling her, "You will not die; for God knows that when you eat of it your eyes will be opened, and you will be like God, knowing good and evil." And so, Eve and Adam disobeyed God, ate, and received knowledge of their nakedness, but not only lost immortality but fellowship with God in the garden. [374]

The serpent told a crafty lie, because it contained some truth; Adam and Eve did become "like" God in that they knew that they were naked, but it wasn't worth breaking the trust of God, being banished from the garden, and dying.

The Internet tempts us in the same way, telling us that we will know all things, and this in itself is a powerful temptation. Never before in human history has a tool been able to give such a staggering amount of information to anyone on a mere request, and only at the cost of a personal computer or smart phone, and an Internet connection.

The Enlightenment always celebrated an increase in knowledge, but knowledge is not wisdom, and a great deal of content on the Internet is either base tribalism or lies with an agenda, as we saw with the Russians meddling in our presidential elections in 2016 and 2020. As St. Paul says, "All things are lawful,' but not all things are beneficial. 'All things are lawful,' but not all things build up."[375]

I remember a few years ago hearing on public radio about "kosher" cell phones. I wondered, how could cell phone components be kosher? But what they meant was that these were not "smart" phones with an Internet connection; all you could do with them was to make and receive actual phone calls. Conservative Jewish parents could communicate with their children, but the children would not have the ability to roam the Internet unsupervised.

I like the idea, partly because most of what I do with my own smart phone is to make and receive calls, but I could see that the many temptations of the Internet would be powerfully seductive to young minds.

When a person become a mature adult, they realize that giving in to temptation has consequences, whether their parents are around to enforce them or not. This takes away a lot of incentive to do naughty things, once we've experienced and paid for the consequences. Gordon Lightfoot, in his song "Try if You Like", looks back on a long life of highs and lows and concludes "No one can lead me astray anymore, you are welcome to try if you like."

Even if young people aren't visiting porn cites or buying things, they don't need with money they don't have, the basic temptation of the Internet is to give your soul to it, just to be able to be "liked" or texted or emailed by "friends", most of whom are trying to insinuate how much better they are living than you.

Studies of Facebook users have shown that those that spend the most time on the platform are in fact *not* happy. In April 2017, Holly B. Shakya and Nicholas A. Christakis published the results of a "more rigorous" social science study than had been done previously, to strengthen the conclusions.

Overall, our results showed that, while real-world social networks were positively associated with overall well-being, the use of Facebook was negatively associated with overall well-being. These results were particularly strong for mental health; most measures of Facebook use in one year predicted a decrease in mental health in a later year. We found consistently that both liking others' content and clicking links significantly predicted a subsequent reduction in self-reported physical health, mental health, and life satisfaction.[376]

If a wave of low self-esteem weren't enough to discourage people from giving more of their time to a virtual "community", the Internet has had a devastatingly negative impact on our national security, from "fake news" spread by the Russians to divide us, to anti-Semitism that inspired the deranged shooting of 18 innocent worshippers at the Tree of Life synagogue in Pittsburgh, with eleven killed and seven wounded, to the Christchurch, New Zealand massacre of 50 Muslims inside a mosque during Friday prayers on March 15, 2019.

According to Wikipedia's entry on the Tree of Life mass shooting, it occurred just after two independent reports from Columbia University and the Anti-Defamation League saw a spike in anti-Semitic activity online, especially on Instagram and Twitter.[377]

The alleged gunman of the synagogue shooting, Robert G. Bowers, had posted on the social network Gab shortly before the shootings that "HIAS [Hebrew Immigrant Aid Society] likes to bring invaders in that kill our people. I can't sit by and watch my people get slaughtered. Screw your optics, I'm going in."[378]

Tribalistic "us" and "them" hate rhetoric on the Internet has not only led to the Tree of Life synagogue shootings, but the violent White supremacist march on Charlottesville in August 2017, and in November of 2018 the FBI reported more than a 17 percent rise in hate crimes across America, the third consecutive year the numbers have increased, showing a yearly spike of almost four times the number of hate crimes just in one year.

The annual report showed there were 7,175 bias crimes, which targeted 8,493 victims based on their race and sexual orientation, reported in 2017. There had been 6,121 hate crimes reported in 2016, 5,850 such offenses in 2015 and 5,479 in 2014. The 17.2 percent spike follows increases of 4.6 percent and 6.7 percent in the previous two years.[379]

It is also an established fact that hateful views spread on social media has been a primary cause for the rise in hate or bias crimes. By April 2019, FBI director Christopher Wray testified to Congress that the Bureau had concluded that the threat of White nationalist violence in the U.S. was "a persistent pervasive threat," a view shared by many in the Department of Justice, but not in the White House.[380]

I won't condemn social media categorically. I'm glad, for example, that Pope Francis has a Twitter account, if only to counter the bad vibes spread by so many others. Just look at his last two tweets as 2018 ended and 2019 began. On New Year's Eve he tweeted, "Let us give thanks to God for the year drawing to an end, recognizing that all the good is His gift." On January 2nd, he tweeted "To make peace is to imitate God, who wants to make peace with us: He sent us his Son, and He has forgiven us." Unfortunately, so few tweets have this godly character.

The false god of the Internet promised that we will have all knowledge available to us for the asking. As Simon Raphael wrote in his novel *After the War,* "I used to love the truth, before I discovered what it was." Eve could have said as much after disobeying God and eating the fruit of the tree of life. How much better off are we, individually and collectively, since we somehow agreed to give our lives to the Internet?

We have learned that the Internet can empower the nasty, deranged, bigoted, and violent, in ways previously not possible for mere mortals. We have learned that, as Jonathan Swift famously said, "a lie can travel halfway around the world while the truth is still putting on its shoes." We have also learned that too many people don't want to hear the truth and would rather believe lies that suit their sensibilities. The Internet didn't create these things, but it has weaponized many evil aspects of human nature.

False Doctrines

There have always been false doctrines, as there have always been false gods. Today in the United States we confront several.

The False Gospel of Prosperity

The Gospel of Prosperity, sometimes known as Health and Wealth gospel or the Gospel of Success, is "a religious belief among some Christians, who hold that financial blessing and physical well-being are always the will of God for them, and that faith, positive speech, and donations to religious causes will increase one's material wealth. Prosperity theology views the Bible as a contract between God and humans: if humans have faith in God, he will deliver security and prosperity. The doctrine emphasizes the importance of personal empowerment, proposing that it is God's will for his people to be happy."[381]

Who can argue that God wants to see us happy and empowered? Won't we be more so if we are healthy and wealthy? Won't he shower us with blessings if we give generously (conflict of interest warning) and since he is all-powerful? You can see how insidious this is; we make a contract with God to worship him, and in return he showers us with blessings. But where is Jesus and His call to leave everything behind and follow Him in this Gospel?

We need to distinguish God's love for us (He certainly wants us healthy to enjoy life and serve Him), from our duty as Christians. It's no accident that this prosperity gospel arose in the United States, with its ever-present emphasis on wealth, combined with the competition between clergy for parishioners (and their offerings). According to Wikipedia, it featured prominently in 1980s televangelism and grew rapidly in the 1990s and early 2000s; by 2006, three of the four largest congregations in the United States were teaching prosperity theology.[382]

Prosperity theology has been criticized by leaders from various Christian denominations, including those within the Pentecostal and Charismatic movements, who maintain that it is irresponsible, promotes idolatry, and is contrary to scripture. Mainstream evangelicalism has consistently opposed prosperity theology as heresy and prosperity ministries have frequently come into conflict with other Christian groups, including those within the Pentecostal and Charismatic movements where it originated.

Prominent evangelical leaders, such as Rick Warren, Ben Witherington III, and the late Jerry Falwell Sr., have harshly criticized the movement, sometimes denouncing it as heretical. Warren proposes that prosperity theology promotes the idolatry of money, and others argue that Jesus' teachings indicate a disdain for material wealth. [383]

It's worth noting that both mainline Protestant churches like Lutherans, Presbyterians, and Methodists and those more closely aligned with conservative political agendas, like some Baptists such as Jerry Falwell Sr., have the same condemnation of the prosperity gospel as a heresy.

In addition to the scripture citations above, I don't think it can be put any plainer than did Jesus in the Gospel of Matthew: "No one can serve two masters; for a slave will either hate the one and love the other, or be devoted to the one and despise the other. You cannot serve God and wealth."[384] This doesn't mean you must despise money; you just have to have your priorities right as a Christian and serve God while respecting money and what it can do for you and others.

Consider what Jesus said to his disciples on the subject of the cost of discipleship, and its rewards.

Peter began to say to him, "Look, we have left everything and followed you." Jesus said, "Truly I tell you, there is no one who has left house or brothers or sisters or mother or father or children or fields, for my sake and for the sake of the good news, who will not receive a hundredfold now in this age—houses, brothers and sisters, mothers and children, and fields, with persecutions—and in the age to come eternal life."[385]

Jesus was speaking of the rewards of gaining a new family of disciples and sharing with them these new things—after the disciples had already made the fateful decision to leave everything and follow him. But he warned also that they would also gain persecutions as well, but "in the age to come, eternal life." That is very different than the grasping sentiment of the Gospel of Prosperity as satirized by Janis Joplin:

Oh Lord, won't you buy me
A Mercedes Benz?
My friends all have Porsche's,
I must make amends.
Worked hard all my life,
No help from my friends.
Oh Lord, won't you buy me
A Mercedes Benz?[386]

The False Gospel of Prosperity vs. the "Gospel of Wealth"

It's important to distinguish the False Gospel of Prosperity from what was called the "Gospel of Wealth" a century ago.

If you'd like to see an admirable example of a socially responsible attitude towards stewardship of financial resources by one of the very wealthy, you can do no better Andrew Carnegie, the steel magnate from the age of Robber Barons. He wrote an editorial in June of 1889 in which he made an eloquent case for social responsibility for his very wealthy colleagues which became known as the "Gospel of Wealth."

The newly rich had concentrated wealth to such an extent that since they could not spend it all but could only pass it on to their heirs who had not earned it, the socially responsible thing to do was to gift it to society at large in thoughtful, responsible ways.

"A man who dies rich dies disgraced," he famously said. Aside from being abstract altruism, he made a point that, in improving society and the common good on earth, one would be rewarded in heaven. To set an example, and to answer critics who disapproved of free handouts to the undeserving, he used his wealth to fund the establishment of public libraries throughout the English-speaking world.

Carnegie became a self-made man through his diligent use of public libraries, and thought that funding an institution which had enabled him to advance in society, he could "Help those who will help themselves, to provide part of the means by which those who desire to improve may do so."[387]

Perhaps Carnegie could feel empathy towards the poor, since he been one of them when he was young. He disapproved of the rich passing on all their wealth to their progeny, who had not earned it themselves and would not know the value of work. Carnegie could empathize with the poor, and made a great and beautiful gesture in a very American way, by providing the means by which any (literate) citizen could avail themselves of his libraries and gain the knowledge to become self-made, as he did.

Now, not everyone had Carnegie's gumption and intelligence, but he left a sterling example for others to follow (although I should add, that Carnegie contributed to the numbers of the poor by refusing to give his steel plant workers wage increases, and locked them out during labor disputes).

We think of ourselves as being so much more enlightened than they were in 1889; when was the last time you heard someone with wealth say, "A man who dies rich dies disgraced?" The parable of Lazarus and the rich one is one which stays in the mind vividly and illustrates the problem of wealth for spiritual health:

There was a rich man who was dressed in purple and fine linen and who feasted sumptuously every day. And at his gate lay a poor man named Lazarus, covered with sores, who longed to satisfy his hunger with what fell from the rich man's table; even the dogs would come and lick his sores. The poor man died and was carried away by the angels to be with Abraham. The rich man also died and was buried. In Hades, where he was being tormented, he looked up and saw Abraham far away with Lazarus by his side. He called out, 'Father Abraham, have mercy on me, and send Lazarus to dip the tip of his finger in water and cool my tongue; for I am in agony in these flames.'

But Abraham said, 'Child, remember that during your lifetime you received your good things, and Lazarus in like manner evil things; but now he is comforted here, and you are in agony. Besides all this, between you and us a great chasm has been fixed, so that those who might want to pass from here to you cannot do so, and no one can cross from there to us.' He said, 'Then, father, I beg you to send him to my father's house—for I have five brothers— that he may warn them, so that they will not also come into this place of torment.' Abraham replied, 'They have Moses and the prophets; they should listen to them.' He said, 'No, father Abraham; but if someone goes to them from the dead, they will repent.' He said to him, 'If they do not listen to Moses and the prophets, neither will they be convinced even if someone rises from the dead.'"[388]

You can feel the misery of Lazarus in his poverty and the opulence of the rich man in his comfort, then the dramatic reversal of fortune after death, when it is too late for the rich man to make amends, even to send Lazarus to warn his brothers. It's also quite vivid to imagine the rich man in his torment looking up to see Lazarus lying in Abraham's bosom. I think this parable was intended to be well-remembered, for unfortunately it will always be relevant on this earth.

I'm happy to say that Andrew Carnegie has at least one follower in these times. On September 15, 2020, *Forbes* magazine announced that Charles "Chuck" Feeney, having amassed a fortune through the retail giant Duty Free Shoppers he founded in 1960, had finally fulfilled a life-long goal: giving away the $8 *billion* he had gained, through his charitable foundation Atlantic Philanthropies, and he gave it all away anonymously. Because of his clandestine, globe-trotting philanthropy campaign, *Forbes* called him the James *Bond of Philanthropy*.[389]

Feeney's idea, which has influenced other billionaire philanthropists like Warren Buffet and Bill Gates, is called "Giving While Living." Feeney summarized his mission in a few sentences. "I see little reason to delay giving when so much good can be achieved through supporting worthwhile causes. Besides, it's a lot more fun to give while you live than give while you're dead."[390]

The False Gospel of Conspicuous Piety (Without Compassion)

I'm not sure where or how it happened, but individually and collectively, it seems that much of Protestant Christianity in the U.S. today seems to be guided by the idea that conspicuous piety proves your right relationship with God, and conveniently distinguishes you from your less pious neighbor.

I've cited Gospel passages earlier where Jesus warns his disciples against conspicuous (and empty) piety; people who fast with loud groanings to show off their piety, or those who make a show of loud and elaborate prayers, or those who even quietly in their hearts, give thanks to God that their station is higher than those below them, and even brag to God of how pious they are.

He also told this parable to some who trusted in themselves that they were righteous and regarded others with contempt: "Two men went up to the temple to pray, one a Pharisee and the other a tax collector. The

Pharisee, standing by himself, was praying thus, 'God, I thank you that I am not like other people: thieves, rogues, adulterers, or even like this tax collector. I fast twice a week; I give a tenth of all my income.' But the tax collector, standing far off, would not even look up to heaven, but was beating his breast and saying, 'God, be merciful to me, a sinner!' I tell you; this man went down to his home justified rather than the other; for all who exalt themselves will be humbled, but all who humble themselves will be exalted."[391]

Piety with compassion is a great blessing, and maybe we don't see enough of it because it is mostly done by those whose motivations are the performing of God's work with their hands, without political posturing, who take seriously Jesus' injunction to give quietly, "so that your alms may be done in secret; and your Father who sees in secret will reward you."[392]

One example of piety without compassion is how some in the Pro-Life (or Anti-Abortion) movement show a contrast between their professed concern for the rights of the unborn with the judgement they pass on pregnant women who do not want to give birth, and on politicians, medical professionals and family planning organizations who do not rule out choosing abortion. "How can a Christian be in favor of abortion, and criticize those who want to save unborn babies," you might ask.

I have several answers to this question. First, I don't know anyone personally who thinks that abortion is a "good idea"; it's better to think of it as a sad choice a woman makes, when forethought, birth control, or saying "no" failed to prevent an unwanted pregnancy.

As with Prohibition, banning abortion may satisfy the sensibilities of a lot of people (many of whom are no longer in a position to be faced with abortion), but will not prevent it from continuing, thanks to human nature, but only drive it underground.

As has been well-documented, women frequently die undergoing illegal (and unsafe) abortions. Surviving women may become disfigured or have debilitating infections. If you think abortion is a bad idea, you haven't considered the gruesome realities of banned abortions.

If you oppose abortion on the grounds that it is murder, what have you done to help sex education and spread the good news of birth control that can not only prevent abortion, but also the spread of STDs? If you oppose abortion *and* birth control, how do you justify that?

If you oppose abortion on the grounds that it is murder, but haven't worked equally hard to limit gun violence in the U.S., how do you justify that? And if you're committed to saving children, what about the children and teens killed each year by gun violence? Remember,

> Those who say, "I love God," and hate their brothers or sisters, are liars; for those who do not love a brother or sister whom they have seen, cannot love God whom they have not seen. The commandment we have from him is this: those who love God must love their brothers and sisters also." – 1 John 4, 18-21.[393]

To those who harass women and their guides who try to visit clinics where abortions are legally offered, or who threaten (and even shoot and kill) doctors who perform these procedures, I would then ask, "How can you claim to love a fetus you have not seen, yet will not love her mother (and respect her autonomy), who you have seen?"

The urge to protect innocent, vulnerable life should apply to *all* human life, which includes migrants, those of different racial and religious backgrounds than ours, the poor and homeless. How are they any less of a priority, especially since they are already in the world, than the unborn?

This brings up the question of why the "pro-life" movement supports President Trump so overwhelmingly, when his record on human rights for anyone other than American White potential voters is terrible. Stephanie Ranade Krider is a pro-life evangelical who until recently served as Director of Ohio Right to Life. "As with most (though not all) people in the pro-life movement, my beliefs are rooted in my Christian faith," she wrote in an op-ed article in the *Washington Post's* Outlook section on Sunday, October 12, 2020.

To many of us, being pro-life means abiding by an ethic that goes well beyond opposition to abortion. It's an ethic committed to protecting the vulnerable, and grounded in the idea that every human deserves dignity, because every human is created in the image of God, including the unborn, Black people, immigrants, the incarcerated and the poor...the Trump administration showed few signs of recognizing that ethic. Instead, it often demonstrated disregard for human dignity—and an appalling willingness to disregard lives not considered politically useful.[394]

Krider notes that in a campaign letter, the president claimed "to have governed as the most pro-life president in history,"[395] but he has not shown evidence of doing this consistently or for the right reasons. In fact, during the 2016 campaign, he said that "there has to be some form of punishment" for women who have abortions. He retracted this statement dramatically just hours later, but not before causing a huge media firestorm.[396]

Krider continues, "The president has frequently claimed to be on the side of God, when in fact what he preaches is a vision of America with himself as savior, as sort of nationalist gospel of his own definition."[397]

The combination of Trump's callousness towards those suffering [from the pandemic] and his indifference towards the Black Lives Matter protests following George Floyd's death made it too difficult for me to stay in my position. The organization I worked for remained silent about the pandemic and racism...I am confident that, in advocating for this president, we will have lost our soul. The church is meant to be known for our unconditional love of others. By supporting Trump, we show only our love of power.[398]

With all the talk of "saving lives" and the value of the lives of the unborn, what has been overlooked is the fact that these unborn, potential children are until birth inseparable from their mother's bodies, and why do we not consider the lives and fates of the mothers, who are already fully functional and autonomous persons? Why do their decisions and circumstances carry no weight among those who insist that abortion is morally unacceptable even in cases of rape or incest? How do the sensibilities and judgments of disinterested parties outweigh the considerations, circumstances and decisions of the (independent and autonomous) persons most involved and affected—the pregnant women themselves?

Also, during this pandemic, the "pro-life" people should be the most prominent in urging everyone to socially distance and wear face coverings in public; are they doing this? For all the emotion about the unborn infants lost to abortion, we now have over a quarter of a million people dead from COVID-19 -19, with a president who claims to have beaten the virus, and conspicuously takes his mask off at rallies.

Let's turn to the Bible (as we so often should) for guidance. Abortion— safe and legal, was unknown then, so let's consider a similar moral dilemma.

The scribes and the Pharisees brought a woman who had been caught in adultery; and making her stand before all of them, they said to him, "Teacher, this woman was caught in the very act of committing adultery. Now in the law Moses commanded us to stone such women. Now what do you say?" They said this to test him, so that they might have some charge to bring against him. Jesus bent down and wrote with his finger on the ground. When they kept on questioning him, he straightened up and said to them, "Let anyone among you who is without sin be the first to throw a stone at her." And once again he bent down and wrote on the ground. When they heard it, they went away, one by one, beginning with the elders; and Jesus was left alone with the woman standing before him. Jesus straightened up and said to her, "Woman, where are they? Has no one condemned you?" She said, "No one, sir." And Jesus said, "Neither do I condemn you. Go your way, and from now on do not sin again." [399]

I think the Pharisees had it in for Jesus because he was more popular than they were, and why not? Everyone who heard him must have known that God was with him. This appealed especially to the powerless and poor, because he had shown that he cared about them. He also was a harsh critic of the Pharisees and scribes, saying "You hypocrites! Isaiah prophesied rightly about you when he said: 'This people honors me with their lips, but their hearts are far from me; in vain do they worship me, teaching human precepts as doctrines.' "[400]

With the woman caught in adultery, the Pharisees (as usual) are only seeking to trap Jesus and prove to him and his listeners that the Law (of which they are the masters) is in charge, not love and mercy.

There are several things I like about this passage. First, it's pretty dramatic, and hard to forget! Second, I think it's funny that the Pharisees declare that this woman "is caught in the very act of adultery," because by definition this must have involved some man, who somehow had disappeared and did not have to answer for this act, as the unfortunate woman had to (my theory is that it was a set-up by the Pharisees). As so often with abortion today, it's the same dynamic; the man is missing but the woman is caught to answer for the seeds he sowed.

I also like that Jesus did not challenge the law of Moses (remember that he said he came to fulfill the law). He put the ball right back in the Pharisees' court by inviting "anyone among you who is without sin be the first to throw a stone at her." I then like that, faced with such a bold invitation, they realized they could not pretend to be without sin, and when they heard it, they went away, one by one, beginning with the elders." The elders had lived long enough to know themselves too well, and were beyond trying to fool themselves or anyone else with bogus piety.

Finally, I like how the passage ends. "Jesus was left alone with the woman standing before him. Jesus straightened up and said to her, "Woman, where are they? Has no one condemned you?" She said, "No one, sir." And Jesus said, "Neither do I condemn you. Go your way, and from now on do not sin again."

Jesus could have just walked away after the crowd departed, but he needed to acknowledge the woman and reassure her that he did not condemn her, but he also urged her "do not sin again." I believe he meant the specific sin of adultery, instead of trying to live perfectly.

No Christian has an excuse to think they are justified by piety in America today, unless that means they are taking up their cross and bearing the burdens of the many victims of violence, poverty and hatred right here in the U.S.A., "daily." And if you have, remember, as Jesus said, "So you also, when you have done all that you were ordered to do, say, 'We are worthless slaves; we have done only what we ought to have done!' "[401]

The False Gospel of Fear

We humans are motivated by many things, but by none as immediately and forcefully as fear. It's our natural survival instinct and serves a purpose. Unfortunately, cynical politicians have discovered that it's more effective to scare people and manipulate them through fear, than to inspire them with a call to their higher nature, especially when these same politicians don't seem to have anything substantial to offer as an alternative.

The False Gospel of Fear finds followers in difficult times when faith in established institutions is fading, people fear for the future, and want an easy answer to explain a lot of complex social and economic chaos. A charismatic politician steps forward and claims that the country is on the verge of collapse, because it is being sabotaged by cultural outsiders.

"I am the only one with the answer that can save this country!" they cry. "Follow me and we'll not only (magically) go back to the Good Old Days, but even surpass them! All we have to do is fight the enemy! The solution is easy! Just follow me, stay afraid, and join me in the fight!"

Does this sound familiar? It should. It's basically the message of Donald Trump in his 2016 presidential campaign in a nutshell; also, interestingly, Hitler and Mussolini, and look where they led their nations.

Christians in America should be asking themselves, "If we really trusted in God, why are we letting ourselves be manipulated by politicians through fear?"

Letting yourself be persuaded that something terrible will happen to you if you don't trust a person or group of people, is letting them have the power to define right and wrong, and also to let them tell you how to feel, and of whom to be afraid of (you'll hate what you fear, of course).

Believe me, I understand that feeling afraid in these times is understandable! This country has seen continual crises since the turn of this century, with both religious and secular terrorism (madmen with many guns) whose acts of violence grow worse by the year, and now we're in the midst of a pandemic, so it's understandable to feel our individual and collective lives are being threatened.

But just because someone tells you to be afraid of any number of things they name, and then tell you they're the "only one" who can save the day, doesn't mean you should just take them at face value without considering whether you're being manipulated to give up thinking for yourself for impulsive fear-based reactions.

> You know, a president once said,
> "The only thing we have to fear is fear itself"
> Now it seems like we're supposed to be afraid.
> It's patriotic, in fact.
> Color-coded,
> What we supposed to be afraid of?
> Why, of being afraid.
> That's what terror means, doesn't it?
> That's what it used to mean.[402]

One of the crazy-making things about life at this moment is that despite the largest pandemic in a century, President Trump and his Republican allies have and continue to make light of the deadly coronavirus, like it's not a big deal, when of course we should be afraid of contracting it and unknowingly giving it to others, especially our friends, family and co-workers.

In the last two weeks of October, 2020, the US had added close to a million new coronavirus cases, averaging 1,000 deaths daily. So, let's have healthy but reality-based fear, but not give in to unlimited and irrational fear.

Let's examine faith, and fear. "Do not be afraid" is a recurring message in the Bible across Old and New Testaments. Let's return to the Garden of Eden and the Fall. Eve eats of the fruit, and gives it to Adam:

Then the eyes of both were opened, and they knew that they were naked; and they sewed fig leaves together and made loincloths for themselves. They heard the sound of the LORD God walking in the garden at the time of the evening breeze, and the man and his wife hid themselves from the presence of the LORD God among the trees of the garden. But the LORD God called to the man, and said to him, "Where are you?" He said, "I heard the sound of you in the garden, and I was afraid, because I was naked; and I hid myself."[403]

The original sin was disobedience, which led to fear; Adam and Eve hid themselves from the Lord, because they had become aware of their nakedness but also because they had disobeyed God. Fear and separation from God go together.

When Joseph discovers that Mary is pregnant, he decides to divorce her quietly, but an angel of the Lord appeared to him and told him "Joseph, son of David, do not be afraid to take Mary as your wife, for the child conceived in her is from the Holy Spirit. She will bear a son, and you are to name him Jesus, for he will save his people from their sins." [404]

Elsewhere in the book of Matthew, Jesus tells his followers that a sparrow doesn't fall from the sky without the Father's knowledge, so "Do not be afraid; you are of more value than many sparrows."[405]

When Jesus came walking to his disciples on the Sea of Galilee during a storm, they thought he was a ghost and cried out in fear, "But immediately Jesus spoke to them and said, "Take heart, it is I; do not be afraid."[406]

When Mary Magdalene and "the other Mary" went to see the tomb on the first day of the week following Jesus' crucifixion, there was an earthquake and an angel of the Lord appeared to them, "and angel said to the women, "Do not be afraid; I know that you are looking for Jesus who was crucified. He is not here; for he has been raised, as he said."[407] When the Mary's run with joy to tell the disciples, they suddenly run into Jesus himself, who says, "Do not be afraid; go and tell my brothers to go to Galilee; there they will see me."[408]

Altogether, the message "Do not be afraid" occurs 63 times in both books of the Bible. Don't you think God is trying to tell us something? During the Great Depression, President Franklin Roosevelt told Americans that "The only thing we have to fear is fear itself."

The New Deal, through the WPA and other programs, put Americans back to work. Their wages not only helped them and their families but stimulated the economy. Most of all, it gave Americans hope that the federal government actually cared about them and their welfare. This gave them the courage to carry on through the long years of the Depression.

My mother told me that when FDR's body was taken on its journey to his final resting place, a man watching the solemn procession was seen weeping by a reporter. When asked if the man had known Roosevelt, he replied "No, but he knew me."

If you "trust in God" only when times are good nationally and economically, what kind of faith is that? Consider the example of Job.

The LORD said to Satan, "Have you considered my servant Job? There is no one like him on the earth, a blameless and upright man who fears God and turns away from evil." Then Satan answered the LORD, "Does Job fear God for nothing? Have you not put a fence around him and his house and all that he has, on every side? You have blessed the work of his hands, and his possessions have increased in the land. But stretch out your hand now, and touch all that he has, and he will curse you to your face." The LORD said to Satan, "Very well, all that he has is in your power; only do not stretch out your hand against him!"[409]

As we know, Job promptly lost livestock, servants and even his own children in short order. His response: "Then Job arose, tore his robe, shaved his head, and fell on the ground and worshiped. He said, "Naked I came from my mother's womb, and naked shall I return there; the LORD gave, and the LORD has taken away; blessed be the name of the LORD." In all this Job did not sin or charge God with wrongdoing."[410]

I'm sure most of us have been afraid of something out of the ordinary in these last 20 years since the year 2000, from fear of losing your job, to fear of the future for your children, to fear of being shot in random violence somewhere, now to fear of the novel coronavirus. How many of us have responded to disaster the way that Job did?

As we know, Job's sufferings continue. Even after his profession of faith, he's inflicted with boils from his head to his feet, and has to scratch himself with a potsherd for relief. His wife urges him to "Curse God and die," but Job replies, "'Shall we receive the good at the hand of God, and not receive the bad?' In all this Job did not sin with his lips."[411]

Here are some Bible verses to consider on fear. "Do not fear those who kill the body but cannot kill the soul; rather fear him who can destroy both soul and body in hell."[412]

"While he was still speaking, some people came from the leader's house to say, "Your daughter is dead. Why trouble the teacher any further?" But overhearing what they said, Jesus said to the leader of the synagogue, "Do not fear, only believe, and she will be saved."[413]

"But even if you do suffer for doing what is right, you are blessed. Do not fear what they fear, and do not be intimidated, but in your hearts sanctify Christ as Lord."[414]

"So, we have known and believe the love that God has for us. God is love, and those who abide in love abide in God, and God abides in them. Love has been perfected among us in this: that we may have boldness on the day of judgment, because as he is, so are we in this world. There is no fear in love, but perfect love casts out fear; for fear has to do with punishment, and whoever fears has not reached perfection in love. We love because he first loved us."[415]

"For it is as if a man, going on a journey, summoned his slaves and entrusted his property to them; to one he gave five talents, to another two, to another one, to each according to his ability. Then he went away. The one who had received the five talents went off at once and traded with them, and made five more talents. In the same way, the one who had the two talents made two more talents. But the one who had received the one talent went off and dug a hole in the ground and hid his master's money. After a long time, the master of those slaves came and settled accounts with them. Then the one who had received the five talents came forward, bringing five more talents, saying, 'Master, you handed over to me five talents; see, I have made five more talents.' His master said to him, 'Well done, good and trustworthy slave; you have been trustworthy in a few things, I will put you in charge of many things; enter into the joy of your master.' And the one with the two talents also came forward, saying, 'Master, you handed over to me two talents; see, I have made two more talents.' His master said to him, 'Well done, good and trustworthy slave; you have been trustworthy in a few things, I will put you in charge of many things; enter into the joy of your master.'

Then the one who had received the one talent also came forward, saying, 'Master, I knew that you were a harsh man, reaping where you did not sow, and gathering where you did not scatter seed; so, I was afraid, and I went and hid your talent in the ground. Here, you have what is yours.' But his master replied, 'You wicked and lazy slave! You knew, did you, that I reap where I did not sow, and gather where I did not scatter? Then you ought to have invested my money with the bankers, and on my return, I would have received what was my own with interest. So, take the talent from him, and give it to the one with the ten talents. For to all those who have, more will be given, and they will have an abundance; but from those who have nothing, even what they have will be taken away. As for this worthless slave, throw him into the outer darkness, where there will be weeping and gnashing of teeth.' [416]

The slaves have done what they could with what they have been given, except for the one slave who was afraid, and went and hid his talent in the ground, then gives it back to the master.

Perhaps he was afraid of failure, or even more, of success and the burden of responsibility it would bring, but he has a bad attitude, telling the master that he was "a harsh man, reaping where you did not sow, and gathering where you did not scatter seed."

Interestingly, the master does not contradict the slave, but points out that through his bad attitude he had disobeyed the master's instructions and intentions. The master could have dug a hole in the ground to hide the talent himself, but he expected active care and stewardship of what he had given the disobedient slave.

We are the slaves who have been given the talents; we are not asked to do more than what we can with what we were given, but we know we will be rewarded by the good master, and if we refuse to put the talents he has given us to work, we will answer to him for it, have our talent taken away, and be "throw him into the outer darkness, where there will be weeping and gnashing of teeth." The disobedient steward's primary fault was not laziness, but fear.

Is fear keeping us from investing the Lord's talents in the world? We should all be asking ourselves of this, and since we have the fate of living in these times, let us not be found lacking when the time of reckoning comes, from our fear, or laziness, in doing the work with our talents on behalf of the Lord.

Finally, as an antidote to fear, consider the fearless example of St. Paul in his letter to the Romans:

Who will separate us from the love of Christ? Will hardship, or distress, or persecution, or famine, or nakedness, or peril, or sword? No, in all these things we are more than conquerors through him who loved us. For I am convinced that neither death, nor life, nor angels, nor rulers, nor things present, nor things to come, nor powers, nor height, nor depth, nor anything else in all creation, will be able to separate us from the love of God in Christ Jesus our Lord.[417]

If we're sincere in our faith, we should trust in God, and act like his children, even in challenging and fearful times. A big part of this means treating others as if we realize they too are God's children even if they don't know it yet. "For the whole law is summed up in a single commandment, 'You shall love your neighbor as yourself.'"[418]

The False Gospel of Guns, or Believing "The Second Amendment Outranks the Fifth Commandment."

The second amendment to the Constitution, originally written to protect local and state militias, has been widely interpreted to mean that any adult American citizen without a criminal record can legally buy any kind of firearms except as further restricted by state law. We have paid a very heavy price as a society for the lack of sensible regulations on the sale of firearms.

Every day, 100 Americans are killed with guns. Every year there are nearly 13,000 homicides from gun violence in the U.S., but nearly twice as many deaths from guns are used in suicides, with the average annual death toll at over 36,000, not counting over 100,000 who are shot and wounded (either intentionally or accidentally). [419]

As we have seen from many horrific school shootings, these statistics are not limited to crime. Firearms are the second leading cause of death for American children and teens and the leading cause of death for Black American children and teens. Guns also play a major role in death and injury from domestic violence.

In an average month, 52 American women are shot to death by an intimate partner, and many more are injured. Nearly one million women alive today have been shot or shot at by an intimate partner. Approximately 4.5 million American women alive today have been threatened with a gun by an intimate partner. Fifty-eight percent of American adults or someone they care for have experienced gun violence in their lifetime, and approximately three million American children witness gun violence every year.[420]

The dollar amount of the costs of all this violence to the American economy is staggering; an estimated $229 billion ($8.6 direct and $221 indirect costs) *per year!*[421] But consider the emotional and spiritual cost behind all these statistics, for the people involved and for the people mourning the victims, including school children.

For many people it seems, firearms are magical; possessing one makes them feel invincible, which is exactly what the gun manufacturers intend. But all that firearms possession guarantees is that you have made your home potentially deadly to someone. How can you guarantee you will out-aim and out-shoot a potential thief, rapist, etc. instead of having the weapon used by, or against, you or your family? You can't. Consider these statistics:

• There are more than 393 million guns in circulation in the United States — approximately 120.5 guns for every 100 people, or 20% more guns than the human population in this country! And these statistics were compiled before the final month of the 2020 presidential campaign, when some gun retailers said they "could not get product" from their suppliers because of overwhelming demand.[422]

• 1.7 million children live with **unlocked, loaded guns** - 1 out of 3 homes with kids have guns.
• In 2015, 2,824 children (age 0 to 19 years) died by gunshot and an additional 13,723 were injured.
• An emergency department visit for non-fatal assault injury places a youth at 40 percent higher risk for subsequent firearm injury.
• Those people that die from accidental shooting were more than three times as likely to have had a firearm in their home as those in the control group.
• Among children, the majority (89%) of unintentional shooting deaths occur in the home. Most of these deaths occur when children are playing with a loaded gun in their parent's absence.[423]

As for those who believe owning guns in the home makes them safer, research published in the New England Journal of Medicine found that living in a home where guns are kept increased an individual's risk of death by homicide by between 40 and 170%.[424]

Christians, who are called to be peacemakers and imitators of Christ, have a responsibility to work in ways to reduce gun violence in the U.S. The NRA and their gun manufacturing allies have essentially thrown down a gauntlet, with the message that the Second Amendment Outranks the fifth commandment (against murder), and millions of Americans have accepted this uncritically, without considering the many scriptural calls for us to be peacemakers.

Let us consider "What would Jesus do?" He said, "Peace be with you," not "A Piece be with you," and it's a world of difference. This is the logical extension of the last section on the false gospel of fear. If you've bought into believing in fear, and your mind is in survival mode, then it makes sense to arm yourself, but why buy into the fear in the first place, if you are a Christian and you trust in the Lord?

Jesus said "Blessed are the peacemakers, for they shall be called the children of God." Peace that comes at the end of a sword (or barrel of a gun) is not genuine or lasting peace, but coercion through fear. Jesus also said, prophetically for us, "Put your sword back into its place; for all who take the sword will perish by the sword."[425] Unfortunately for us, too many who perish by guns were not the ones who made the decision to take them up.

In Oct. 2017, the deadliest mass shooting in America took place in Las Vegas, with 59 killed and 500 injured, when Stephen Craig Paddock opened fire from the 32nd floor of a hotel during a concert. Investigators found 23 firearms in Paddock's room at Mandalay Bay Resort and Casino and 19 more at his home.[426]

Amazingly, Paddock's weaponry, which included high-capacity magazines capable of holding 100 rounds each, .223-caliber AR-15-type semi-automatic rifles, .308-caliber AR-10-type rifles, and bump stocks (essentially converting semi-automatic rifles to automatic machine guns) which through rifle recoil enabled their triggers to fire at a rate of 90 rounds in 10 seconds, were all purchased legally.[427]

This massacre was followed by the Stoneman Douglass High School mass shooting in Parkland, Florida on Valentine's Day 2018 (ironically also Ash Wednesday), with 17 deaths and 17 injuries, the deadliest attack in an American high school.[428]

A week apart in early May 2019, two students saved many of their peers in sacrificing themselves by bravely facing active shooters in schools. Kendrick Castillo died after lunging at the shooter in STEM School Highlands Ranch, near Denver, giving others at enough time to hide. Eight other students were injured in the shooting. The previous week at the University of North Carolina at Charlotte, Riley Howell died after tackling a gunman.

As Americans, and Christians, what kind of society do we want to live in or hope that our children grow up in, and not get randomly killed due to gun violence? Are we too apathetic or just too cynical to care enough to see this as a matter of faith as well as the common good, and public safety? Do you consider that scores of dead, innocent people, victims of American gun violence, reflect the quality of your life, if you've done nothing to attempt to change it?

If we react to this issue out of our sensibilities, this seems like an intractable issue, but if we consider what makes sense for the common good, we can at least start to solve the problem. First, as Christians, affirm that the fifth commandment is a higher law than the second amendment, and hold politicians to account for their votes on this. Second, most gun owners support common-sense gun control like high-tech trigger locks, a ban on semi-automatic assault rifles (and now, also, "bump" stocks converting rifles to automatic status).

A legal limit on buying only one handgun per month was passed in Virginia in the 1990s; why not press for that in every state? And why was the national ban on semi-automatic rifles allowed to expire in the mid-2000s? Let's get to work to make the country safer. A country that allows gun violence as a matter of course, but also claims to be a "Christian nation", has not examined the contradiction between Judeo-Christian morality and laissez-faire firearms availability, and its awful cost for the millions of innocent victims.

There are arguments on the other side, but why should those with anti-government paranoia and a claim to entitlement of gun ownership without consequences to themselves, determine what happens to others with the deadly availability of guns in this country? There is no issue of such pressing urgency (besides the current pandemic) as public safety in the face of random gun violence such as we saw in Las Vegas, Sandy Hook and the Parkland Florida school shooting.

Any member of Congress claiming to be a Christian and who opposes safer gun legislation should be asked to explain themselves in Christian terms. "What would Jesus do?" is an entirely legitimate question in this context. When Peter drew his sword and cut off the ear of the chief priest's slave in the Garden of Gethsemane, Jesus told him to put it up; "He who lives by the sword will perish by the sword."

 But in America today, he who lives by guns enables the deaths of thousands of others annually, without paying a personal price himself. That is neither just, Christian, nor sustainable. President Trump (who was careful to call the Parkland shooting tragedy an "event", not a "shooting") suggested arming "trained" teachers in schools who could theoretically shoot someone using a gun in schools. That's the problem with seeing society through a gun sighting; pretty soon every problem looks like a gun target.

Christians can work with anyone of goodwill who wants to live in a safer society; Christ is the Prince of Peace, but a coalition of all religions or persons of conscience without a religion to solve this problem would be blessed by Him.

The survivors of the Marjory Stoneman Douglas High School massacre in Parkland, FL. have had the courage to stand up and demand positive change in sensible limits on guns in America, inspiring thousands of their peers across the country to do the same.

E.J. Dionne Jr., reported on February 26, 2018 on the proceedings of the Conservative Political Action Conference of four days earlier. He pointed out that Wayne LaPierre, executive director of the National Rifle

Association at the time, responded to calls for more gun control (just after the Parkland massacre) by calling those voices "saboteurs" and "socialists", warning that "our American freedoms could be lost and our country could be changed forever."

Change is one thing, but how could it be worse than parents being powerless to prevent a mentally deranged person from shooting their children in school, or at a movie theater? Our country has already been changed for the worse, thanks to increasing de-regulation of firearms.

Is this an appropriate Christian response to the grief and anger of survivors of a deadly attack on students and teachers? Ted Nugent, an N.R.A. board member, personally insulted the students who organized the March for Our Lives movement, saying that the "kids are liars," "poor, mushy-brained children," and even "soulless" during an interview on March 30, 2018 with *The Joe Pags Show*, a nationally syndicated conservative radio show.[429]

As if insulting the victims wasn't enough, he continued "All you have to do now is not only feel sorry for the liars, but you have to go against them and pray to God that the lies can be crushed and the liars can be silenced so that real measures can be put into place to actually save children's lives," Nugent said. What kind of a god does Nugent worship? And what kind of lies does he claim the Parkland students are telling?

As Americans, we value freedom. As members of a civilized society, we accept that there are limitations on our individual behavior for the common good. We can't drive through red lights without breaking the law, with risk to ourselves and others, and if we're caught driving above the legal blood alcohol limit, we can be thrown in jail.

Why do we not have sensible limitations on firearms, since every day 100 people are killed by guns in this country, and too frequently, schools, movie theaters and other public places are turned into slaughterhouses by deranged madmen?

It is as if we worship the god of unlimited individual freedom, including the freedom to purchase, carry and use firearms with virtually no limits. The price for worshipping this god is the blood sacrifice of 36,000 innocent American lives annually, their bodies piled on an obscene altar to the false god of unlimited "freedom."

As a Christian, I reject the lie that the second amendment outranks the fifth commandment, and am willing to work with any reasonable people to bring solutions into law to save innocent lives. I encourage every Christian to ask themselves, whom do you serve; Jesus, or guns? You can be a Christian and a gun owner, like you can be a Christian and an American, but which one is Lord? "No one can serve two masters; for a slave will either hate the one and love the other, or be devoted to the one and despise the other.[430]"

No one concerned with "national security" should excuse themselves from considering gun violence a top public health and safety threat.

Remember, fear is the enemy, and fear enables people to convince themselves that arming themselves will magically make them invincible over their enemies. The price that 100 people per day pay with their lives for gun owners' second amendment rights is a disgrace to this nation and its laws.

Let's turn again to the Bible for guidance. When God decided to flood the earth, he did so because his creation had become marred by violence; "And God said to Noah, "I have determined to make an end of all flesh, for the earth is filled with violence because of them; now I am going to destroy them along with the earth."[431]

"The fruit of the righteous is a tree of life, but violence takes lives away."[432]

"The LORD tests the righteous and the wicked, and his soul hates the lover of violence."[433]

Do not enter the path of the wicked, and do not walk in the way of evildoers...For they eat the bread of wickedness and drink the wine of violence. But the path of the righteous is like the light of dawn, which shines brighter and brighter until full day."[434]

The False God of Tribalism

As Americans, our tribe has traditionally been one of a diverse collection of peoples from many other nations, united in a common set of ideas: the sovereignty of the people, government that is accountable to the voters, the Constitution and its checks and balances on power, on a foundation of Judeo-Christian values.

The genius, and strength, of this "tribe" is that it is based on ideas instead of ethnicity or race. As Thomas Jefferson wrote in the Declaration of Independence, "We hold these truths to be self-evident, that all men are created equal, and are endowed by their creator with unalienable rights to life, liberty and the pursuit of happiness."

It would take until 1919, a century ago, for not only all men, but all adults of both genders, to gain the right to vote, but until very recently the United States has been gradually moving towards greater social justice and inclusion.

The equality of all persons before the law, and the freedom to pursue one's destiny, and an identification with ideals instead of ethnicity, are the genius of the American experiment. Admired worldwide, our core set of values, as President Madison said, "Mean nothing if they only exist on paper."

Unfortunately, our identification as fellow Americans who identify with shared values has been under attack since 2016 by a White nativism which is hostile towards cultural outsiders, whether foreigners, or American minorities.

The presidential candidacy of Donald Trump was based on an unabashed and coarse "us versus them" rhetoric. He called Mexicans thieves and rapists, attempted to ban Muslims from entering the U.S., mocked the Black Lives Matter movement, and offered to pay the legal fees of any of his supporters arrested for beating up protesters at his rallies.

In normal times all this would have been condemned and dismissed, but Republican party leaders soon realized Trump was leading in the polls, and aside from three or so Republican Congressmen, did and said nothing to distinguish themselves from him and his hateful rhetoric.

Through his example, he gave his supporters permission to be nasty to anyone he defined as "the enemy", from Mexicans and Muslims to members of the media (we've already seen how hate/bias crimes have risen sharply in the last few years according to the FBI).

Demonizing groups of people as being "other" and "the enemy", and greenlighting violent behavior towards them, are not only non-Christian behaviors, they also are hallmarks of fascist dictators against whom American soldiers have fought and died to save democracy for other nations, and not only us. Christians should be in the forefront of action for social justice and peace.

Do not lie to one another, seeing that you have stripped off the old self with its practices and have clothed yourselves with the new self, which is being renewed in knowledge according to the image of its creator. In that renewal there is no longer Greek and Jew, circumcised and uncircumcised, barbarian, Scythian, slave and free; but Christ is all and in all![435]

As Christians and Americans, we are all heirs to life in Christ and share a common set of national values. We sin if we consider that a group, we happen to feel comfortable with is somehow more worthy, more Christian or American than any other, and that includes levels of income.

My brothers and sisters, do you with your acts of favoritism really believe in our glorious Lord Jesus Christ? For if a person with gold rings and in fine clothes comes into your assembly, and if a poor person in dirty clothes also comes in, and if you take notice of the one wearing the fine clothes and say, "Have a seat here, please," while to the one who is poor you say, "Stand there," or, "Sit at my feet," have you not made distinctions among yourselves, and become judges with evil thoughts? Listen, my beloved brothers and sisters... You do well if you really fulfill the royal law according to the scripture, "You shall love your neighbor as yourself." But if you show partiality, you commit sin and are convicted by the law as transgressors.[436]

Here is a case where being a good American and a good Christian has no contradiction.

Some False Tribal Gods

• Serving Country Before God

We need to stay vigilant and be clear on the differences between authentic patriotism and bigoted nativism, and not allow Christianity to be defined by those who would twist both to unholy ends. I personally agree with the Seventh Day Adventists who refuse to pledge allegiance to the flag, and it's something every Christian should consider. Remember the First Commandment: "I am the Lord God...you shall have no other gods before me." That includes any country on this earth, and also their symbols.

Ever since the end of World War II, many if not most American Christians have taken it for granted that "God is on our side." Certainly, the totalitarian governments of Russia and China and the old Soviet Union have no fear of God and His commandments and have a long record of human suffering to answer for.

On the other hand, it was a tragic mistake during the Cold War to assume that the fight against Communism should be an actual war fought by our troops against the people of other countries (as with Vietnam). Some prominent Christians, from Billy Graham to Hubert Humphrey, did not bother to consider the consequences, for Americans as well as Vietnamese, of conflating the Cold War with some idea of a Christian Holy War, and as a result over 58,000 American troops were killed, and about two million Vietnamese on both sides, yet the "bad guys" still won.

George W. Bush directed the U.S. military to invade Iraq in the spring of 2013, claiming on November 1, 2001 that "you're either with us or against us in the fight against terror," using the absolutist language of scripture ("Whoever is not with me is against me")[437] to justify starting a land war in Asia, all based on false intelligence. The consequences have been tragic, and on an epic scale.

Accordingly, we should be hesitant and skeptical when any politician (or clergy member) tells us that we have the chance to support a "good" war, or should "defeat Satan", or use other language appropriating the words of scripture for the ends of war which put lives at risk.

If it comes down to it, every American Christian should be ready to choose Jesus as the Prince of Peace instead of those clamoring for a "just" or "patriotic" war. There are times (World War II) when there is plenty of time to assess the nature and intent of an enemy who is overrunning our allies' countries, and to do our part to help them, but things are rarely that cut-and-dried these days.

- **Male Domination**

As the #MeToo movement has revealed, too many men like the combination of sex and power, and abuse their professional positions to achieve them. We saw from the Gospel of John that it was the woman who was brought before Jesus who was caught "in the very act of adultery"; her partner went free and unaccountable.

The church is not living a faithful witness if it duplicates the worldly order of making women subservient to men instead of holding them as co-equal humans and Christians. When Roy Moore ran for an open Senate seat in Alabama vacated by Jeff Sessions in 2017, he was enthusiastically endorsed by local White evangelicals, despite allegations by *five* women that Moore sexually pressured them when he was in his 30s and they were all underage.

President Trump endorsed Moore, and the Republican National Committee followed suit, leading many to observe that if a political party could be said to have a soul, the Republicans had sold it to the devil in a (failed) bid to hold a senate seat. On November 13th, 2017, Miguel De la Torre, writing an opinion piece in the online Baptist News Global, said "No greater proof is needed of the death of Christianity than the rush to defend a child molester in order to maintain a majority in the U.S. Senate."

Moore had "devout" supporters shameless enough to use scripture to justify his actions "Take Joseph and Mary. Mary was a teenager and Joseph was an adult carpenter. They became parents of Jesus," Alabama State Auditor Jim Zeigler told *The Washington Examiner*. "There's just nothing immoral or illegal here. Maybe just a little bit unusual."[438]

Jesus was a feminist. He always treated women with respect, including the Samaritan woman he met at the well.

Now as they went on their way, he entered a certain village, where a woman named Martha welcomed him into her home. She had a sister named Mary, who sat at the Lord's feet and listened to what he was saying. But Martha was distracted by her many tasks; so, she came to him and asked, "Lord, do you not care that my sister has left me to do all the work by myself? Tell her then to help me." But the Lord answered her, "Martha, Martha, you are worried and distracted by many things; there is need of only one thing. Mary has chosen the better part, which will not be taken away from her."[439]

One of the Pharisees asked Jesus to eat with him, and he went into the Pharisee's house and took his place at the table. And a woman in the city, who was a sinner, having learned that he was eating in the Pharisee's house, brought an alabaster jar of ointment. She stood behind him at his feet, weeping, and began to bathe his feet with her tears and to dry them with her hair. Then she continued kissing his feet and anointing them with the ointment. Now when the Pharisee who had invited him saw it, he said to himself, "If this man were a prophet, he would have known who and what kind of woman this is who is touching him—that she is a sinner."

Jesus spoke up and said to him, "Simon, I have something to say to you." "Teacher," he replied, "speak." "A certain creditor had two debtors; one owed five hundred denarii, and the other fifty. When they could not pay, he canceled the debts for both of them. Now which of them will love him more?" Simon answered, "I suppose the one for whom he canceled the greater debt." And Jesus said to him, "You have judged rightly." Then turning toward the woman, he said to Simon, "Do you see this woman? I entered your house; you gave me no water for my feet, but she has bathed my feet with her tears and dried them with her hair. You gave me no kiss, but from the time I came in she has not stopped kissing my feet. You did not anoint my head with oil, but she has anointed my feet with ointment. Therefore, I tell you, her sins, which were many, have been forgiven; hence she has shown great love.[440]

While he was at Bethany in the house of Simon the leper, as he sat at the table, a woman came with an alabaster jar of very costly ointment of nard, and she broke open the jar and poured the ointment on his head. But some were there who said to one another in anger, "Why was the ointment wasted in this way? For this ointment could have been sold for more than three hundred denarii, and the money given to the poor." And they scolded her. But Jesus said, "Let her alone; why do you trouble her? She has performed a good service for me. For you always have the poor with you, and you can show kindness to them whenever you wish; but you will not always have me. She has done what she could; she has anointed my body beforehand for its burial. Truly I tell you, wherever the good news is proclaimed in the whole world, what she has done will be told in remembrance of her."[441]

Meanwhile, standing near the cross of Jesus were his mother, and his mother's sister, Mary the wife of Clopas, and Mary Magdalene. When Jesus saw his mother and the disciple whom he loved standing beside her, he said to his mother, "Woman, here is your son." Then he said to the disciple, "Here is your mother." And from that hour the disciple took her into his own home.[442]

Many women were also there, looking on from a distance; they had followed Jesus from Galilee and had provided for him. Among them were Mary Magdalene, and Mary the mother of James and Joseph, and

Richard G. Leahy

the mother of the sons of Zebedee... Mary Magdalene and the other Mary were there, sitting opposite the tomb. [443]

Early on the first day of the week, while it was still dark, Mary Magdalene came to the tomb and saw that the stone had been removed from the tomb. So, she ran and went to Simon Peter and the other disciple, the one whom Jesus loved, and said to them, "They have taken the Lord out of the tomb, and we do not know where they have laid him."

Then Peter and the other disciple set out and went toward the tomb. The two were running together, but the other disciple outran Peter and reached the tomb first. He bent down to look in and saw the linen wrappings lying there, but he did not go in. Then Simon Peter came, following him, and went into the tomb. He saw the linen wrappings lying there, and the cloth that had been on Jesus' head, not lying with the linen wrappings but rolled up in a place by itself.

Then the other disciple, who reached the tomb first, also went in, and he saw and believed; for as yet they did not understand the scripture, that he must rise from the dead. Then the disciples returned to their homes. But Mary stood weeping outside the tomb. As she wept, she bent over to look into the tomb; and she saw two angels in White, sitting where the body of Jesus had been lying, one at the head and the other at the feet. They said to her, "Woman, why are you weeping?" She said to them, "They have taken away my Lord, and I do not know where they have laid him."

When she had said this, she turned around and saw Jesus standing there, but she did not know that it was Jesus. Jesus said to her, "Woman, why are you weeping? Whom are you looking for?" Supposing him to be the gardener, she said to him, "Sir, if you have carried him away, tell me where you have laid him, and I will take him away." Jesus said to her, "Mary!" She turned and said to him in Hebrew, "Rabbouni!" (which means Teacher). Jesus said to her, "Do not hold on to me, because I have not yet ascended to the Father. But go to my brothers and say to them, 'I am ascending to my Father and your Father, to my God and your God.'" Mary Magdalene went and announced to the disciples, "I have

211

seen the Lord"; and she told them that he had said these things to her.[444]

I'm personally moved by all of these passages, because they demonstrate that Jesus showed no partiality towards women, just as he showed no partiality to people based on class or social station, even though women were held in low regard in Jewish society of the day. In return, these women treat Jesus with more respect (in some cases) than he is given by people of high social station.

Mary the mother of Jesus, his mother's sister, Mary the wife of Clopas, Mary Magdalene and Mary the mother of James and Joseph, through love that overcame fear (though all the male disciples had run away except for John), were faithful enough to stay with Jesus until the bitter end. Mary Magdalene's faith and devotion made her the first witness of the Resurrection, going to the tomb before dawn.

Who can doubt that these brave and faithful women will be great in the kingdom of heaven? Who can then justify thinking of women as second-best, or means to an end, instead of fully equal children of God?

- **Racism**

Racism is the false belief, turned into doctrine by the Nazis, Southern slavery apologists, and the former apartheid system in South Africa, that the White (Caucasian) race is somehow "superior" to all others, most especially to sub-Saharan Africans and their descendants. It has been used to justify kidnapping of Africans from their native lands, chaining and transporting them across the Atlantic in conditions that ensured many would die from disease, then selling the survivors into slavery to White masters with the aim of turning their coerced labor into profit.

Racism has also been used as an excuse to separate, and keep separate, Africans and "brown" peoples (such as Indians), from White Europeans, to the extreme of shipping European Jews to concentration (and death) camps during the Holocaust.

Since this was impossible to justify as treatment of equal human beings, the racists had to de-humanize the victims with all kinds of fake "science" and lies. De-humanizing migrants by calling them "animals" as President Trump has done, is another example of racism.

> For in Christ Jesus you are all children of God through faith. As many of you as were baptized into Christ have clothed yourselves with Christ. There is no longer Jew or Greek, there is no longer slave or free, there is no longer male and female; for all of you are one in Christ Jesus.[445]

There really needn't be any other scripture verse to show that racism is un-Christian, and should be renounced and rejected by all Christians, but I'll add a couple more:

> But to all who received him, who believed in his name, he gave power to become children of God, who were born, not of blood or of the will of the flesh or of the will of man, but of God."[446]

> "For God so loved the world that he gave his only Son, so that everyone who believes in him may not perish but may have eternal life."[447]

The persistence of racism is front and center in American public life today in the continued violence against Black Americans by the police, and we'll examine the issue in more detail in a separate chapter.

- **Homophobia**

The same verses used above to show the grace of God's love being offered to, and transforming, all the world, erasing all man-made distinctions of rank and hierarchy, applies to those in the LGBTQ (lesbian, gay, bi-sexual, trans-gender and queer) community as much as to straight, White men and women.

The members of this community have been reviled, abused, discriminated against and even killed for their sexual orientation, which they did not choose, just as those of us who are straight did not choose that either. Since we did not choose it, we cannot claim any kind of moral superiority for it (and ourselves); we also have no right to judge others who did not claim their differing sexuality, most especially if they hear the calling of the Holy Spirit to join the Christian community.

I was shocked when, after the 9/11 attacks, Rev. Jerry Falwell, speaking on fellow evangelist Pat Robertson's "700 Club" television show, blamed the terrorist attacks on gays, feminists, the ACLU, and "abortionists"

"The abortionists have got to bear some burden for this because God will not be mocked. And when we destroy 40 million little innocent babies, we make God mad. I really believe that the pagans, and the abortionists, and the feminists, and the gays and the lesbians who are actively trying to make that an alternative lifestyle, the ACLU, People for the American Way, all of them who have tried to secularize America, I point the finger in their face and say, 'You helped this happen.' " To which Mr. Robertson said: "I totally concur, and the problem is we have adopted that agenda at the highest levels of our government."[448]

I doubt if Falwell Sr. was aware of the irony that the Al Qaeda terrorists behind the 9/11 attacks had themselves condemned America for many of the same reasons. In other words, besides the difference in clothes, English vs. Arabic, and the use of violence, what is the real difference between Falwell's hateful sanctimony and that of Al Qaeda?

In this instance, the Black evangelical church, no less than the White evangelical church, has much to answer for in letting cultural taboos against homosexuality gain credibility within the church as reasons to denigrate, exclude and condemn an entire group of people. I write this on Martin Luther King, Jr. Day, who said that a person should be judged not by the color of his skin, but by the content of their character. To that I would add, "nor be judged by their sexual orientation."

Here it is important to distinguish between our sensibilities and comfort levels (we all have them), and our call as Christ's disciples to "love one another as I have loved you."[449] As St. Paul has made clear above, it is not our place to make value judgments on other people, especially those who want and have a right to stand among God's people as equal heirs of His love and mercy.

In the world at large we may feel more comfortable with some groups of people than others, or some peoples' sexual orientation may make us squeamish. Why is it any of our business, and how can we use our sensibilities as an excuse to justify excluding anyone from God's grace?

Some people will say, "They are sinners!" Surely, just as we all are. But do you think you're better just because you were born a heterosexual? And as Christians, we can't hide behind the sensibilities and prejudices of our culture; we have a higher call. Christians, like physicians, should act as if they had taken the Hippocratic Oath, to do no harm. That is not always possible, but almost always it is.

How we betray the witness and sacrifice of Christ who died for all, if we come along some 2000 years later and say that persons who are homosexual in orientation or otherwise LGBTQ are unworthy of Christ or Christianity? After all, if its pleased God to make salvation available to the Gentiles, why stop at sexual orientation?

Similarly, many people tend to believe myths about their own ethnicity as being somehow superior to that of others; this is cultural prejudice and has no place being attached to Christianity.

These examples of tribalism have something in common: they are all artificial distinctions to label some groups of people inferior as judged by other groups of people. This is a human tendency, but God's grace and generosity are not to be limited by human prejudice.

Sadly, mistaking our sensibilities for gods to be worshipped means that they can become more important than worshipping God and loving our neighbors. In the late winter of 2019 at a special session of the General Conference, the United Methodist Church, the second largest Protestant denomination in the U.S., voted by 53% to uphold and strengthen bans on gay marriage and on the ordination of LGBTQ persons.

Hannah Adair Bonner, a (self-described) queer Methodist minister who was also a delegate to the conference, described how one opponent of gay ordination justified it by quoting Jesus' warning about those who would harm or lead innocent children astray; "If any of you put a stumbling block before one of these little ones who believe in me, it would be better for you if a great millstone were fastened around your neck and you were drowned in the depth of the sea."[450],[451]

This is an example of trying to use scripture to discredit and disrespect other people. Since when does having a particular sexual orientation or preference mean a person (especially a pastor) is therefore depraved? What about all the heterosexual pastors who have seduced women or abused children? Were they suspect just because of their sexual orientation? If it's absurd in one direction, it has to be so in the other direction.

What would happen if you worshipped in a church where everyone didn't have to pretend to be someone else to avoid offending others' sensibilities, where the disabled and people of any race and nationality were considered as equals before God, and we could forget all the tribal and judgmental distinctions of the world? It would be a lot like the kingdom of God. To put this in perspective, let's ponder the words of John Prine as sung by Kris Kristofferson in "Jesus Was a Capricorn":

Jesus was a Capricorn,
He ate organic foods.
He believed in love and peace
And never wore no shoes.
Long hair, beard and sandals
And a funky bunch of friends,
Reckon we'd just nail him up
If he came down again.

[Chorus]
'Cause everybody's gotta have somebody to look down on,
Who they can feel better than at any time they please.
Someone doin' somethin' dirty decent folks can frown on,
If you can't find nobody else, then help yourself to me.[452]

I also think it's good to consider the "three surprises" of heaven that I heard in a sermon once: "The first surprise will be the people you see. The second surprise will be the people you do not see. The third surprise will be that you are there."

False Prophets

For those of you who turned to this page right away to see which names I'll be naming here, so you can tweet or squawk etc. about them on social media, that's not what this section is about, so turn back to the very beginning of this book.

As we've been reading lately, there are a number of false doctrines and false gods in American culture today that have been important to distinguish, so we can avoid confusing them with the Gospel.

There's a temptation to name names when writing about false prophets (just think of the many people who have been accused of being the Antichrist), but individuals are mere mortals who are here today and gone tomorrow. It's much more important to ponder what scripture tells us in general about false prophets, their habits and how to know them, so that we can apply this wisdom widely, from the national political and cultural arenas to our own communities when necessary.

As always, scripture is our guide, and scripture is non-political as concerns our tribes and ideologies today. What does scripture tell us about false prophets and how to know them?

First and foremost, now that we've had a chance to examine false gods and false doctrines, it follows that false prophets include those who preach them, and tell others to, instead of pointing to God's grace as a gift for all people regardless of gender, race, ethnicity, citizenship status or sexual orientation.

One sign of a false prophet is one who preaches the false gospel of complacency. Every godly person of any faith should be noted for their personal humility, for the more we know God, the more aware we should be of our own unworthiness (yet, by grace through faith, we can let God guide us). So, when you hear that you can be saved through works, or that you need not repent of anything, or that the lives of the faithful should be carefree and blessed, you are being flattered into carefree complacency; what Dietrich Bonhoeffer called "cheap grace."

This is a temptation in our egotistical society. The prophet Jeremiah shows us that it is a universal human temptation, but his words seem startingly relevant to the American situation today:

> Both prophet and priest are ungodly; even in my house I have found their wickedness, says the LORD. Therefore, their way shall be to them like slippery paths in the darkness, into which they shall be driven and fall; for I will bring disaster upon them in the year of their punishment, says the LORD. In the prophets of Samaria, I saw a disgusting thing: they prophesied by Baal and led my people Israel astray. But in the prophets of Jerusalem I have seen a more shocking thing: they commit adultery and walk in lies; they strengthen the hands of evildoers, so that no one turns from wickedness; all of them have become like Sodom to me, and its inhabitants like Gomorrah.

> Therefore, thus says the LORD of hosts concerning the prophets: "I am going to make them eat wormwood, and give them poisoned water to drink; for from the prophets of Jerusalem ungodliness has spread throughout the land." Thus says the LORD of hosts: Do not listen to the words of the prophets who prophesy to you; they are deluding you. They speak visions of their own minds, not from the mouth of the LORD. They keep saying to those who despise the word of the LORD, "It shall be well with you"; and to all who stubbornly follow their own stubborn hearts, they say, "No calamity shall come upon you."[453]

As with many things, one way to distinguish a false prophet is to clarify the difference between his/her words and their deeds.

> Beware of false prophets, who come to you in sheep's clothing but inwardly are ravenous wolves. You will know them by their fruits. Are grapes gathered from thorns, or figs from thistles? In the same way, every good tree bears good fruit, but the bad tree bears bad fruit. A good

tree cannot bear bad fruit, nor can a bad tree bear good fruit. Every tree that does not bear good fruit is cut down and thrown into the fire. Thus, you will know them by their fruits.[454]

Let us contrast the fruits of the Spirit with the fruits of evil, to help clarify what we can expect from how a person's words and actions reveal of their character.

Now the works of the flesh are obvious: fornication, impurity, licentiousness, idolatry, sorcery, enmities, strife, jealousy, anger, quarrels, dissensions, factions, envy, drunkenness, carousing, and things like these. I am warning you, as I warned you before: those who do such things will not inherit the kingdom of God.[455]

Are there public figures, politicians or self-styled religious leaders who demonstrate even some these fruits on a regular or even daily basis? If so, how can we believe they represent God's will?

By contrast, the fruit of the Spirit is love, joy, peace, patience, kindness, generosity, faithfulness, gentleness, and self-control. There is no law against such things. And those who belong to Christ Jesus have crucified the flesh with its passions and desires. [456]

We all sin and need God's grace, but the extent to which a person's life reflects a dominance of one set of fruits versus the other will tell you about their character, how closely they follow the Commandments, and whether they have earned our trust for what they have to say.

In St. John's first letter, we have more to consider on how a person's life matches their profession of faith:

Now by this we may be sure that we know him, if we obey his commandments. Whoever says, "I have come to know him," but does not obey his commandments, is a liar, and in such a person the truth does not exist; but whoever obeys his word, truly in this person the love of God has reached perfection. By this we may be sure that we are in him: whoever says, "I abide in him," ought to walk just as he walked.[457]

You may say, "I don't want a Christian as our leader; I want a bad-ass who will wreak destruction on our enemies." Remember the example of Hitler; many naïve Christians (both Catholics and Protestants), having been seduced by the false gospel of fear, decided they needed to put their faith in the Nazis who indeed wreaked havoc on all Germany's neighbors.

Then, they needed to find and punish internal "enemies", and the suspension of any independent judiciary meant that anyone could be declared an enemy of the state with no due process. Martin Niemöller was a German Protestant clergyman and social activist who left us a famous poem about the dangers of passive apathy in the face of government with evil policies.

> First, they came for the Jews,
> and I did not speak out because I was not a Jew.
>
> Then they came for the Communists,
> and I did not speak out because I was not a Communist.
>
> Then they came for the trade unionists,
> and I did not speak out because I was not a trade unionist.
>
> Then they came for me,
> and there was no one left to speak out for me.[458]

Even the most ardent pro-Nazi German nationalists paid an awful price for putting their faith and their livelihoods in the hands of a madman leading a party of murderous pagans. Because they did not surrender to the Allies, Germany was invaded, its cities were bombed, its men were killed, its women were raped, and the remaining population was starving and homeless by the end of the war. This is the price of putting faith in godless men and armaments instead of in God and in His faithful servants, or even god-fearing persons of other faiths.

For example, suppose we had a President who lied on a daily basis, threw temper tantrums several times a week, did and said nothing to discourage violent White nationalists, was obsessed with himself and his popularity and alleged greatness, whose personal life was a litany of sleaze, megalomania and lust, and who appeared to be a walking advertisement for the Seven Deadly Sins? How could we expect that anything good could come from the sinful example of such an ungodly leader?

"And if anyone says to you at that time, 'Look! Here is the Messiah!' or 'Look! There he is!'—do not believe it. False messiahs and false prophets will appear and produce signs and omens, to lead astray, if possible, the elect. But be alert; I have already told you everything."[459]

In American history, there has been an interesting phenomenon since the 19th century: the belief that the end of the world, and the Second Coming, are near. During the second Great Awakening in 1831 William Miller, a Baptist convert, began to preach that the Second Coming of Jesus would occur somewhere between March 1843 and March 1844, based on his interpretation of the book of Daniel. His prophecy was so persuasive that he attracted thousands of followers from many Protestant denominations.

By the summer of 1844, some of Miller's followers promoted the date of October 22nd. They linked the cleansing of the sanctuary in the book of Daniel with the Jewish Day of Atonement, believed to be October 22 that year. "By 1844, over 100,000 people were anticipating what Miller had called the 'Blessed Hope'. On October 22 many of the believers were up late into the night watching, waiting for Christ to return and found themselves bitterly disappointed when both sunset and midnight passed with their expectations unfulfilled. This event later became known as the Great Disappointment."[460]

This was perhaps the largest example of its kind, but for some reason many American evangelicals are impatient for an end to this boring and trying earthly existence, and continue to let themselves be fooled that some new preacher has "the answer" to when the world will end. Around 1980, there were dire predictions of the eminent end of the world in evangelical circles, followed by the same thing at the millennium.

Harold Camping was a radio preacher and long-time head of the Family Radio, a California-based radio station group that broadcasts to more than 150 markets in the U.S. Camping became famous in 2011 when he predicted that Jesus Christ would return to Earth on May 21, 2011, whereupon the saved would be taken up to heaven in the rapture, and that there would follow five months of fire, brimstone and plagues on Earth, with millions of people dying each day, culminating on October 21, 2011, with the final destruction of the world. (He had previously predicted that Judgment Day would occur on or about September 6, 1994.)[461]

Here follows a list of headlines from National Public Radio documenting the chronology of his predictions and their aftermath over a year and a quarter:

Jan. 3, 2011. For Some Believers, May 21 Is Judgment Day
May 20, 2011. Update: The Rapture Supposedly Starts Tonight
May 21, 2011. Judgment Day? Not According to The Evidence
May 23, 2011. 'Rapture' Prophet Harold Camping Says He Had 'A Really Tough Weekend'
May 24, 2011. 'Rapture' Prophet Camping: "Did I Say May 21? I Should Have Said Oct. 21."
Oct. 15, 2011. 'Rapture' Prophet Camping: World Will 'Probably' End Quietly Next Friday
March 9, 2012. Doomsday Prophet Camping Says Predictions Were 'Incorrect and Sinful'

NPR pointed out that "Religion News Service says Camping's warnings were convincing to 'thousands of followers.' A few sold their possessions. Others fell victim to entrepreneurs selling such services as after-rapture pet care." I vividly remember driving on a highway in southern Virginia, with large billboards every mile or so. In an ironic sequence, one billboard would tout the imminent end of the world, followed by the next from a business saying, "We buy gold."

The next year, 2012, saw New Age version of the End of the World prediction, with the erroneous belief that the end of one cycle of the Mayan (Mesoamerican) "long count" calendar would mean the end of the world.

In fact, it only means the start of a new cycle of the "long count" calendar.[462]

Let us remember, returning to scripture, what Jesus told his disciples:

"But about that day and hour no one knows, neither the angels of heaven, nor the Son, but only the Father. For as the days of Noah were, so will be the coming of the Son of Man. For as in those days before the flood they were eating and drinking, marrying and giving in marriage, until the day Noah entered the ark, and they knew nothing until the flood came and swept them all away, so too will be the coming of the Son of Man. Then two will be in the field; one will be taken and one will be left. Two women will be grinding meal together; one will be taken and one will be left. Keep awake therefore, for you do not know on what day your Lord is coming."[463]

Now concerning the times and the seasons, brothers and sisters, you do not need to have anything written to you. For you yourselves know very well that the day of the Lord will come like a thief in the night. When they say, "There is peace and security," then sudden destruction will come upon them, as labor pains come upon a pregnant woman, and there will be no escape! But you, beloved, are not in darkness, for that day to surprise you like a thief; for you are all children of light and children of the day; we are not of the night or of darkness. So then let us not fall asleep as others do, but let us keep awake and be sober.[464]

Sobriety is partly intellectual and spiritual. The idea that the Second Coming is imminent has become so common in evangelical circles that it has led to highly irresponsible behavior, like selling one's possessions and succumbing to charlatans hawking post-Rapture pet care services.

Martin Luther is reputed to have said, "If I knew the world would end tomorrow, I would plant a tree." The saying does not appear in his collected works, but it's the sort of thing Luther could have said, maybe even should have said. It's very similar to a Jewish saying, "If you have a sapling in your hand and they tell you that the Messiah has arrived, first plant the sapling and then go out to greet him."[465]

Concluding Prayer for This Chapter

Lord, keep us steadfast in your Word, so we may not be led astray by false gospels, false doctrines or false prophets. It is a confusing, chaotic world, more now than ever with the influence of the Internet and its temptations. Keep us also from the many temptations of tribalism and imagining other people to be beneath us. As your children, give us faith, courage and discipline to focus on being your disciples and trusting that we can be in the world doing your will, without being overwhelmed by doubt or fear, since we know you are with us always. Help us to acknowledge that the United States belongs to all of its citizens and to remember our tradition of welcoming those who, like us or our ancestors, wanted to work to contribute to the common good. Help us to make sensible decisions in our politics, in prioritizing the common good.

Chapter Twelve: Christian Love:

"The Journey is the Destination."

"And I say to you, I have also decided to stick to love. For I know that love is ultimately the only answer to mankind's problems. And I'm going to talk about it everywhere I go. I've seen hate on the faces of too many Klansmen and too many White Citizens Councilors in the South to want to hate myself, because every time I see it, I know that it does something to their faces and their personalities and I say to myself that hate is too great a burden to bear. I have decided to love." –Dr. Martin Luther King, Jr.[466]

After all we've learned and reflected on in this book, the appropriate place to conclude is reflecting on how we can grow in practicing and demonstrating love, which is the aim of the Christian life. Since, even though we are saved by grace, our human default is selfishness, we can't achieve perfection in the Christian life on this earth, but that does not excuse us from the obligation to actively live in that intention.

Beloved, let us love one another, because love is from God; everyone who loves is born of God and knows God. Whoever does not love does not know God, for God is love. God's love was revealed among us in this way: God sent his only Son into the world so that we might live through him. In this is love, not that we loved God but that he loved us and sent his Son to be the atoning sacrifice for our sins. Beloved, since God loved us so much, we also ought to love one another. No one has ever seen God; if we love one another, God lives in us, and his love is perfected in us.[467]

M. Scott Peck, in his landmark self-help book *The Road Less Traveled,* points out that "love is not a feeling." Rather, it is demonstrated in actions taken by people, individually and collectively, motivated by love. Instead of sappy sentimentality, which is passive, love is proven in action taken to care for others.

As an example, Peck describes an alcoholic who, holding forth on a barstool, tells the bartender how much he loves his family, who desperately need his love in the form of his presence and active care. He is absent from them, but is deluded into mistaking passive sentiment for active love.

Perhaps the most famous bible verse for Christians is John 3:16, but let's look at it through verse 17: "For God so loved the world that he gave his only Son, so that everyone who believes in him may not perish but may have eternal life. Indeed, God did not send the Son into the world to condemn the world, but in order that the world might be saved through him."[468]

Once again, let's reflect on 1 John 11: "Beloved, since God loved us so much, we also ought to love one another." Let's hear how St. Paul describes love in action in Romans chapter 12, in a section titled by the editors "Marks of the True Christian":

> Let love be genuine; hate what is evil, hold fast to what is good; love one another with mutual affection; outdo one another in showing honor. Do not lag in zeal, be ardent in spirit, serve the Lord. Rejoice in hope, be patient in suffering, persevere in prayer. Contribute to the needs of the saints; extend hospitality to strangers.[469]

I like how St. Paul gets specific in how to live out a commitment to love, and that this does not only apply to other Christians whom you know, but to strangers. This shows that there is no biblical justification for the idea that living a Christian life means only taking care of your friends, family and fellow church parishioners.

Holy Thursday is also called Maundy Thursday, from the Latin word for "mandate". At the Last Supper and Jesus' institution of Holy Communion, he told his disciples this: I give you a new commandment, that you love one another. Just as I have loved you, you also should love one another. By this everyone will know that you are my disciples, if you have love for one another.[470]

We are not just suggested to "try on love", Jesus *commands* us to love one another, in part to demonstrate to the world how His love is perfected in us. Jesus also showed us throughout his short life on earth that love is not sentiment, but action, towards God (prayer) and towards anyone in need, especially the lowliest whom the world scorns and rejects.

St. Paul again speaks on living love, using Christ as the example to follow:

Let each of you look not to your own interests, but to the interests of others. Let the same mind be in you that was in Christ Jesus, who, though he was in the form of God, did not regard equality with God as something to be exploited, but emptied himself, taking the form of a slave, being born in human likeness. And being found in human form, he humbled himself and became obedient to the point of death— even death on a cross.[471]

On the one hand, to undertake the authentic Christian path is very difficult, because we are exhorted to "look not to your own interests, but to the interests of others," which is most certainly *not* the way of the world. Also, the Christian path of living in love is never complete, because there is always more to do and more to learn. We are called to love others, just as God loved us, for otherwise how can he live in us?

The book of Acts was not called the book of Opinions or Doctrines or Statutes. It was called the book of Acts because it documents the apostles in action, testifying bravely to the Gospel and spreading the Good News, and ministering to the people of God. We are called to Christian lives of action, as St. James reminds us:

But be doers of the word, and not merely hearers who deceive themselves. For if any are hearers of the word and not doers, they are like those who look at themselves in a mirror; for they look at themselves and, on going away, immediately forget what they were like. But those who look into the perfect law, the law of liberty, and persevere, being not hearers who forget but doers who act—they will be blessed in their doing."[472]

Any study of Christian love should include St. Paul's immortal words from his first letter to the Corinthians; they are an inspiration on modeling an attitude of love, as well as a reliable way of distinguishing sincere Christians from those who claim to be Christian but whose lives do not show that love is their aim.

If I speak in the tongues of mortals and of angels, but do not have love, I am a noisy gong or a clanging cymbal. And if I have prophetic powers, and understand all mysteries and all knowledge, and if I have all faith, so as to remove mountains, but do not have love, I am nothing. If I give away all my possessions, and if I hand over my body so that I may boast, but do not have love, I gain nothing.

Love is patient; love is kind; love is not envious or boastful or arrogant or rude. It does not insist on its own way; it is not irritable or resentful; it does not rejoice in wrongdoing, but rejoices in the truth. It bears all things, believes all things, hopes all things, endures all things. Love never ends. But as for prophecies, they will come to an end; as for tongues, they will cease; as for knowledge, it will come to an end. For we know only in part, and we prophesy only in part; but when the complete comes, the partial will come to an end.

When I was a child, I spoke like a child, I thought like a child, I reasoned like a child; when I became an adult, I put an end to childish ways. For now, we see in a mirror, dimly, but then we will see face to face. Now I know only in part; then I will know fully, even as I have been fully known. And now faith, hope, and love abide, these three; and the greatest of these is love.[473]

As is often true with a spiritual path, "the journey is the destination." We are not called to perfection in this life, just to being on the path of living love in action. It's well to remember the twin aspects of Jesus' call to us. First, he said to them all, "If any want to become my followers, let them deny themselves and take up their cross daily and follow me. For those who want to save their life will lose it, and those who lose their life for my sake will save it.[474]

As we've noted before, "taking up the cross" means denying your own needs and pleasures for the work of God, and the good of others. It does not mean putting up with people or things you don't like; that's just "life."

Note that Jesus asks us to "take up their cross *daily*," so just showing up once a week on Sundays isn't even enough. But second,

> Costly grace confronts us as a gracious call to follow Jesus, it comes as a word of forgiveness to the broken spirit and the contrite heart. Grace is costly because it compels a man to submit to the yoke of Christ and follow him; it is grace because Jesus says: "My yoke is easy and my burden is light."[475]

This book was partly inspired by the spiritual discipline and writings of the Lutheran pastor Dietrich Bonhoeffer who wrote the quote above, and most especially by his faithful example. In 1933 he was offered a parish post in Berlin but turned it down out of protest against National Socialism and its pressure on the church in Germany. He accepted a two-year appointment as a pastor of two German-speaking Protestant churches in London: the German Lutheran Church in Dacres Road, Sydenham and the German Reformed Church of St Paul's in Whitechapel.[476]

He was rebuked by his colleague the Swiss theologian Karl Barth for leaving his duty to the German church. While he could easily have kept out of Germany for the rest of Nazi rule, and even got a coveted invitation to study non-violence with Gandhi, he decided to return to Germany in 1935 in order to help train still-faithful pastors in an underground seminary, having to move often and stay off the radar. During this time, he wrote his most influential work, *The Cost of Discipleship,* which helped inspire this book, and is still considered a classic of modern Christian thought.

As the Germans were in the process of preparing for war and shutting down the underground seminary, Bonhoeffer once again was able to leave Germany at the invitation of Union Theological Seminary in New York, but felt guilty at having achieved safety while the German church was still at the mercy of the Nazis. He wrote to his friend and fellow Lutheran theologian Reinhold Niebuhr the following, before returning to Germany on the last scheduled steamer to travel east across the Atlantic before the war:

Christians in Germany will have to face the terrible alternative of either willing the defeat of their nation in order that Christian civilization may survive or willing the victory of their nation and thereby destroying civilization. I know which of these alternatives I must choose but I cannot make that choice from security. [477]

On his return, Bonhoeffer joined the Abwehr, the German military intelligence service, but secretly was working for the German resistance. He was arrested in April 1943 and imprisoned, but in 1944, after the failed plot to assassinate Hitler, Abwehr documents were found incriminating him in the plot, and he was transferred to the Flossenburg concentration camp.

Bonhoeffer was condemned to death by a kangaroo court and was executed at dawn on April 9, 1945 along with his Abwehr co-conspirators including its former head, Wilhelm Franz Canaris. Tragically, in just two more weeks, the Nazis would surrender.

Bonhoeffer's thinking about the church and the world was influenced by his time in the U.S. In 1930, while attending Union Theological Seminary on a teaching fellowship, a fellow seminarian introduced him to the Abyssinian Baptist Church in Harlem, at that time the largest Protestant church in the country, where he was influenced by the sermons of Adam Clayton Powell, Sr. on social justice and the Gospel, and he saw how Black Americans experienced segregation and discrimination While in the underground seminary in Germany, Bonhoeffer helped German Jews escape to Switzerland. [478]

Bonhoeffer's example of faithful sacrifice had great influence and inspiration on Christians across broad denominations and ideologies, such as Martin Luther King Jr. and the Civil Rights Movement in the United States, the anti-communist democratic movement in Eastern Europe during the Cold War, and the anti-Apartheid movement in South Africa.[479]

Actual martyrdom is not a necessary requirement of honest Christianity, but I believe the willingness to follow Jesus that far is. "For those who want to save their life will lose it, and those who lose their life for my sake will find it. For what will it profit them if they gain the whole world but forfeit their life? Or what will they give in return for their life?" [480]

After His resurrection when Jesus had appeared to the disciples, they seemed to return to their former way of life. Peter tells six of the disciples that he is going fishing on the Sea of Galilee. They sat in the boat all night but didn't catch anything. Jesus comes to them on the shore in disguise, and asks them if they've caught anything, and when they say no, he tells them to put their nets on the right side of the boat and they'd catch some; when they do, the entire net is full of fish, and John tells Peter "It is the Lord."[481]

When they had finished breakfast, Jesus said to Simon Peter, "Simon son of John, do you love me more than these?" He said to him, "Yes, Lord; you know that I love you." Jesus said to him, "Feed my lambs." A second time he said to him, "Simon son of John, do you love me?" He said to him, "Yes, Lord; you know that I love you." Jesus said to him, "Tend my sheep." He said to him the third time, "Simon son of John, do you love me?" Peter felt hurt because he said to him the third time, "Do you love me?" And he said to him, "Lord, you know everything; you know that I love you." Jesus said to him, "Feed my sheep."[482]

We know that Peter would be the leader of the new church, and Jesus was reminding him of his responsibilities for the spiritual care of his flock. But with the brokenness of our world and the constant need for tending to those who are sick, or hungry, or naked, or in prison, isn't Jesus also exhorting us to tend to people with these needs? What will we say when we stand before Him on that last day, and we remember what we did, or did not do, to "feed my sheep?"

In the beginning of *The Cost of Discipleship*, Bonhoeffer points out that Jesus had exhorted Peter "Follow me" twice; once, at the start of their relationship and Jesus' earthly ministry, and then after His resurrection.

Between the two calls lay a whole life of discipleship in the following of

Christ. Half-way between them comes Peter's confession, when he acknowledged Jesus as the Christ of God. Three times Peter hears the same proclamation that Christ is his Lord and God—at the beginning, at the end, and at Caesarea Philippi. Each time it is the same grace of Christ which calls to him "Follow me" and which reveals itself to him in his confession of the Son of God. Three times on Peter's way did grace arrest him, the one grace proclaimed in three different ways. This grace was certainly not self-bestowed. It was the grace of Christ himself, now prevailing upon the disciple to leave all and follow him, now working in him that confession which to the world must sound like the ultimate blasphemy, now inviting Peter to the supreme followship of martyrdom for the Lord he had denied, and thereby forgiving him all his sins. In the life of Peter grace and discipleship are inseparable. He had received the grace which costs.[483]

May we hear Jesus' call to us to follow Him, wherever that call may take us, to minister to the many needs of many peoples, so we may be confident on the Last Day that He will count us among those who saw Him naked and clothed him, saw Him hungry and thirsty and fed him and gave him drink, saw Him in prison and visited him, saw Him a stranger and welcomed Him, saw him sick and took care of Him. And let us pray for God's grace that, despite our many faults, we still have the faith, courage and love to take His yoke upon us.

Notes

All bible citations are from Harper Bibles, NRSV Bible, HarperCollins. Kindle Edition.

---

[1] Chandelis Duster, "'You just don't do that, Mr. President': Televangelist Pat Robertson condemns Trump's 'law and order' response to protests," CNN, June 3, 2020.

[2] Victor Hugo's last written words, cited by Marva Bennett in her biography of Hugo, "To Love is to Act."

[3] Carolyn Kormann, "Georgia Postcard: Field Research", *The New Yorker,* June 29, 2020.

[4] Peter Baker, "Trump Tweets and Golfs, but Makes No Mention of Virus's Toll," *The New York Times,* May 24, 2020.

[5] Carolyn Kormann, "Georgia Postcard: Field Research", *The New Yorker,* June 29, 2020.

[6] The above details are from Wikipedia's detailed entry on the death of George Floyd.89

[7] The phrase "when the looting starts, the shooting starts" was used by Walter E. Headley, the police chief of Miami, Florida, who said it in response to an outbreak of violent crime during the 1967 Christmas holiday season, accusing "young hoodlums, from 15 to 21", of taking "advantage of the civil rights campaign" that was then sweeping the United States. Having ordered his troopers to combat the violence with shotguns, he told the press that "we don't mind being accused of police brutality." Headley's phrase and similar language threatening police use of deadly force in the United States was also used by other public officials in 1967-68. Wikipedia entry on the origin of "when the looting starts, the shooting starts."

[8] Tweet from @realDonaldTrump May 29, 2020.

[9] Philip Bump, "Timing: The Clearing of Lafayette Square", June 5th, 2020, *The Washington Post.*

[10] Philip Rucker and Ashley Parker, "Lafayette Square clash, still reverberating, becomes an iconic episode in Donald Trump's presidency", *The Washington Post,* June 13, 2020.

[11] Ibid.

[12] Account of her experience as the police in riot gear overran a peaceful demonstration in Lafayette Square on June 1st, by Rev. Virginia Gerbasi on her Facebook page, as reported by Joe Heim in the *Washington Post,* "Episcopal

priest describes being gassed and overrun by police at Lafayette Square church", June 2, 2020.

[13] Twitter postings of bishop Mariann Budde, @MeBudde, on June 1, 2020.

[14] Sarah Pulliam Bailey and Sarah Pulliam Bailey," Catholic archbishop of Washington slams Trump's visit to John Paul II shrine," *The Washington Post,* June 2, 2020.

[15] Chandelis Duster, "'You just don't do that, Mr. President': Televangelist Pat Robertson condemns Trump's 'law and order' response to protests," CNN, June 3, 2020.

[16] Wikipedia entry on George Floyd protests in Portland, OR.

[17] Hannah Fry, Luke Money, "Orange County public health officer resigns in coronavirus controversy," *Los Angeles Times,* June 9, 2020.

[18] Justin Carrisimo, "Who is Rayshard Brooks, 27-year old Black man killed by Atlanta police?" CBS News, June 16th and June 18th.

[19] Adam Gabbatt, "Trump defends officer who shot Rayshard Brooks as police call in sick," *The Guardian,* June 18, 2020.

[20] Joshua Partlow and Josh Dawsey, "Workers removed thousands of social distancing stickers before Trump's Tulsa rally, according to video and a person familiar with the set-up," *The Washington Post,* June 27, 2020.

[21] Newsbreak, "Why don't all cities with high rates of crime get the same Trump treatment?" msn.com, August 2, 2020.

[22] Meg Wagner, Melissa Macaya, Mike Hayes and Veronica Rocha, "Fauci, Redfield testify on Trump's coronavirus response," edition.cnn.com, June 23, 2020.

[23] Heather Cox Richardson, blog entry in https://heathercoxrichardson.substack.com/, June 23, 2020.

[24] Ibid.

[25] Heather Cox Richardson, "Letters from an American" blog, June 24th, 2020.

[26] Ibid, June 26th, 2020.

[27] World Health Organization dashboard on COVID-19-19 worldwide statistics 6/28/20, https://COVID-1919.who.int/.

[28] J. David Goodman and Patricia Mazzei, Florida Smirked at New York's Virus Crisis. Now It Has Its Own, *The Washington Post,* June 26, 2020.

[29] Karen Attiah, Global Opinions Editor, "I Thought I'd Be Safe Waiting Out the Coronavirus in Texas. I Was Wrong," The *Washington Post*, June 26, 2020.

[30] Patrick Svitek, "Gov. Greg Abbott orders Texas bars to close again and restaurants to reduce to 50% occupancy as coronavirus spreads", *Texas Tribune,* June 26, 2020.

[31] Scott Neuman, "Arizona Issues New Shutdown Order as Coronavirus Cases Spike," NPR.

[32] Charlie Savage, Eric Schmidt and Michael Schwirtz, "Russia Secretly Offered Afghan Militants Bounties to Kill U.S. Troops, Intelligence Says", *The New York Times*, June 26, 2020.

[33] Heather Cox Richardson, "Letters from an American" blog, June 29th, 2020.

[34] Carol E. Lee and Kristen Welker, "Trump's 'White power' retweet sets off 'five-alarm fire in White House", *NBC News,* June 29, 2020.

[35] Heather Cox Richardson, "Letters of an American," June 29, 2020.

[36] James Laporta, "White House Aware of Russian Bounties in 2019", Associated Press, June 30, 2020.

[37] Susan Rice, "Why Does Trump Put Russia First?", *The New York Times,* June 30, 2020.

[38] Philip Rucker and Seung Min Kim, "Republican leaders now say everyone should wear a mask — even as Trump refuses and has mocked some who do," *The Washington Post,* June 30, 2020.

[39] *The Washington Post,* "Coronavirus Updates", July 1, 2020.

[40] https://www.worldometers.info/coronavirus/#countries.

[41] https://www.cnn.com/world/live-news/coronavirus-pandemic-06-30-20-intl/index.html.

[42] Heather Cox Richardson, "Letters from an American" blog, 6/30/2020.

[43] Meg Wagner, Mike Hayes, Veronica Rocha and Melissa Macaya, "Fauci, Redfield testify on COVID-19-19 reopening as cases rise", CNN politics, June 30, 2020.

[44] Heather Cox Richardson, "Letters from an American" blog, 7/1/2020.

[45] Tim Elfrink, "Kansas GOP official apologizes for cartoon comparing mask mandate to the Holocaust," *The Washington Post,* July 6, 2020.

[46] Roni Caryn Rabin and Chris Cameron, "Trump Falsely Claims '99 Percent' of Virus Cases Are 'Totally Harmless'", *The New York Times,* July 5, 2020.

[47] "Health experts push back on Trump's false claim that 99 percent of U.S. infections are 'totally harmless,'" Coronavirus Update, *The New York Times,* July 5, 2020.

[48] Christina Maxouris, Holly Van, Amir Vera, "U.S. is still 'knee-deep' in first wave of pandemic, Dr. Fauci warns," CNN, July 6, 2020.

[49] Emily Rauhala, Karoun Demirjian and Toluse Olorunnipa, "Trump administration sends letter withdrawing U.S. from World Health Organization over coronavirus response," *The Washington Post,* July 7, 2020.

[50] "George Floyd protests in Portland, Oregon," Wikipedia entry.

[51] Lauren Egan, "Trump says coronavirus crisis will probably 'get worse before it gets better,' repeats it will 'disappear', NBCnews.com, July 22, 2020.

52 John Wagner, Brittany Shammas, Lateshia Beachum, Hannah Denham, Adam Taylor, Marisa Iati, Hannah Knowles and Meryl Kornfield, "U.S. coronavirus cases double in just six weeks, to 4 million," *The Washington Post,* July 23, 2020.

53 Coronavirus updates, *The Washington Post,* July 27, 2020.

54 Anneken Tappe, "US economy posts its worst drop on record", CNN.com.

55 Devan Cole, "White House chief of staff: 'We are not going to control the pandemic,'" CNN, October 25, 2020.

56 Jessie Yeung, Adam Renton, Zamira Rahim, Vasco Cotovio, Melissa Macaya and Meg Wagner, "The latest on the coronavirus pandemic,"CNN https://www.cnn.com/world/live-news/coronavirus-pandemic-10-30-20-intl/index.html.

57 Matthew S. Schwartz, "U.S. adds almost 100,000 new coronavirus cases in 1 day as colder weather sets in," NPR, October 31, 2020.

58 Jessie Yeung, Adam Renton, Zamira Rahim, Vasco Cotovio, Melissa Macaya and Meg Wagner, "The latest on the coronavirus pandemic,"CNN https://www.cnn.com/world/live-news/coronavirus-pandemic-10-30-20-intl/index.html.

59 Grace Segers, "McConnell urged White House not to make a deal on stimulus bill ahead of election," October 20, 2020.

60 Nicholas Fandos, "Senate Confirms Barrett, Delivering for Trump and Reshaping the Court," *The New York Times,* October 26, 2020.

61 Abraham Lincoln, "Annual message to Congress, concluding remarks", 1862.

62 Polly Mosendz, "Dylann Roof Confesses: Says He Wanted to Start 'Race War'", *Newsweek, June 19, 2015.*

63 Kristen Gelineau and Jon Gambrell, *Associated Press,*3/15/19, reported by chicagotribune.com.

64 Jonathan Lemire, *Associated Press,* 3/15/19, as reported by chicagotribune.com.

65 Catherine E. Shoichet, Inside the search for the parents of 545 children separated at the border, October 22, 2020, CNN.com.

66 Kris Mamula, Andrew Goldstein, Paula Reed Ward, Liz Navratil And Shelly Bradbury, "Eleven dead, six wounded in massacre at Squirrel Hill synagogue," Pittsburgh Post-Gazette, October 27, 2018.

67 Exodus 22, 18: "Thou shalt not suffer a witch to live." (King James version).

68 Romans 13: 1-2. Harper Bibles. NRSV Bible. Kindle.

69 Romans 13: 3-4. Harper Bibles. NRSV Bible. Kindle.

70 Acts 5: 29. Harper Bibles. NRSV Bible. Kindle.

71 *Los Angeles Times,* by Gatineau Molly Hennessy-Fiske, Houston Bureau Chief, May 24, 2019.

72 Ed Pilkington, "'It is serious and intense:' white supremacist domestic terror threat looms large in US," *The Guardian,* October 19, 2020.

73 Ibid.

74 Pew Research Center, "America's Changing Religious Landscape", May 2015, www.pewforum.org.

75 Ibid.

76 Wikipedia, entry on Martin Luther.

77 Brecht, Martin. *Martin Luther*. tr. James L. Schaaf, Philadelphia: Fortress Press, 1985–93, 1:48, cited by Wikipedia.

78 Wikipedia, entry on Martin Luther.

79 Kittelson, James. *Luther The Reformer*. Minneapolis: Augsburg Fortress Publishing House, 1986, 79, cited by Wikipedia.

80 Hillerbrand, Hans J. "Martin Luther: Indulgences and salvation," *Encyclopedia Britannica*, 2007, cited by Wikipedia.

81 Wikipedia entry on Martin Luther.

82 Brecht, Martin. Martin Luther. tr. James L. Schaaf, Philadelphia: Fortress Press, 1985–93, 1:204–205. Cited by Wikipedia.

83 Ephesians 2: 8-9. Harper Bibles, NRSV Bible.

84 Bouman, Herbert J. A. "The Doctrine of Justification in the Lutheran Confessions", *Concordia Theological Monthly*, 26 November 1955, No. 11:801, cited by Wikipedia.

85 Luther, Martin. "The Smalcald Articles," in *Concordia: The Lutheran Confessions*. Saint Louis: Concordia Publishing House, 2005, 289, Part two, Article 1, cited by Wikipedia.

86 Roland H. Bainton, Here I Stand: A Life of Martin Luther, New York: Mentor, 1955, OCLC 220064892, 81, cited by Wikipedia.

87 Richard Marius, *Luther*, London: Quartet, 1975, ISBN 0-7043-3192-6, 87–89; Bainton, Roland. *Here I Stand: A Life of Martin Luther*. New York: Penguin, 1995, 82, cited by Wikipedia.

88 Marius, 93; Bainton, Mentor edition, 90.

89 G. R. Elton, Reformation Europe: 1517–1559, London: Collins, 1963, OCLC 222872115, 177.

90 Brecht, Martin. (tr. Wolfgang Katenz) "Luther, Martin," in Hillerbrand, Hans J. (ed.) *Oxford Encyclopedia of the Reformation*. New York: Oxford University Press, 1996, 2:463, cited by Wikipedia.

91 Brecht, 1:460.

92 Bratcher, Dennis. "The Diet of Worms (1521)," in The Voice: Biblical and Theological Resources for Growing Christians.

[93] Reformation Europe: 1517–1559, London: Fontana, 1963, 53; Diarmaid MacCulloch, Reformation: Europe's House Divided, 1490–1700, London: Allen Lane, 2003, 132.

[94] Lohse, Bernhard, Martin Luther: An Introduction to his Life and Work, translated by Robert C. Schultz, Edinburgh: T & T Clark, 1987, ISBN 0-567-09357-3,112–17; Wilson, 183; Bainton, Mentor edition, 258.

[95] Daniel Weissbort and Astradur Eysteinsson (eds.), Translation—Theory and Practice: A Historical Reader, Oxford: Oxford University Press, 2002, ISBN 0-19-871200-6, 68.

[96] Marius, 163–64.

[97] Schaff, Philip. "Luther's Marriage. 1525.", History of the Christian Church, Volume VII, Modern Christianity, The German Reformation. § 77, rpt. Christian Classics Ethereal Library. Mullett, 180–81.

[98] Brecht, 2:273; Bainton, Mentor edition, 263

[99] Marty, Martin. Martin Luther. Viking Penguin, 2004, 123; Wilson, 278.

[100] Mullett, 186. Quoted from Luther's preface to the Small Catechism, 1529; MacCulloch, 165.

[101] Harper Bibles. NRSV Bible, I John 1:8-10. Kindle.

[102] Wikipedia, entry on Martin Luther.

[103] Jaroslav J. Pelikan, Hilton C. Oswald, Luther's Works, 55 vols. (St. Louis and Philadelphia: Concordia Pub. House and Fortress Press, 1955–1986), 46: 50–51.

[104] Erlangen Edition (Erlangener Ausgabe: "EA"), comprising the Exegetica opera latina – Latin exegetical works of Luther, v. 59, p. 284.

[105] Luther, On the Jews and Their Lies, Luthers Werke. 47:268–271.

[106] "Declaration of the ELCA to the Jewish Community", 1994.

[107] Luke 18: 18-1918 Harper Bibles. NRSV Bible (Kindle Locations 51248-51249).

[108] Letters and Other Writings of James Madison, v. III, 1816-1828, 242, J.P. Lippencott, 1865., cited by Wikipedia.

[109] Locke, John, On the Difference between Civil and Ecclesiastical Power, in The Life and Letters of John Locke, Lord King, Henry G. Bohn, London, 1858, p. 300, cited by Wikipedia.

[110] "Martin Luther and the Long March to Freedom of Conscience", National Geographic, October, 2017. https://news.nationalgeographic.com/2017/10/martin-luther-freedom-protestant-reformation-500/

[111] During the 2004 presidential election season, the faith organization Sojourners put out a bumper sticker with these words: "God Is Not a Republican, or a Democrat," https://sojo.net/articles/god-still-not-republican-or-democrat.

[112] Winters, Michael Sean, "How the Ghost of Jerry Falwell Conquered the Republican Party", *The New Republic,* March 2012.

[113] Wikipedia, entry on "Treaty of Tripoli".

[114] Wikipedia entry on Roger Williams.

[115] Barry, John M. (January 2012). "God, Government and Roger Williams' Big Idea". *Smithsonian*, cited by Wikipedia.

[116] Lemons, Stanley. "Roger Williams Champion of Religious Liberty". Providence, RI City Archives, cited by Wikipedia.

[117] https://billofrightsinstitute.org/founding-documents/primary-source-documents/danburybaptists/.

[118] http://tjrs.monticello.org/letter/199, letter by Thomas Jefferson to the Baptists of Danbury, 1/2/1802.

[119] Burr, George Lincoln, ed. (1914) *Narratives of the Witchcraft Cases, 1648-1706.* C. Scribner's Sons, p. 197, cited by Wikipedia's entry on Salem witch trials.

[120] University of Virginia archives, virginia.edu, Salem Witch Trials 004 0001 and 033 0001.

[121] Ephesians 2:8-9, Harper Bibles. NRSV Bible. Kindle.

[122] Ephesians 2:10, Harper Bibles. NRSV Bible. Kindle.

[123] Harper Bibles. NRSV Bible, Romans 3: 22-25. Kindle.

[124] Luke 3:8, Harper Bibles. NRSV Bible. Kindle.

[125] Matthew 5:4-16, Harper Bibles. NRSV Bible. Kindle.

[126] Matthew 21:28-31.

[127] Mark 10: 42-45, Harper Bibles. NRSV Bible. Kindle.

[128] Philippians 2:3-9, Harper Bibles. NRSV Bible. Kindle.

[129] Matthew 6:2, NRSV Bible (Kindle Location 47948). Kindle.

[130] Mark Twain, *Letter to the Earth,* "Office of the Recording Angel", in *Letters from the Earth: Uncensored Writings by Mark Twain,* Harper & Row, 1962, edited by Bernard DeVoto, p.117-119.

[131] Brecht, Martin. (tr. Wolfgang Katenz) "Luther, Martin," in Hillerbrand, Hans J. (ed.) *Oxford Encyclopedia of the Reformation*. New York: Oxford University Press, 1996, 2:7–9, cited by Wikipedia's article on Martin Luther.

[132] Martin Luther, "Let Your Sins Be Strong," a Letter From Luther to Melanchthon, August 1521, Project Wittenberg, cited by Wikipedia's article on Martin Luther.

[133] Luke 7:39-50, Harper Bibles. NRSV Bible. Kindle.

[134] Matthew 5:17-20, Harper Bibles. NRSV Bible. Kindle.

[135] Matthew 5:21-23, 27-28, 31-32, Harper Bibles. NRSV Bible (Kindle Locations 47911-47929). Kindle.

[136] Matthew 18: 21-22, Harper Bibles. NRSV Bible. Kindle.

[137] Matthew 18: 31-35, Harper Bibles. NRSV Bible. Kindle.

[138] Mark 2:24, Harper Bibles. NRSV Bible. Kindle.

[139] Mark 2: 27-28, Harper Bibles. NRSV Bible. Kindle.

[140] Mark 3: 1-6, Harper Bibles. NRSV Bible. Kindle.

[141] Psalm 51, 10-12, Harper Bibles. NRSV Bible. Kindle.

[142] James, 1:27 Harper Bibles. NRSV Bible. Kindle.

[143] John 10: 1-10, Harper Bibles. NRSV Bible. Kindle.

[144] Mark Twain, *The Innocents Abroad.*

[145] Luke 20:25, Harper Bibles. NRSV Bible. Kindle.

[146] John 18:36, Harper Bibles. NRSV Bible. Kindle.

[147] Isaiah 53:3. Harper Bibles. NRSV Bible, Kindle.

[148] From the film production of *Cold Comfort Farm* by Stella Gibbons, produced by Universal Pictures, 1995, cited by www.quotes.net.

[149] Luther's small catechism, preface, 1-3, cited by Timothy Wengert in *Martin Luther' Catechisms, Forming the Faith,* Fortress Press, 2009, p. 14.

[150] Luther, Martin. *Luther's Works*. Philadelphia: Fortress Press, 1971, 50:172–73; Bainton, Mentor edition, 263, cited in the Wikipedia entry on Martin Luther.

[151] "Acting in God's Love by Francine Knowles, in *Living Lutheran,* November 6, 2018.

[152] Gary Simpson, "How Luther helps today's citizens", in *Living Lutheran,* 10/16.

[153] Ibid.

[154] Ibid.

[155] Laurie Goodstein, "Falwell: blame abortionists, feminists and gays," *The New York Times,* 9/19 2001.

[156] Joe Heim, "Jerry Falwell Jr. can't imagine Trump 'doing anything that's not good for the country', 1/1 2019, *The Washington Post.*

[157] Harper Bibles, NRSV Bible, Luke 4: 16-19. Kindle.

[158] Matthew 22:21, Harper Bibles. NRSV Bible. Kindle.

[159] Joe Heim, interview with Jerry Falwell, Jr., 1/1 2019, *The Washington Post.*

[160] Wikipedia on the quotations of Edmund Burke, noting that it cannot be documented that he ever made this famous quote.

[161] "Martin Luther King Honorary Degree Ceremony", Newcastle University, as referenced by Wikipedia's entry on Dr. Martin Luther King, Jr.

[162] The Martin Luther King, Jr. Research and Education Institute, "Poor People's Campaign," Stanford University.

[163] Ibid.

[164] Rev. William Barber II, "America's moral malady," *The Atlantic,* https://www.theatlantic.com/magazine/archive/2018/02/a-new-poor-peoples-campaign/552503/.

[165] Ibid.

[166] https://www.poorpeoplescampaign.org/about/.

[167] Ephesians 2:10, Harper Bibles. NRSV Bible (Kindle Location 56383). Kindle.

[168] Derek Hawkins, Felicia Sonmez, Laura Meckler and Marisa Iati, "Florida shatters single-day infection record with 15,300 new cases", *The Washington Post,* July 12, 2020.

[169] Steve Almasy, Jay Croft, Faith Karimi and Amanda Watts, "Fauci implores state and local leaders to be as forceful as possible with mask orders," CNN, July 17, 2020.

[170] Derek Hawkins, Felicia Sonmez and Laura Meckler, "Coronavirus update: Florida shatters single-day infection record with 15,300 new cases," *The Washington Post,* July 12, 2020.

[171] Heather Cox Richardson, "Letters from an American," October 13, 2020.

[172] Ibid.

[173] Anneken Tappe, "US economy posts its worst drop on record", CNN.com.

[174] Harper Bibles. NRSV Bible, Matthew 28:20. Kindle.

[175] Harper Bibles. NRSV Bible, Psalm 46, 1-3. Kindle.

[176] Reinhold Niebuhr's Serenity Prayer, cited by Wikipedia.

[177] Robert Earl Keene, lyrics from "The Road Goes on Forever."

[178] Morris Fiorina of Stanford University, quoted by Dana Milbank in "The Great American Crackup is underway," *The Washington Post,* June 19, 2020.

[179] Luther's Small Catechism, Digireads.com. Kindle.

[180] Laura Vozzella, "Angst in Appalachia", *The Washington Post,* September 6, 2020.

[181] Kate Manne, "In Trump's world, real men never wear masks," *The Washington Post,* October 12, 2020.

[182] Ibid.

[183] Ibid.

[184] Ibid.

[185] Lori Wagoner, as told to Eli Saslow, 'No mask, no entry. Is that clear enough? That seems pretty clear, right?', *Voices from the Pandemic, The Washington Post,* July 19, 2020.

[186] Eric Todisco, "Woman Who Refused to Wear Mask at Starbucks Wants Half of the $100K Raised for Barista She Shamed Online," people.com, July 16, 2020.

[187] Laura Vozzella, "Angst in Appalachia", *The Washington Post,* September 6, 2020.

[188] Patty Wright, "Sanford School Run by Church With COVID-19-19 Outbreak Will Open Next Week Amid Community Concern", Mainepublic.org, September 3, 2020.

[189] Ibid.

[190] Chief Rabbi Jonathan Sacks, *Morality: Restoring the Common Good in Divided Times,* quoted by Jane Eisner in her review, *The Washington Post,* November 29, 2020.

[191] Harper Bibles. NRSV Bible, Galatians 5:13-14, Kindle.

[192] Ibid.

[193] Veronica Stracqualursi and Karl de Vries, "Herman Cain dies from coronavirus," CNN, July 30th, 2020.

[194] Rebecca Shabad, 'Reckless and selfish': Nevada Gov. Sisolak slams Trump for holding big indoor rally, violating state rules, NBC News, September 14, 2020.

[195] Martin Luther, Luther's Works, Vol. 43: Devotional Writings II, ed. Jaroslav Jan Pelikan, Hilton C. Oswald, and Helmut T. Lehmann, vol. 43 (Philadelphia: Fortress Press, 1999), 119–38. Cited by Lutheran Witness blog, https://blogs.lcms.org/wp-content/uploads/2020/03/Plague-blogLW.pdf.

[196] Ibid.

[197] Avivah Wittenberg-Cox, "What Do Countries with The Best Coronavirus Responses Have in Common? Women Leaders," *Forbes,* April 13, 2020.

[198] Ibid.

[199] Our World in Data, Daily and total confirmed COVID-19-19 deaths per million, August 5, 2020, ourworldindata.com.

[200] Derek Hawkins and Marisa Iati, "No way to spin that,' a critical Romney says of deaths under administration," *The Washington Post,* August 16, 2020.

[201] "The curve bends the wrong way", editorial, *The Washington Post*, July 12, 2020.

[202] ABC News, as cited by "The curve bends the wrong way", editorial, *The Washington Post*, July 12, 2020.

[203] World Health Organization coronavirus dashboard, Data last updated: 2020/7/12, 4:49pm CEST, https://COVID-1919.who.int/.

[204] Poynter, "'We have it totally under control.' A timeline of President Donald Trump's response to the coronavirus pandemic," https://www.poynter.org/fact-checking/2020/.

[205] Matilda Coleman, "Trump, coronavirus and the politics of a pandemic," upnewswire.com, March 14, 2020.

[206] Ibid.

[207] Ibid.

[208] NBC News, "Trump says coronavirus crisis will probably 'get worse before it gets better,' repeats it will 'disappear'," July 22, 2020.

[209] Jamie Gangel, Jeremy Herb and Elizabeth Stuart, 'Play it down': Trump admits to concealing the true threat of coronavirus in new Woodward book,' CNN, September 9, 2020.

[210] Doyle MacManus, "Trump's strange coronavirus show", *Los Angeles Times,* March 22, 2020.

[211] Gov. Larry Hogan, "Fighting alone," editorial, *The Washington Post,* July 19, 2020.

[212] "The curve bends the wrong way", editorial, *The Washington Post*, July 12, 2020.

[213] CDC, COVID-19-19 mortality rate, July 12, 2020; https://www.cdc.gov/coronavirus/2019-ncov/COVID-19-data/COVID-19view/ index.html.

[214] Advisory Board, https://www.advisory.com/daily-briefing/2020/06/02/COVID-19-health-effects.

[215] Coronavirus Updates, *The Washington Post,* July 24, 2020.

[216] CNN morning news, August 18, 2020.

[217] Derek Hawkins, Felicia Sonmez and Laura Meckler, "Coronavirus update: Florida shatters single-day infection record with 15,300 new cases," *The Washington Post,* July 12, 2020.

[218] "U.S. reports a record 500,000-plus new coronavirus cases in a week," *The New York Times,* October 27, 2020.

[219] "New Coronavirus Cases Stay Elevated," *The Wall Street Journal,* October 27, 2020.

[220] Luke Mogelson, "Nothing to lose but your masks", *The New Yorker,* August 24, 2020.

[221] Melissa Quinn, "Feds bust alleged plot to kidnap Michigan Governor Gretchen Whitmer", CBS News online, October 9, 2020.

[222] Ibid.

[223] Kimberlee Kruesi, Associated Press, as reported in *The Washington Post,* July 4, 2020.

[224] Tom Frieden, Jeffrey Koplan, David Satcher, Richard Besser, "We ran the CDC. No president ever politicized its science the way Trump has," *The Washington Post,* July 14, 2020.

[225] As reported by CNN, By Veronica Stracqualursi and Paul LeBlanc, "Georgia governor sues Atlanta mayor over city's mask mandate, July 16, 2020.

[226] Reese Oxner, "Texas bar owners file $10 million federal lawsuit against Gov. Greg Abbott, the second suit over the shutdown in two days," Texastribune.org, June 30, 2020.

[227] Ibid.

[228] President Trump on Twitter, March 22, 2020.

[229] Alan Judd, "For health care 'heroes,' death toll keeps rising," *Atlanta Journal-Constitution*, August 14, 2020

[230] Abha Bhattari, "Once heroic, they now feel debased," *The Washington Post,* August 16, 2020.

[231] Ibid.

[232] Lateshia Beachum, John Wagner, Brittany Shammas, Miriam Berger, Taylor Telford, Reis Thebault, Michael Brice-Saddler, Felicia Sonmez and Colby Itkowitz, "Trump shifts tone on coronavirus, says it will probably 'get worse before it gets better', *The Washington Post,* July 21, 2020.

[233] Reese Oxner, "Texas bar owners file $10 million federal lawsuit against Gov. Greg Abbott, the second suit over the shutdown in two days," Texastribune.org, June 30, 2020.

[234] Hendrik Hertzberg, "Biggus Buckus", *The New Yorker,* November 2, 2009.

[235] The Lutheran Hymnal, Hymn #283, Text: Ps. 16:6. Author: Nikolai F. S. Grundtvig, 1817, Translated by: Ole G. Belsheim, 1909, Titled: "Guds Ord det er vort Arvegods" Composer: Fritz Reuter, 1916, Tune: "Reuter".

[236] *Arblaster, Paul; Juhász, Gergely; Latré, Guido, eds. (2002), Tyndale's Testament,* Brepols, ISBN 2-503-51411-1, in Wikipedia's entry on German Bible translations.

[237] Derek Wilson (2007). *Out of the Storm: The Life and Legacy of Martin Luther,* p.183. London: Hutchinson. ISBN 9780091800017, cited in Wikipedia's entry on Martin Luther.

[238] Richard Marius, *Luther,* London: Quartet, 1975, ISBN 0-7043-3192-6,162, cited in Wikipedia's entry on Martin Luther.

[239] https://www.huffingtonpost.com/bernard-starr/why-christians-were-denied-access-to-their-bible-for-1000-years_b_3303545.html.

[240] Ibid.

[241] 1 John 4:8, Harper Bibles. NRSV Bible. Kindle.

[242] Matthew 28:21, Harper Bibles. NRSV Bible. Kindle.

[243] John 3:17, Harper Bibles. NRSV Bible (Kindle Location 51943). Kindle.

[244] Oberman, Heiko, *Luther: Man Between God and the Devil*, New Haven: Yale University Press, 2006, ISBN 0-300-10313-1, 238, cited by Wikipedia's entry on Martin Luther.

[245] Brecht, Martin. *Martin Luther*. tr. James L. Schaaf, Philadelphia: Fortress Press, 1985–93, 2:329, cited by Wikipedia.

[246] From the Formula of Concord, 1577, cited by Wikipedia's entry on sacramental union.

247 Ronald D. Witherup, S.S., "The Use and Abuse of the Bible," American catholic.org, archived by Catholic Association of Religious and Family Life Educators of Ontario, https://carfleo.com/2017/07/06/summer-reading-2/.
248 Ibid.
249 Ibid.
250 Ibid.
251 Ibid.
252 Ibid.
253 Romans 9:13, Harper Bibles. NRSV Bible. Kindle.
254 Leviticus 19:22 Harper Bibles. NRSV Bible. Kindle.
255 Harper Bibles. NRSV Bible, Leviticus 11: 20-21. Kindle.
256 Harper Bibles. NRSV Bible, Leviticus 19:18. Kindle.
257 Romans 13: 1-2. Harper Bibles. NRSV Bible, Kindle.
258 CNN, "When Romans 13 was used to justify evil", https://www.cnn.com/2018/06/22/opinions/jeff-sessions-bible-verse-nazi-germany-opinion-weber/index.html, by Thomas Weber, 6/22/18.
259 Acts 5: 29. Harper Bibles. NRSV Bible. Kindle.
260 Harper Bibles, NRSV Bible, Matthew 5:46-48. Kindle.
261 Harper NRSV Bible, Luke 10:25-37. Kindle.
262 Harper Bibles. NRSV Bible, John 5:48. Kindle.
263 Harper Bibles. NRSV Bible, Revelation 22:18-19, Kindle.
264 Harper Bibles. NRSV Bible, Matthew 5:19. Kindle.
265 Harper Bibles. NRSV Bible, Matthew 13:4-9, 18-23. Kindle.
266 Harper Bibles, NRSV Bible, James 2:19. Kindle.
267 Geoffrey Layman, "Where is Trump's evangelical base? Not in church," *Washingtonpost.com,* March 29, 2016.
268 Harper Bibles, NRSV Bible, Revelation 3: 14-19. Kindle.
269 Wikipedia, entry on "Seven Social Sins".
270 Bonhoeffer Dietrich, *The Cost of Discipleship*, page 43. Kindle.
271 Ibid, pages 43-45.
272 Harper Bibles, NRSV Bible, Luke 3: 4-6. Kindle.
273 Harper Bibles, NRSV Bible, Luke 3:3. Kindle.
274 Harper Bibles, NRSV Bible, Luke 3:7-14. Kindle.
275 Harper Bibles, NRSV Bible, Ephesians 2:8-10. Kindle.
276 Mark 8: 31–38, cited by Dietrich Bonhoeffer, *The Cost of Discipleship* (p. 86). Touchstone. Kindle.
277 Bonhoeffer, Dietrich. *The Cost of Discipleship* (p. 87-88). Touchstone. Kindle.
278 Harper Bibles, NRSV Bible, Isaiah 53:3. Kindle.
279 Harper Bibles, NRSV Bible, Luke 9:57-62. Kindle.

[280] Bonhoeffer, Dietrich. *The Cost of Discipleship* (pp. 88-90). Touchstone. Kindle.

[281] Ibid, pp. 90-91.

[282] Ibid, p. 91.

[283] Harper Bibles, NRSV Bible, Psalm 111:10. Kindle.

[284] Harper Bibles, NRSV Bible, Matthew 7:21. Kindle.

[285] Harper Bibles, NRSV Bible, 2nd Corinthians, 5:10. Kindle.

[286] Harper Bibles, NRSV Bible, Luke 12:48. Kindle.

[287] Harper Bibles, NRSV Bible, Matthew 25:31-46. Kindle.

[288] Harper Bibles, NRSV Bible, Matthew 7:22-23. Kindle.

[289] Harper Bibles, NRSV Bible, James 2:14-24, 26. Kindle.

[290] Martin Luther King, Jr., from "I have a dream" speech at the Lincoln Memorial, August 28, 1963.

[291] Slogan of the British-American abolitionist movement in the late 18th century, next to an image of a chained Black man kneeling, http://www.bbc.co.uk/history/british/abolition/.

[292] Rosa Brooks, "Bob Woodward's revelations are hardly shocking anymore," *The Washington Post,* Outlook, September 13, 2020.

[293] Andrew Solender, "Trump Launches 'Patriotic Education' Commission, Calls 1619 Project 'Ideological Poison', *Forbes,* September 17, 2020.

[294] Historicjamestown.org.

[295] Wikipedia, History of slavery in Virginia.

[296] Ibid.

[297] Ibid.

[298] Ibid.

[299] Wikipedia, *Loving v. Virginia.*

[300] Peter Carlson, "Strom Thurmond meets his daughter," History.net.

[301] Ibid.

[302] Mary C. Curtis, contributor, She the People, *The Washington Post,* February 5th, 2013.

[303] Equal Justice Institute, Lynching Report, p. 4.

[304] Ibid, p. 5.

[305] Congressional Record Volume 153, Number 175 (Tuesday, November 13, 2007)] [House] [Pages H13836-H13839] From the Congressional Record Online through the Government Publishing Office.

[306] Randy Newman, *Rednecks,* from "Good Old Boys", 1974.

[307] Equal Justice Institute, Lynching Report, p. 4.

[308] Wikipedia entry on *Birth of a Nation.*

[309] Wikipedia entry on "Tulsa Race Massacre/Riots."

[310] Ibid.

[311] Ibid.

[312] Ibid.

[313] Ibid.

[314] Ibid.

[315] Ibid.

[316] Ibid.

[317] Ibid.

[318] Ibid.

[319] Sulzberger, A. G. (June 19, 2011). "As Survivors Dwindle, Tulsa Confronts Past". *The New York Times*. Archived from the original on June 22, 2011, cited by the Wikipedia entry on "Tulsa Race Massacre/Riots."

[320] Wikipedia entry on "Tulsa Race Massacre/Riots."

[321] Ibid.

[322] "Trump dismisses controversy over Tulsa rally, says it will be a 'celebration' of his campaign", *USA Today,* June 12, 2020.

[323] Gina Barton, "'That's the shooter': Witnesses describe the night Kyle Rittenhouse opened fire in Kenosha," Milwaukee Journal Sentinel, cited by USA Today, August 31, 2020.

[324] Associated Press Wire Content, June 15, 2020.

[325] Clyde W. Ford, "Opinion: The immigration crisis and the racism driving it have roots in Hitler's 'bible'", *The Los Angeles Times,* January 7, 2020.

[326] Ibid.

[327] "The Faithful Church Abolished Slavery," 8/12/17, on www.thefaithfulchurch.com.

[328] Sarah McCannon, "In Charlottesville, Religious Leaders Try to Comfort Residents," NPR, August 13, 2017.

[329] Harper Bibles. NRSV Bible, Colossians 3:15. Kindle.

[330] Harper Bibles. NRSV Bible, Galatians 3, 27-29. Kindle.

[331] Alexander Hamilton. *The Federalist Papers* (p. 350). Chios Classics. Kindle.

[332] Wikipedia, entry on Commonwealth.

[333] Harper Bibles. NRSV Bible, I Corinthians 12, 4-7. Kindle.

[334] Alexander Hamilton. *The Federalist Papers* (p. 179). Chios Classics. Kindle.

[335] Harper Bibles. NRSV Bible, Zechariah 7, 10. Kindle.

[336] Harper Bibles. NRSV Bible, Jeremiah 22:3. Kindle.

[337] Harper Bibles. NRSV Bible, Exodus 22, 21-27. Kindle.

[338] Harper Bibles. NRSV Bible, Deuteronomy 10, 17-19. Kindle.

[339] Harper Bibles. NRSV Bible Deuteronomy 27, 19. Kindle.

[340] Harper Bibles. NRSV Bible Job 22, 5-9. Kindle.

[341] Harper Bibles. NRSV Bible Exodus 22: 22-24. Kindle.

[342] Pam Fessler, "U.S. Census Bureau Reports Poverty Rate Down, But Millions Still Poor", NPR, September 10, 2019.

[343] Ibid.

[344] The U.S. Bureau of Economic Analysis.

[345] Center on Budget and Policy Priorities, Chart Book: Tracking the Post-Great Recession Economy, updated September 4, 2020.

[346] Ibid.

[347] Sophie Lewis, "Coronavirus model projects U.S. deaths will surpass 400,000 by end of year," CBS News, September 5, 2020.

[348] Harper Bibles. NRSV Bible, Luke 20:25. Kindle.

[349] Harper Bibles. NRSV Bible, James 1:27. Kindle.

[350] Harper Bibles. NRSV Bible, Luke 10:7. Kindle.

[351] Harper Bibles. NRSV Bible, Psalm 24:1-2. Kindle.

[352] Andrew Rafferty and Ali Vitali, "Trump: It's 'Disgraceful' for Pope to Question My Christianity," NBC News, Feb. 18, 2016.

[353] Harper Bibles. NRSV Bible, Matthew 7:15-20. Kindle.

[354] Harper Bibles. NRSV Bible, Galatians 5:16-23. Kindle.

[355] Wikipedia entry on Internet Research Agency.

[356] U.S. Department of Justice, Report on The Investigation into Russian Interference in the 2016 Presidential Election.

[357] Julian Barnes, "Russia Continues Interfering in Election to Try to Help Trump, U.S. Intelligence Says," nytimes.com, August 7, 2020.

[358] This actually happened in 2016 accusing Hillary Clinton and John Podesta, her campaign manager; the Internet troll haven 4Chan circulated this fake story; significantly, it was picked up and pushed by then-candidate Trump and alt-right media supporters like Alex Jones, in the weeks before the election. The rumor got such wide circulation that employees of the Comet Ping Pong pizzeria in Washington, D.C. feared for their safety, and in fact, a gunman, after bursting in with an assault rifle, fired at least one shot in the restaurant to demand an end to "child suffering". Nobody was hurt, and the gunman later apologized sincerely in a written statement.

[359] League of Women Voters, "How to Judge a Candidate," https://www.lwv.org/blog/how-judge-candidate.

[360] Dan Mangan, "President Trump told Lesley Stahl he bashes press 'to demean you and discredit you so … no one will believe' negative stories about him," CNBC, MAY 22, 2018.

[361] Harper Bibles, NRSV Bible, 1 Timothy 6:9-10. Kindle.

[362] Harper Bibles. NRSV Bible, Luke 1:42. Kindle.

363 Harper Bibles. NRSV Bible, Luke 1: 46-55. Kindle.

364 Harper Bibles. NRSV Bible, Luke 4: 18-21. Kindle.

365 Harper Bibles. NRSV Bible, James 2:5-7. Kindle.

366 Harper Bibles. NRSV Bible, Mark 9:17-25. Kindle.

367 Harper Bibles. NRSV Bible, John 18:36. Kindle.

368 "Being Rich Damages Your Soul", Charles Mathewes and Evan Sandsmark, *The Washington Post,* 7/30/17.

369 Harper Bibles, NRSV Bible, Matthew 4:8-10. Kindle.

370 Harper Bibles. NRSV Bible, Matthew 6:24. Kindle.

371 Bob Dylan, "Gotta Serve Somebody", on "Slow Train Coming", Columbia Records, 1979.

372 Harper Bibles, NRSV Bible, Exodus 20:17. Kindle.

373 Harper Bibles, NRSV Bible, Matthew 6:31-33. Kindle.

374 Harper Bibles, NRSV Bible, Genesis 3:4-6. Kindle.

375 Harper Bibles, NRSV Bible, I Corinthians 10: 23-24. Kindle.

376 Holly Shakya and Nicholas Christakis, A New, More Rigorous Study Confirms: The More You Use Facebook, the Worse You Feel, *Harvard Business Review,* April 10, 2017.

377 Wikipedia's entry on the "Pittsburgh Synagogue Shooting."

378 Levenson, Eric; Sanchez, Ray (October 27, 2018). "Mass shooting at Pittsburgh synagogue". CNN, cited in reference by Wikipedia.

379 David K. Li, "Hate Crimes in America Spiked 17% Last Year, Says FBI," NBC News, 11/13/18.

380 Jane Costen, "FBI director: White nationalist violence is a "persistent, pervasive threat," *Vox,* April 4, 2019.

381 Wikipedia entry on "Prosperity Theology"

382 Ibid.

383 Ibid.

384 Harper Bibles, NRSV Bible, Matthew 6:24. Kindle.

385 Harper Bibles, NRSV Bible, Mark 10: 28-30. Kindle.

386 Janis Joplin / Bob Neuwirth / Michael McClure, Mercedes Benz lyrics © Strong Arm Music, WIXEN MUSIC PUBLISHING OBO STRONG ARM MUSIC.

387 Andrew Carnegie, "The Gospel of Wealth, published in *North American Review,* 1889, cited in Wikipedia's "Gospel of Wealth" entry.

388 Harper Bibles. NRSV Bible, Luke 16: 19-31. Kindle.

389 Steven Bertoni, "Exclusive: the billionaire who wanted to die broke, is finally broke," *Forbes,* September 15, 2020.

390 Ibid.

391 Harper Bibles, NRSV Bible, Luke 18: 9-21. Kindle.

392 Harper Bibles, NRSV Bible, Matthew 6:4. Kindle.

393 Harper Bibles. NRSV Bible, 1 John 4, 18-21. Kindle.

394 Stephanie Ranade Krider, "I'm a pro-life evangelical. Our movement sold its soul for Trump," *The Washington Post,* October 12, 2020.

395 Ibid.

396 Emily Crockett, Donald Trump: "There has to be some form of punishment" for women who have abortions," Vox, March 30, 2016.

397 Stephanie Ranade Krider, "I'm a pro-life evangelical. Our movement sold its soul for Trump," *The Washington Post,* October 12, 2020.

398 Ibid.

399 Harper Bibles, NRSV Bible. John 8: 3-11. Kindle.

400 Harper Bibles, NRSV Bible. Matthew 15: 7-9. Kindle.

401 Harper Bibles. NRSV Bible. Luke 17:10. Kindle.

402 Randy Newman, "A Few Words in Defense of Our Country," Nonesuch Records, 2008.

403 Harper Bibles. NRSV Bible, Genesis 3: 7-10. Kindle.

404 Harper Bibles. NRSV Bible, Matthew 1: 20-22. Kindle.

405 Harper Bibles. NRSV Bible, Matthew 10: 31. Kindle.

406 Harper Bibles. NRSV Bible, Matthew 14: 27. Kindle.

407 Harper Bibles. NRSV Bible, Matthew 28: 5-6. Kindle.

408 Harper Bibles. NRSV Bible, Matthew 28: 10. Kindle.

409 Harper Bibles. NRSV Bible, Job 1:5-7. Kindle.

410 Harper Bibles. NRSV Bible, Job 1:20-22. Kindle.

411 Harper Bibles. NRSV Bible, Job 2:9-10. Kindle.

412 Harper Bibles. NRSV Bible, Matthew 10:28. Kindle.

413 Harper Bibles. NRSV Bible, Luke 8, 49-50. Kindle.

414 Harper Bibles. NRSV Bible, I Peter 3:14-15. Kindle.

415 Harper Bibles. NRSV Bible, I John 4: 16-19. Kindle.

416 Harper Bibles. NRSV Bible, Matthew 25: 14-30. Kindle.

417 Harper Bibles. NRSV Bible, Romans 8:36, 38-39. Kindle.

418 Harper Bibles. NRSV Bible, Galatians 5:14, St. Paul quoting Leviticus 19:18.

419 Everytown for Gun Safety, https://everytownresearch.org/gun-violence-america/ and https://lawcenter.giffords.org/facts/statistics/ citing statistics from the Center for Disease Control and Prevention.

420 Everytown for Gun Safety, https://everytownresearch.org/gun-violence-america/.

421 Giffords Center to Prevent Gun Violence, https://lawcenter.giffords.org/facts/statistics/.

422 Marc Fisher, "With Election Day looming, an anxious nation hears rumblings

of violence," *The Washington Post,* October 31, 2020.

[423] Children's Hospital of Philadelphia Research Institute Center for Injury Research and Prevention, https://injury.research.chop.edu/violence-prevention-initiative/types-violence-involving-youth/gun-violence/gun-violence-facts-and#.XLp6-ehKiyJ.

[424] Garen J. Wintemute, *Guns, Fear, the Constitution, and the Public's Health,* 358 New England J. Med. 1421-1424 (Apr. 2008), cited by the Giffords Law Center to Prevent Gun Violence.

[425] Harper Bibles. NRSV Bible, Matthew 26:52. Kindle.

[426] NBC News, 10/2/17, https://www.nbcnews.com/storyline/las-vegas-shooting/las-vegas-police-investigating-shooting-mandalay-bay-n806461.

[427] Wikipedia's entry on the Las Vegas shooting, https://en.wikipedia.org/wiki/2017 _Las_Vegas_shooting#Weaponry.

[428] Wikipedia's entry on Parkland, Florida, https://en.wikipedia.org/wiki/Parkland, Florida.

[429] Ted Nugent, speaking on *The Joe Pags Show*, March 30, 2018.

[430] Harper Bibles. NRSV Bible, Matthew 6:24. Kindle.

[431] Harper Bibles, NRSV Bible, Genesis 6:13. Kindle.

[432] Harper Bibles. NRSV Bible, Proverbs 11:30. Kindle.

[433] Harper Bibles. NRSV Bible, Psalm 11:5. Kindle.

[434] Harper Bibles. NRSV Bible, Proverbs 4: 13, 17-18. Kindle.

[435] Harper Bibles. NRSV Bible, Colossians 3: 9-11. Kindle.

[436] Harper Bibles. NRSV Bible, James 2: 1-4, 8-9. Kindle.

[437] Harper Bibles. NRSV Bible, Matthew 12:30. Kindle.

[438] Michelle Boorstein, "Alabama state official defends Roy Moore, citing Joseph and Mary: 'They became parents of Jesus', *The Washington Post,* 11/12/17.

[439] Harper Bibles. NRSV Bible, Luke 10: 38-42. Kindle.

[440] Harper Bibles. NRSV Bible, Luke 7: 36-47. Kindle.

[441] Harper Bibles. NRSV Bible Mark 14: 3-9. Kindle.

[442] Harper Bibles. NRSV Bible, John 19: 25-26. Kindle.

[443] Harper Bibles. NRSV Bible, Matthew 27: 55-56, 61. Kindle.

[444] Harper Bibles. NRSV Bible, John 20: 1-18. Kindle.

[445] Harper Bibles. NRSV Bible, Galatians 3:25-28. Kindle.

[446] Harper Bibles. NRSV Bible, John 1: 12-13. Kindle.

[447] Harper Bibles. NRSV Bible, John 3: 16. Kindle.

[448] Laurie Goodstein, *The New York Times,* Wed. 19 Sep 2001.

[449] Harper Bibles. NRSV Bible, John 15:12. Kindle.

[450] Harper Bibles. NRSV Bible, Matthew 18:6-7. Kindle.

[451] Hannah Adair Bonner, "We queer clergy begged our fellow Methodists to

love us. They voted no," *The Washington Post,* March 1, 2019.

[452] Kris Kristofferson (lyrics by John Prine), "Jesus was a Capricorn", Monument Records, 1972.

[453] Harper Bibles. NRSV Bible, Jeremiah 23:11-18. Kindle.

[454] Harper Bibles. NRSV Bible, Matthew 7:15-20. Kindle.

[455] Harper Bibles. NRSV Bible, Galatians 5:19-21. Kindle.

[456] Harper Bibles. NRSV Bible, Galatians 5:22-24. Kindle.

[457] Harper Bibles. NRSV Bible, I John 2:3-7. Kindle.

[458] Martin Niemöller, first spoken in a speech he gave on January 6, 1946, to the representatives of the Confessing Church in Frankfurt, cited by Wikiquotes.

[459] Harper Bibles. NRSV Bible, Mark 13:21-23. Kindle.

[460] Wikipedia entry on the history of the Seventh Day Adventist history, under the heading "Millerite."

[461] Wikipedia entry on Harold Camping.

[462] Wikipedia entry on the Mayan calendar.

[463] Harper Bibles. NRSV Bible, Matthew 24:36-42. Kindle.

[464] Harper Bibles. NRSV Bible, I Thessalonians 5:1-6. Kindle.

[465] Jason Byasse, Faithandleadership.com, on "Eschatological Innovation," 8/3/09.

[466] From King's "Where do we go from here?" speech at the 11th Southern Christian Leadership Conference, August 16th, 1967, Atlanta, GA.

[467] Harper Bibles. NRSV Bible, 1 John 4:7-12. Kindle.

[468] Harper Bibles. NRSV Bible, John 3:16-17. Kindle.

[469] Harper Bibles. NRSV Bible, Romans 12:9-13. Kindle.

[470] Harper Bibles. NRSV Bible, John 13:34-35. Kindle.

[471] Harper Bibles. NRSV Bible, Philippians 2:4-8. Kindle.

[472] Harper Bibles. NRSV Bible, James 1:22-25. Kindle.

[473] Harper Bibles. NRSV Bible I Corinthians 13:1-13. Kindle.

[474] Harper Bibles. NRSV Bible, Luke 9:23-24. Kindle.

[475] Bonhoeffer, Dietrich. *The Cost of Discipleship* (p. 45). Touchstone. Kindle.

[476] Wikipedia, from the entry on Dietrich Bonhoeffer.

[477] Eberhard Bethge, *Dietrich Bonhoeffer: Eine Biographie*, p. 736, cited in Wikipedia's entry on Bonhoeffer.

[478] Wikipedia, from its entry on Bonhoeffer.

[479] Ibid.

[480] Harper Bibles. NRSV Bible, Matthew 16: 24-26. Kindle.

[481] Harper Bibles. NRSV Bible John 21:4-7, Kindle.

[482] Harper Bibles. NRSV Bible, John 21:15-17. Kindle.

[483] Bonhoeffer, Dietrich. *The Cost of Discipleship* (pp. 45-46). Touchstone. Kindle.

Made in the USA
Middletown, DE
13 January 2021